HIGH

HIGH

*Drugs, Desire, and
a Nation of Users*

INGRID WALKER

UNIVERSITY OF WASHINGTON PRESS

Seattle and London

Printed and bound in the United States of America
Design by Katrina Noble
Composed in Minion Pro, typeface designed by Robert Slimbach
21   20   19   18   17   5   4   3   2   1

UNIVERSITY OF WASHINGTON PRESS
www.washington.edu/uwpress

Library of Congress Cataloging-in-Publication Data
Names: Walker, Ingrid, author.
Title: High : drugs, desire, and a nation of users / Ingrid Walker.
Description: 1st Edition. | Seattle : University of Washington Press, [2017] |
    Includes bibliographical references and index. |
Identifiers: LCCN 2017019448 (print) | LCCN 2017032832 (ebook) |
    ISBN 9780295742335 (ebook) | ISBN 9780295742311 (hardcover : alk. paper) |
    ISBN 9780295742328 (pbk. : alk. paper)
Subjects: LCSH: Drug abuse—United States.
Classification: LCC HV5825 (ebook) | LCC HV5825 .W38123 2017 (print) |
    DDC 362.290973—dc23
LC record available at https://lccn.loc.gov/2017019448

For Dante Tenzin, my star

There is not one but many silences, and they are an integral part of the strategies that underlie and permeate discourses.

MICHEL FOUCAULT, *THE HISTORY OF SEXUALITY*

CONTENTS

PREFACE

Breaking User Silence

When I was seven years old, I had my first hit of marijuana at my father's invitation and to my mother's horror. To be fair, my father had thought I might take him up on his offer a decade later. My mother thought that he had lost his mind. My parents remember that I talked for over an hour about the endless stars I saw out of the berth window in our Volkswagen bus. The moment's politics are those of the decade: the liberal hippie parents living the scene in Los Angeles. The adventurous father who did not want to limit his precocious daughter in any way. The cautious, conservative mother whose position was quite understandable. My drug pedigree begins here; the culture had opened Pandora's box and my dad held it out to me. I was a long-haired California girl and it was 1971. Of course I inhaled.

Despite a natural reluctance given the social milieu and my sense of privacy, it would strain credibility in writing a book about drug use to be coy about my experience with and predisposition toward the subject. While this project has nothing to do with an aspiration to confess my behavior to unknown readers, it has everything to do with breaking a cultural silence about drug use. One of the greatest strengths of the US domestic war on drugs has been its effective silencing of users. That vacuum has allowed for a relatively unchallenged social discourse dominated by the aggressive ideologies of drug warriors. The absence of other voices has, among other things, mischaracterized the experience of a minority of users who abuse drugs as the full spectrum of drug use. Speaking up about practices of controlled drug use is, for me, the initial step in asserting the reality and validity of various kinds of drug use.

Several authors of academic books about drugs have written about their former drug experiences, ones safely in the past. For some, drug use was and may still be a part of their story. For others, the experience was notable as an experience in their lives, maybe as an experiment in youth, or even a struggle with addiction. This is not one of those books. This is a book by what I will call a controlled drug user. By *controlled*, I mean many things: nonabusive or moderate; regular, episodic, or sometimes even rare. My use practice has never been anywhere near a "problem" as measured by a psychologist or physician. I have never struggled with abuse or addiction. In other words, drugs were and are, for me, normalized. Perhaps they are like your glass of wine or cup of coffee. Or maybe not, as it seems to me that most users enjoy both of those substances more than I do.

Over the last few decades, I have realized that my experience with drugs is both typical in terms of my use of various substances and atypical in my knowledge of particular drug cultures. The use of illicit and licit drugs and the effects of drug economies and the US war on drugs have, at key times, been in the foreground or close periphery of my experience. I am well acquainted with most use practices but am not the frequent user I once was. I have never needed or abused a particular substance. In fact, frequently many years pass by without drugs, although I do engage in occasional recreational use. I have tried almost every category of drug, and most licit and illicit drugs available, and that means nearly all of them with the exception of a few difficult to find psychedelics and newer synthetics. I appreciate many drugs, having learned which are useful and fun for me in particular contexts; I have made use of some of them part of my life practice. I continue to be more interested in marijuana and hallucinogens than stimulants or opiates. For example, alcohol has always been a less favored drug; my body does not metabolize it well. So I am an infrequent, moderate drinker. On the other hand, I enjoy marijuana and try to fit in a hallucinogenic trip at least once a year because it adjusts my thinking in a positive way. In this sense, I may be a classic example of a controlled user: I am a tenured professor, a parent, and a community member—a successful person by American social standards. I know when to work and when to play and display none of the stereotypical behaviors of the war on drugs's caricature of a "drug user." Drugs are, for me, one small element in a world of people, nature, ideas, art, travel, exercise, spirituality, work, and play. Drugs are, as many other things, part of a productive pattern in my life. They provide opportunities and pleasure, just as food, running, art, music, and community provide opportunities and pleasures.

This book proposes a reasoned response to the cultural imperative for drug users to remain silent and underground. I am committed to speaking honestly from informed experience (my own and others') about all aspects of drug use to draw attention to cultural misconceptions about drug practices and the significant social problems they have produced in the United States. We need to hear all kinds of user stories, but especially those relating experiences other than addiction and recovery, because nonaddiction stories represent the majority of users. Let me repeat this critical fact: people who use psychoactive substances in ways that are not destructive to their lives or others'—in other words, controlled users—constitute the vast majority of users. Breaking the silence around all types of drug use will open a more accurate public dialogue about the full spectrum of drug use in the United States.

However, my personal experience and understanding of various drug cultures is not the driver of this study. Rather, the conflict between my perspective and dominant drug discourses and popular representations inspired me to pose a series of research questions about the origins of US drug discourses and narratives. The resulting research, across various professional domains, contextualized and clarified a set of cultural dynamics in the United States, answering many of my questions. At the same time, my study has raised other questions. Sharing my research and sometimes surprising conclusions offers the potential to engage others in more questions and more research. I propose that we will not address issues like the considerable long-term damage of the drug war or the current concern with opiate abuse, for example, without considering the cultural biases, misinformation, and skewed expectations that construct current cultural norms about drug use. A better-informed dialogue is not just long overdue, it is desperately needed in order to change the terms of the conversation and to address the many social conflicts created because of our misconceptions about drugs and their users.

NOTE ABOUT THE DATA

The data used in this book are derived from various national agencies and organizations and include statistics about drug arrests and conviction, drug use and abuse, and rates of drug prescription, as well as industry data about pharmaceutical drug advertising. For consistency, I used the most recent data available across those various sources at the time the manuscript was completed. Thus, data throughout the book represent available statistics through 2014.

Since then, the United States has been engaged in a public debate about an increase in opiate-related deaths. Among the challenges of this crisis are understanding what, exactly, has contributed to the quadrupling of overdoses since 1999. It is a complex issue, one that engages many of the discourses and cultural assumptions discussed in this book. I would have liked to include recent data on this trend but find that we still struggle to grasp the variety of factors that have led to this spike in deaths. Related factors include overprescription of opiates, a related increase in the use of heroin, counterfeit synthetic drugs like fentanyl being passed off as OxyContin or heroin, unexpected drug interactions such as that of benzodiazepines with opiates, and unsatisfactory treatment of pain. Because death certificate data does not clarify causal factors in the presence of multiple drugs, or simply at all in 20 percent of overdose deaths, it is impossible to confidently cite more current data regarding the factors involved in opiate abuse and the cause of the spike in opiate overdose deaths. The Centers for Disease Control and Prevention, which has the most up-to-date information about this increase in opioid overdoses, notes some of the complicating factors listed above (see www.cdc.gov/drugoverdose/data/analysis.html). It is likely that we will struggle with this crisis of overdose deaths until we begin to address the multifaceted dynamics that inform and frame drug use and abuse.

ACKNOWLEDGMENTS

My deepest appreciation to all of you who supported me along the way. Special thanks to:

The Vox contributors, whose voices are the backbone of this book.

The early believers: Michael Berubé, Anthony Vital, and Trish Moore.

Colleagues in writing: Natalie Jolly, Alexine Fleck, Emma Rose, Josh Tenenberg, Renee Smith Nyberg, Dan Turner, Russ Castronovo, and Melissa McEuen.

Elin Björling for many patient and informed discussions about national data.

Alyssa Ng for her research and unflagging bibliographic support.

Narayan Singh for his graphical support.

Aaron Stevens and the Broadway Center for the Performing Arts for the invitation to explore desire in a TEDx Talk.

Ana Reyes for her many kindnesses.

Andrew Penn for his broad professional expertise.

Ranjit Arab for his collaboration and mad skills at conversing through song lyrics.

Paul Bearden for many conversations and voyages.

Scott Fields for his wit, friendship, and many explorations.

KPR, for the promise of a life-after-book.

My parents, Pat Wood, Larry Wood, and Bob Walker, for their unconditional support and love.

My sister, Erin Walker Kelly, for laughter and love.

My son, Dante Fields, who, despite a childhood spent with this project, survived intact as a funny, insightful, and curious soul. His patience, love, and support made this possible.

Gretel Katze, who kept me company and reminded me to play.

To all who work for reform in health care, drug policy, sentencing, and user social justice. Most especially, to those who speak the truth about the wages of our ignorance about drugs and users.

Support and funding for parts of this project came from:

The University of Washington Royalty Research Fund and sabbatical support.

The School of Interdisciplinary Arts and Sciences, University of Washington, Tacoma.

The University of Washington libraries and librarians, especially Suzanne Klinger.

The Whiteley Center, University of Washington.

HIGH

INTRODUCTION

WE ARE ALL USERS

That humanity at large will ever be able to dispense with Artificial
Paradises seems very unlikely.

—ALDOUS HUXLEY, *THE DOORS OF PERCEPTION*

AMERICANS LOVE TO CONSUME AND THEY ESPECIALLY LOVE TO
alter consciousness. Standing in a convenience store at 6:00 p.m. on a Friday
evening, I witness over a dozen people rush the liquor isle in less than twenty
seconds. Each individual carries away at least a bottle of wine or a six-pack
of beer. This moment signifies a cultural practice—the intentional transition
from the workweek to the weekend. Judging from their purchases, these
users seek the relaxation of a drink or two or, maybe, the buzz guaranteed
by having quite a few more. Because drinking is not only legal but is also an
American pastime, this scene is not noteworthy—unless you are thinking,
as I am, about the many ways Americans use psychoactive drugs in their
daily lives.[1] You are probably one of millions of Americans who starts the
day with caffeine. Maybe you stimulate your brain's endocannabinoids by
regularly running, swimming, or cycling.[2] You might be a student who stocks
up on either legal or illegal stimulants to fuel study sessions. Or, perhaps
you enjoy happy hour with colleagues and friends. In these and other ways,
Americans indulge in psychoactive drugs of all sorts, whether prescribed
or proscribed—including substances and practices that they do not even
acknowledge alter consciousness. The United States is a nation of users in a
culture of self-management and self-medication. From caffeine, alcohol, or
nicotine to energy drinks, pharmaceuticals, or street drugs, most Americans
regularly use a drug to manage their moods. A long history of substance use
demonstrates that a "drug-free America" is a fantasyland that most Americans do not want to inhabit.

CONFLICTING DRUG NARRATIVES

Despite widespread and varied drug-use practices, Americans live in a
cultural context of conflicting ideologies about psychoactive drug use.

Dominant public discourses of drug addiction and criminalization have so effectively characterized and marginalized certain kinds of drug use that you might assume that "drug use" has nothing to do with you.[3] While Americans enthusiastically endorse the regular, pleasurable use of some substances, they sanction an all-out war on others. Why? To begin with, Americans have accepted oversimplified narratives about licit and illicit drugs, narratives that promote misconceptions about drugs and users. Stereotypical representations of users of "good" and "bad" drugs persist because of the effective legislative lobbies of special interests, substantial funding and profiteering, by the private prison industry, for example, and targeted media campaigns that are pro-pharmaceutical and anti-illicit drugs. Most importantly, misconceptions about drugs and users endure because they've become connected to professional communities that have framed how Americans think about drug use and users.

Differentiated thinking about drug use in the United States is grounded in parallel cultural developments in the twentieth and twenty-first centuries: the coevolution of well-funded domestic drug interdiction (facilitated by law enforcement, the criminal justice system, and a growing prison industry), and the integration of the medical and psychiatric professions with an expanding pharmaceutical industry.[4] These two cultural dynamics have greatly influenced Americans as drug users. Drug control's expansion into an active mandate—a "war on drugs"—not only criminalized particular drugs but specifically targeted and penalized users of those psychoactive substances. This is evident in US arrests for illicit drug possession alone, which rose by 80 percent from 1990 to 2010.[5] At the same time, health care's growing reliance on pharmaceutical therapies to treat a variety of ailments has medicalized or expressed medical authority over greater aspects of individuals' lives, fundamentally changing how mental and physical health is understood.[6] Primary among those changes is the direct association of achieving or preserving health with pharmaceutical intervention. Not surprisingly, Americans' use of psychoactive prescription drugs increased 22 percent from 2001 to 2010, with about half of Americans now taking at least one prescription drug and 10 percent of Americans taking three or more.[7] The dominant effect of prohibiting some drugs in a culture that also widely prescribes pharmaceutical drugs has been to divide the politics of drug use by either criminalizing or medicalizing (and sometimes both) the users of various psychoactive substances. Even as the culture has whole-heartedly endorsed the use of pharmaceutical drugs, the United States has severely penalized millions of users of drugs such as heroin, methamphetamine, and marijuana. While the psychoactive elements in some of those drugs are not substantially different (e.g., OxyContin and heroin are both opiates), how Americans conceive of these drugs, their users and providers, and their respective regulatory environments contrasts dramatically.

How did the United States come to have such polarized thinking about drugs—and what are its effects on American culture? *High: Drugs, Desire, and a Nation of Users* examines how criminalization and medicalization have shaped understanding of illicit and licit drug use practices in the United States. By tracing key factors that have informed problematic thinking about drugs and users across various disciplines, professions, and constituencies, this study focuses on the significant outcomes of this polarization. Further, the book includes a critical element that is missing in US drug discourse: the recognition of a range of drug use practices that constitute what I call controlled drug use—or drug use that does not fall into categories of abuse or addiction. Though it is the most prevalent experience motivating the vast majority of drug users, pleasure in controlled use is almost entirely absent in US drug discourses. Although researchers cite different statistics depending on whether they refer to specific drugs or overall psychoactive drug use, the consensus is that less than 10 percent and possibly only 2.5 percent of users of all drugs except cigarettes become addicted. (See chapter 3, figs. 3.1 and 3.2.) Another way of saying that is that the great majority of psychoactive drug users, recreational and otherwise, are controlled users. Yet so much public discourse is about addiction, as if it were a much more widespread dilemma. The consequences of the exclusion of controlled use are myriad, but perhaps the most fundamental among them are the silencing effects of criminalization and medicalization on those controlled users and thus the continued cultural devastation of drug policies that do not fit actual use patterns. If conversations about drugs, policy, and public health do not include the experiences of the majority of drug users, then the United States and drug users will continue to incur the costs of those misconceptions. This book undertakes a discussion of user experience and incorporates the perspectives of a variety of users and people in the drug war whose reflections fill in the gaps in US narratives about drugs and users. Recognizing a wider range of users and their experiences offers an alternative to oversimplified thinking about drug use, the kind of thinking that not only blinds Americans to the broad realities of psychoactive drug use in the United States, but also continues to perpetuate social inequities.

CULTURAL CONTEXT: CONTROL

Drugs and alcohol have constituted a contested ground for political and social control in the United States since the late nineteenth century, when the second wave of the temperance movement took root and states and cities began to pass laws to curb the use of opium, heroin, and morphine. By the early twentieth century, federal efforts to control drugs and alcohol resulted in the Harrison Narcotics Tax Act of 1914 (designed to control drug use through the regulation and distribution of coca and opium products) and the Eighteenth Amendment and subsequent Volstead Act (intended to regulate and control the sales and strength of alcoholic products). While federal alcohol prohibition was quickly repealed, national drug control has expanded over the last hundred years with, among other factors, massive budget growth, arrest and seizure quotas, mandatory minimum penalties for users, and the authority of drug courts to mandate treatment. Still, we struggle in the United States to control drugs in many contexts. Sports organizations attempt to identify and ban the use of performance-enhancing substances for athletes. The Food and Drug Administration (FDA) monitors many substances but cannot effectively regulate the ever-growing dietary and herbal supplement market. Even with widespread antismoking policies across the country, the tobacco industry continues to promote and sell nicotine products. The secondary, illicit market for pharmaceutical drugs thrives, with street prices as high as thirty dollars per thirty-milligram oxycodone tablet.[8] Many former prescription-opiate users switch to heroin to avoid oversight and expense. This inability to control drugs in a culture of drug control demonstrates Americans' active use of many kinds of psychoactive substances—and that they are conflicted about how to manage the many ways in which they consume them.

Over the last forty years, this tension has deepened. The declaration and waging of the "war on drugs" has been the most visible factor in shaping divided cultural drug discourses. When President Richard Nixon declared war in 1971, he announced that the "public enemy number one in the United States is drug abuse. In order to fight and defeat this enemy, it is necessary to wage a new, all-out offensive."[9] While drug interdiction has been an utter failure in achieving the policy goal of eradicating illicit drug distribution and use in the United States, it has had colossal, long-lasting sociopolitical impact. By 2009, the United States had spent over $1 trillion on law enforcement, extensive media campaigns, and antidrug education.[10] The conviction and incarceration of hundreds of thousands of people with extreme sentences for low-level drug offenses has had a devastating impact across particular ethnic and socioeconomic demographics. Persistent misapprehensions about illicit drugs and their users have facilitated a disproportionate and unjust war in which *users*—not drug abuse—have become the enemy.

Just as antidrug policies and their effects have permeated the culture, the dominance of pharmaceutical drugs in healthcare has created influential new health norms. The proportion of Americans diagnosed with disorders such as depression, anxiety, or attention deficit disorder who are prescribed pharmaceutical treatment has grown massively. By 2010, at least one in five Americans was taking psychotherapeutic drugs, with an increase across all ages.[11] It is now common to start children of elementary school age on these drugs—pharmaceutical therapies that may continue for life. Although the pervasiveness of pharmaceutical drug use may be less apparent as a cultural practice, propharmaceutical influences have succeeded in making Americans the most medicated population in history.

In the four decades of the war on drugs, the effects of criminalization and medicalization have also been manifest in US attitudes toward the utility of different drugs (as well as those who are imagined as their users). Media campaigns authorized by Congress and designed by advertising firms have been astonishingly successful in directly informing our attitudes about drug use. From the war on drugs' antidrug public-service announcement (PSA) campaigns to direct-to-consumer (DTC) pharmaceutical advertisements, drug media has found credulous audiences. The Office of National Drug Control Policy (ONDCP) has invited striking advertising campaigns by award-winning creative firms, following what would become its associate media organization, the Partnership for a Drug Free America, and its infamous 1987 antidrug PSA.[12] That original thirty-second television spot featured a deceptively simple three-part narrative. A man holding an egg declared: "This is your brain." The egg cracked into a hot frying pan, then sizzled loudly, demonstrating "your brain on drugs." The actor's concluding query, "Any questions?" was, of course, rhetorical. Regardless of the ad's accuracy as a statement about the risks of recreational drug use, the metaphor's threat—having one's brain "fried by drugs"—could not have been more memorable. While this early example seems almost quaint by the standards of todays' graphic, shock-based antidrug tactics (see chapter 1), it is difficult to overstate the cultural dominance of antidrug PSAs' negative characterizations of using and users. The drug war's discourse about illicit substances has effectively formed the frameworks through which American legislation, criminal justice, medical diagnosis and treatment, drug reform, and popular culture imagine and discuss users.

Similarly, medicalization's counter discourse about the necessity and benefits of pharmaceutical interventions in our lives has influenced medical and psychiatric practices, as well as Americans' acceptance of mental health issues. In the same year as the fried-egg PSA, a Ritalin-SR print advertisement featured a seven-year-old boy focusing on his schoolwork with the tagline "Let the ADD child leave his medicine at home." Far from suggesting that the child should go unmedicated, the ad promised that an extended-release formula of the drug would liberate parents and schools from the difficulty of medicating children repeatedly throughout the school day. A Prozac advertising campaign of this same period featuring a smiling woman promised a similar kind of liberation, delivering what it called "the therapeutic triad: convenience, confidence, and compliance."[13] Both ads assure patients that they will achieve or restore good health, well-being, and lifestyle convenience through a specific pharmaceutical intervention—outcomes that are seen as desirable and socially if not medically necessary. The unmistakable lesson of these cultural drug narratives is that the experience of one's brain on drugs entirely depends on whether you have been prescribed pharmaceutical drugs by a physician or you choose to crack open your brain with street drugs. Most social narratives that address psychoactive drug use reflect this fervent difference, distinguishing between hazardous or "bad" drugs and beneficial or "good" drugs. These dual narratives have currency not just in government PSAs and health-care campaigns, but especially in media culture, which more often than not amplifies and perpetuates such divergent characterizations. Importantly, these discourses signal specific assumptions about user control or user agency. The prevailing assumption is that if you use illicit drugs, they control you. If you use licit drugs, you regain control over your life.

THE SILENT MAJORITY

Despite conflicting discourses that have shaped cultural perceptions about drugs and users, Americans continue to use drugs in ways that plot a broad spectrum of substances, use practices, and users. The sort of psychoactive substances used may change with trends and availability, but the practice and desire to use drugs remains constant. Americans are not unique in this tendency: human behavior across time and cultures suggests that substance use, especially pleasure-seeking use, is a fundamental desire—what physician Andrew Weil calls "a basic human appetite." If "[a]ll cultures use drugs that influence the brain," as neuroscientist David Linden declares, then perhaps this behavior is not merely a superfluous, recreational aspect of our lives. In fact, Ronald K. Siegel, a psychopharmacologist, argues that the universal desire for intoxication among humans and other primates is a fourth biological drive.[14] Why and what people use, and how they conceive of those practices, present a complex set of issues. While most people use some substance or practice to intentionally alter consciousness, they may not consider themselves users. In a culture like the United States, so attuned to particular depictions of using (whether the drug is Xanax or heroin), it is important to explore the origins of drug discourses, their expressed ideologies and consequences, and what they preclude. Examining how criminalization and medicalization have constrained and moralized our capacity for understanding the desire to alter consciousness is fundamental to more accurately grasping and appreciating the roles of pleasure and intoxication in our lives. The recognition of using in this wider sense is critical to rethinking drug policy in a culture that has arbitrary and conflicted notions about the users of psychoactive substances.

Many of the recent reforms to our drug policies, from decriminalization to cutting mandatory minimum prison sentences, have been inspired by people who have rightly and necessarily focused our attention on the injustices caused by the war on drugs, specifically the consequence of a carceral culture that has imprisoned and decimated specific communities, predominantly people in lower socioeconomic, urban areas, and people of color.[15] Similarly, much of the rethinking about the medicalization of recreational users has been inspired by reformers who recognize the realities of users most at risk and seek to reduce those more extreme users' potential for harm. These are pressing drug issues that should be addressed at every level—whether to redress systemic racism, to reduce outsized penalties for drug possession, or to address addictions and their complicating social factors. To leave it at that, however, would be to perpetuate the binary thinking about drug use that has led to drug criminalization and medicalization. In order to successfully disentangle the roots of issues underlying criminalization, the cultural dynamics and effects of medicalization must also be acknowledged and addressed. As a significant but somewhat unseen element of drug discourse, medicalization complicates notions of drug use by focusing on some kinds of drug use as abuse or addiction and other kinds of drug use as medically necessary. This polarized thinking about drugs and users is influential for many reasons, as much because of what it precludes as what it emphasizes.

At the heart of all drug use, and what Americans tend to avoid talking about, is one very simple thing: desire. American drug-use practices reveal a great deal about the desire for pleasure and the various ways people want to feel good, maintain a particular psychological state, or get high. In other words, their practices reveal how people want to live. To avoid discussion about the connection between drugs and pleasure is to maintain that most drug use comes from uncontrollable need and/or addiction, or that the majority of people are not drug users. Neither of those assumptions is accurate. Most psychoactive drug practice occurs in controlled ways that make us feel better—or even very good—and takes place in normalized contexts. Another way of saying this is that most users can and do express agency: the ability to choose whether or not to use. These users are the silent majority, the users that go unnoticed in our drug discourses.

For example, drinking alcohol in the United States is so normalized that you may not notice how deeply embedded it is in our general culture. Use of alcohol varies widely, but it is worth noting that there are some social occasions at which it is not only acceptable but also somewhat expected to drink. Drinking to the point of drunkenness so typifies alcohol use that Americans have developed social norms to address it. From designated drivers to alcohol education about alcohol percentages and body mass, Americans have found ways to support people in using alcohol safely. Americans play drinking games both in person and on social media to engage with events like political debates. A popular television program, *Drunk History,* features episodes of US history narrated by people who get "drunk enough" to tell a good story.[16] All of this is possible because alcohol is readily available, regulated, legal—and the majority of people who drink in the United States drink responsibly. The majority of drinkers express user agency in a variety of ways, but for the most part, American drinkers practice controlled use. Of the 52 percent of Americans who use alcohol, only 6.4 percent struggle with alcoholism, binge drinking, or episodic excessive use. Alcohol is but one example, but it is the most frequently and broadly used drug that Americans generally enjoy in a controlled, normalized manner.

Similarly, other psychoactive drugs are also used within a range of practices and expressions of agency—predominantly manifesting as controlled, nonproblematic use that fulfills many needs and desires. If this is the case, why are pleasure and the concept of user agency so absent in American drug discourses? One reason is that for illicit drugs in particular, normative or controlled drug use—the very idea of user agency—has been eclipsed by what has come to be the centerpiece of drug discourse: addiction. Broadly defined as an inability to control substance use, addiction has so dominated public policy, research, and treatment that it seems to be the only outcome of the use of some kinds of drugs. Indeed, addicts are the most visible users within the contexts of criminalization and medicalization. On the one hand, this makes sense: law enforcement, criminal justice actors, social workers, and health-care professionals tend to come in contact with addicted users most often, because these are the users who may be penalized for drug possession and use, convicted of other related crimes, have health issues, or need social services. But, on the other hand, users of various drugs are ideologically labeled as addicts whether or not that is an accurate assessment. When is the last time you heard about a controlled methamphetamine user? Addiction is a culturally dominant narrative about particular users both because it is real *and* because where it is not present, it is more often than not presumed. What are the effects of this overpromotion of addiction as the outcome of most drug use? The motivations, experiences, and needs of psychoactive substance users are misunderstood or misperceived, along with indicators of user choice. To examine user agency, one must ask: where is psychoactive drug use normalized? What is known about nonaddicted users—that is, the majority of users? And how might it change the drug war and other drug policy if more were known about controlled users?

The challenge is to try to determine the line between normalized use and addiction. Is someone who has four cups of coffee a day an addict? Are you an alcoholic if you have several glasses of wine most days? What if you smoke marijuana habitually? While an inability to control one's drug use is the basis of most definitions of addiction, none of those behaviors, alone, qualifies as addiction. The American Psychological Association (APA) and the American Medical Association (AMA) list a considerable series of qualifying behaviors and conditions, with the presence of a significant subset of these required to diagnose addiction. So the question of what is "acceptable" drug use is a complicated topic. To make controlled use practices visible, the question might be not where is the bright line designating "dangerous" drug use (which is, again, comprised of many variable factors) but, what do users do regularly that is recognized as nonproblematic use? In other words: what are Americans' actual use practices? Most users' experiences bear witness to a spectrum of drug-use practices and not a bright line denoting use and abuse.

Acknowledging controlled drug-use practices may be the most important foothold in dismantling fallacies about drug use and users. Although this understanding is just emerging in the United States, it is better recognized outside our cultural echo chamber. In its inaugural report in June 2011, an independent Global Commission on Drug Policy (GCDP) emphasized that the proportion of drug addicts to casual users is grossly overstated. Based on World Health Organization (WHO) data, the report stresses that of the estimated 250 million drug users worldwide, less than 10 percent are addicts—a figure that parallels US data. Further, the GCDP maintains that "the majority of people who use drugs do not fit the stereotype of the 'amoral and pitiful addict,'" and calls for a challenge to, rather than a reinforcement of, common misperceptions about drug markets, users, and dependence.[17] One way of challenging such thinking is to recognize that the spectrum of use stretching between abstinence and addiction is broad and varied. That middle ground constitutes a significant population, *all the other users,* a majority of Americans who use either illegal and legal drugs, or both, but do not suffer the consequences of abuse, dependence, or addiction. While it may be debatable whether normalized or controlled users self-medicate or suffer serious consequences of their use, the assertion that majority of users do not suffer the consequences of abuse, dependence, or addiction is based on data from users, research clinicians, and health-care providers.[18] There are many different kinds of users with various reasons for using who employ a wide range of substances to manage moods and experiences. A key outcome of oversimplified drug discourse is that it leaves Americans with little accurate information about such users. Understanding those experiences and *why* Americans use is as important as understanding what is used. Acknowledging how and why psychoactive substances are used radically changes cultural thinking about using—and is likely to encompass a more extensive category of substances than those on the controlled-substances schedules. Journalist Nick Gillespie writes, "Far from our drugs controlling us, by and large *we control our drugs*; as with alcohol, the primary motivation in taking drugs is to enjoy ourselves, not destroy ourselves. . . . There is such a thing as responsible drug use, and it is the rule, not the exception."[19] This trend of reasoning, to imagine and effect a sustainable socialization of controlled use, is the means to a more realistic and authentic approach to drug users.

RETHINKING DRUG USE

It is simple to posit the socialization of controlled drug use but difficult to propose how to get there. I argue that one begins by becoming aware of and demystifying highly conditioned thinking. Over a decade ago, when a student was arrested for allegedly manufacturing methamphetamine, the community's responses were nearly uniform in classifying meth as a "bad" or dead-end drug. A close friend who is a regular user of various legal and illegal drugs commented, "Meth is destroying Appalachia along with OxyContin, but at least Oxy is a *good* drug." Good drugs. Bad drugs. These are words that serve as codes for legal versus illegal, prescribed versus proscribed. Psychoactive drugs are neither bad nor good—more accurate distinctions might be made between their elements, purposes, and effects. Such responses are ones of ignorance in the most literal sense; in many ways, we learn about the experiences we have not known through stories. People without firsthand experience of an activity have limited understanding with which to filter, much less reconsider, the pervasive cultural narratives about those activities that dominate our media.

In that sense, we are in a serious knowledge deficit. The information we have with which to appraise and understand drugs is shaped by polarized cultural attitudes and contributes to this deficit. Drugs create chemical reactions in our brains and bodies, but they also are greatly affected by context, culture, and individual psychology—what researchers and users have come to know as "set and setting".[20] Each drug should be understood within this array of factors. Current scheduling of controlled substances in the United States does not accurately reflect their pharmacological nature, known potential for harm, or phenomenological effects. A well-researched taxonomy of drugs that discerns between substances by describing their various effects and potential applications would be influential.[21] But that is just a beginning; understanding users' various experiences and their applications of these substances is an important but missing secondary body of knowledge. Exploring the *desire* to use as intrinsic to use practices, and conceiving of it beyond our medicalization and addiction paradigms, is critical to deepening that body of empirical knowledge. Some of those issues are explored in this book, including the desire to get high, the social realities of using substances of all kinds, and how the dysfunction of addiction is part of a broader set of user experiences.

To address the gaps in cultural drug discourses, *High: Drugs, Desire, and a Nation of Users* examines how drug-use practices in the United States have been framed by the pervasive and enduring cultural influences of criminalization and medicalization in the twentieth and twenty-first centuries. This study contextualizes the social construction and constraint of drug use by looking across prevalent discourses that frame our understanding of drugs and users—through US drug policy and law enforcement, medical research, and health-care practice and recovery cultures, as well as popular culture and user narratives, plus advertising and other media campaigns. The assumptions and conventions underlying public drug discourses are surfaced and contextualized within various academic and professional epistemological domains, in order to consider their implications. For example, this study explores how health professionals express user agency almost exclusively as either iatric (directly related to medical treatment) or addictive (a user's uncontrolled use or use outside medical treatment). This analysis incorporates the most profound factor missing in most user characterizations: that the urge for pleasure through getting high is ubiquitous in human culture. The widespread practices of substance use and other pursuits that alter consciousness indicate a valid and undeniable desire. To better understand drug-use practices, this study considers how users express this pursuit in their lives. The spectrum of using is varied and complex: from abstinence to addiction with many other points plotted along the way.

Demystifying cultural discourses around drugs and users begins with an examination of the origins and cultural currency of strategic user characterizations. Misconceptions about drugs and users have a long and well-documented history.[22] While the cultural problematization of drug users stretches back through this longer history, the key antecedents for the issues I will focus on took shape in the mid-twentieth century with the Kennedy and Nixon administrations' efforts to specify drug abuse as a problem and to overtly declare a war on drugs. Specifically, I focus on the outcomes of an escalation of drug-war policy from the Reagan era to the present. Chapter 1, "Picture a Drug User," analyzes significant representations of drug users in American popular media, as well as the legislation and funding behind contemporary drug advertising that shaped these depictions. This chapter considers how propharmaceutical advertising and antidrug PSAs (from the 1980s to the present) established the characterizations of drugs and their users that provide our baseline for public drug discourse. Continuing with an analysis of film and television representations of drugs and users, this chapter explores how iconic representations of users from popular culture reflect and inform how Americans understand drug use and users in real life. User caricatures such as the drug lords, lost youth, and paragons of drug excess that populate fiction, television, and film have staying power in US popular culture. Consider how the excessive violence and madness of *Scarface*'s cocaine kingpin Tony Montana and the inner-city crack dealer in films like *New Jack City* or *Clockers* depict one kind of enemy in the drug war. The empty lives of the users in *Drugstore Cowboy* or *Leaving Las Vegas* represent a commonly imagined dead-end drug experience. Still, the heroes of drug use and excess, like Hunter S. Thompson, the Big Lebowski, Cheech and Chong, and Harold and Kumar, serve to romanticize particular drug practices. These and other characterizations become even more significant as we see them reproduced in public discourses about drugs and users in policy making, funding, law enforcement, medical research, and health care.

The popular representation of drugs and users promoted in PSAs by the ONDCP and affiliated groups has both informed and depicted the criminal prosecution not just of drug distributors—the drug war's specified target—but especially drug users. Chapter 2, "Criminalization: Winning the Crusade but Losing the War," examines how public drug discourse has been shaped by war as a social policy. When the Reagan administration escalated Nixon's domestic war on drugs, establishing a basis for ongoing increases in funding and oversight, it set a course for what has become the United States' largest mobilization of law-enforcement and criminal-justice resources. By the 1990s, however, the ONDCP found that the war on drugs would not be won but had, instead, become an unending crusade against a limitless source of crime. In 2001, a direct parallel to the war on terror was made almost immediately by George W. Bush's administration in a media campaign directly connecting drug use to funding terrorism. Yet the explicit mission of drug prohibition—to eradicate drug supply and demand—belied the tenuous nature of what, in practice, the drug war has most often policed: low-level drug possession, prosecuting individuals for possessing as little as a single hit of acid, a couple of tabs of Ecstasy, or less than an eighth of an ounce of marijuana. This chapter argues that the war on drug possession has served as a proxy for the actual act of *using* the drug—particularly the users of the drug. More often than not, the drug war has prosecuted victimless crimes by criminalizing users as ambiguous social offenders. From the crack epidemic to the meth epidemic and, now, a heroin epidemic, criminalization has perpetuated a culture of moral panic. The tangible effects of that cultural anxiety and attendant policies and laws have been well documented.[23] This analysis considers the cultural politics of a set of policies that seated a new drug czar and his considerable budget at the helm of an all-out war on drug users. The chapter tracks the implications of criminalizing certain drug users with increasingly militarized enforcement practices, tracks who is affected by criminalization's direct support of the prison industry, and how the mandate to eradicate drugs in the United States became a mandate to eradicate certain drug users.

Perhaps the major obstacle to decriminalizing and equitably addressing the recreational use of drugs is a moralistic conceptualization of illicit drug use. Medical and psychological research into the effects of illicit and/or recreational drug use have shaped a broad characterization of drug use as addiction by conceptualizing nearly all recreational drug use as abuse. Cultural historian Stuart Walton argues that, during the period of US drug regulation, the medicalized version of altered consciousness has come to stand in for the entire spectrum of the experience of intoxication.[24] Chapter 3, "Medicalization: Defining Drug Use," explores how a medicalized culture has affected a cultural sense of health, expressly, how health is or is not maintained through drug use. Health-care professions have established the authority to prescribe and monitor substance use. Users who practice outside of that authority— the user of illicit drugs, and the uncontrolled or unauthorized recreational user of either illicit or licit drugs—have come to represent what health care identifies as "drug users." Just as the term "antidrug" is an artifact of criminalization that specifically references illicit drugs, a "drug user," in the context of medicalization, is someone whose drug practice is not the result of medical prescription or oversight. By examining how this identification of the user has coevolved within the language of research models and diagnostic definitions that identify drug use as addiction, I trace various medical communities' particular construction of user agency. Because addiction, or an inability to control drug use, is overestimated and has so dominated public drug discourse, the reality of controlled or normative use of all psychoactive drugs has all but been eclipsed. The implications of this skewed perspective are staggering, influencing research, diagnosis and health care, drug-use penalties, harm reduction, and all users. The notion that most drug use is about a loss of control, disease, or both obscures the possibility that users choose to use for a variety of reasons—many of them quite rational and functional. Further, conceiving of some pursuits of altered consciousness as problematic and dysfunctional but others as medically sanctioned is not only confusing and illogical, but also misleading.

The user-as-addict characterization maintained by medicine, law enforcement, the criminal justice system, legislation, and often popular culture defines the desire to alter consciousness as damaging personally as well as socially. By framing some users and the use of some substances as a disorder, the medicalization of using has missed the significance of desire—and pleasure—altogether. That is not surprising; although Americans spend an inordinate amount of time anticipating, pursuing, and relishing pleasure, they have an uneasy relationship with it. Chapter 4, "Why We Use: The Pleasure and the Eros of Drugs," focuses on pleasure as a critical aspect of psychoactive substance use. In drug discourse, pleasure is a concept that, as cultural studies scholar David Lenson notes, stands out by its very absence.[25] This chapter proposes that the pathway to a better-informed, more realistic social dialogue about the nature of illegal and legal drugs is one that entertains the joys, perils, and many experiences of getting high. Health and sexuality scholar Kane Race argues for the possibility of pleasure as a need that informs the lives of marginalized users as a form of agency and self-understanding.[26] By virtue of the very act of using, illicit and recreational drug users enact a form of civil disobedience with many implications. Coming to understand users' motivations and the meanings that they attach to using is a rich area to be explored outside the confines of legal frameworks, moralism, and medical rationality. This chapter's discussion of the social construction of pleasure focuses on its centrality to user identity and agency through cultural theory, user narratives, and studies, recentering user experience as critical to understanding drug-use practices.

LISTENING TO USERS: VOX

In addition to a cultural-studies-based analysis across various fields of drug research, this project is directly informed by an unorthodox first-person, participant-observer perspective—my own and others'. In two decades of reflecting on how United States culture discusses and represents drug use, I have come to realize that while many academic drug scholars are concerned with the same issues I undertake here, few explicitly bring their own empirical knowledge to the project.[27] In this vacuum, first-hand awareness of the often erroneous nature of public drug discourse is useful, especially in illuminating how various blind spots created by communities can be replicated in drug research and scholarship. I recognize that in reaching across different professional and epistemic contexts, I risk misconstruing issues and concepts. At the same time, I hope to bring an informed outsider perspective that can illuminate what has been greatly overshadowed by the politics and practices of prohibition as well as its collateral cultural effects in some of these areas. My experiences, both individual and sociopolitical, provide a space from which to consider issues of user agency and the silence and silencing of users. This particular user history (and present) has resulted in kinds of knowledge that dispute some of the prevailing assertions about substances and using. The aperture offered by that perspective has helped me inquire further, noting how discourses shape responses and how various disciplines, in doing their very good work, have reinforced ways of knowing that should be questioned. This is a dynamic and mutable topic; I do not claim to have the most valid perspective or one that offers more answers than another. Rather, I contend that looking across the domains of knowledge in this book from a controlled user's perspective evokes a missing aspect of the cultural dialogue about drug use. It raises different questions about substances and their use, questions researchers and readers should be asking.

Talking about my drug use raises the dilemma of those whose use practices include illicit drugs or recreational pharmaceuticals in a culture of criminalization and medicalization. When I disclose my use, I risk being misread. The sheer ugliness with which Americans have characterized the use of some of the drugs that I happen to use can come up. Yet, a controlled user lifestyle is not unusual. Of the over 27 million marijuana users in this country, many are not merely marijuana users. This point is worth emphasizing because a typical strategy among writers critical of the war on drugs is to distinguish between "soft" and "hard" drug to sidestep the stickier issue of the use of other drugs, especially those associated with psychological and physical addiction. Many users, users who are not addicted, consume drugs besides marijuana with regularity and/or moderation—from MDMA (Ecstasy) or methamphetamine to heroin and prescription opiates. National and international studies show that far more people than imagined (from 75 to 95 percent of users) use many of these drugs with some frequency and suffer none of the problems the antidrug or medical establishments insist are their logical end. (See chapter 3.) This inconsistency between experience and social discourse is a significant issue in accurately understanding drug use and users.

If using psychoactive drugs is a normative behavior, what does using psychoactive substances mean for various people, and what does it represent in their lives? What can be learned from users' experiences, motivations, and reflections on their use? The "Vox" narratives in this book offer a platform to users of the silent majority. Their voices are privileged because Americans are very familiar with narratives of addiction, but less so with the narratives of other users. For the most part, although not entirely, the Vox narratives cover other experiences of using, including the normalization of drug use and its varied facets. American culture has much to learn about the diverse experiences of people who use all kinds of drugs. While any drug use may provide the fuel for self-destructive behavior, most recreational users are stable, functioning individuals. They are productive. They raise families. They are your neighbors and colleagues. The Vox accounts offer the stories and experiences of users as alternative ways of understanding drug use within mainstream American culture. These narratives personify, contextualize, and examine drug use. Vox narrators are thoughtful about not only the experience of using but also about the sociopolitical contexts in which they use. Vox pieces express different perspectives about using—from ritual and practice to recreation and creation, as well as drug subcultures and mainstream cultures. The Vox contributors represent a range of people with varied user and life experiences, including business owners, industry workers, educators, artists, and professionals in health care, information technology, and law enforcement. Their stories describe use practices from the commonplace to the spiritual, driven by everything from a health-care need to the celebration or the *alterity* of using in what writer Aldous Huxley calls "one of the principal appetites of the soul."[28] In their Vox narratives, users speak into a cultural silence about particular kinds of drug use, often surfacing the issues underlying value judgments expressed in public drug discourses.

While the stories and voices in the Vox section are authentic and written by these users, pseudonyms have been used to protect authors' privacy and to shield them from other repercussions. The Vox authors are people who, when they became acquainted with my project, had a story to share. They represent a range of American backgrounds and use experiences. All Vox pieces appear with the permission of the authors. I am grateful to them for their voices and their stories.

The consequences of the US war on drugs have been costly, and its policy goal of a drug-free America is unrealizable, because the eradication of street drugs is a straw man. In addition to acknowledging the failure of drug policy, recognizing the effects of cultural biases toward certain drug users is critical to a more realistic and accurate conversation about using and drug control. Understanding that medical drug use is on the rise fills in a broader picture. Culturally, the United States is at a point at which it either begins to interrogate, inform, and clarify the bases of cultural understanding of substance use, or it will likely further amplify a costly, bifurcated set of drug policies and practices. This effort has created a two-tiered system that pushes some substances and punishes the use of others—with little benefit to individual and social well-being. Americans are inundated with ideologies that operate as cultural norms and make it difficult to see how these concepts shape our perceptions. The project of this book is to initiate and broaden a public conversation about drug use across various fields of drug research, health care, and policy making. One primary goal of this conversation is to fill in various gaps—to complicate oversimplified notions of drug use and users, and to make explicit the ways in which user narratives have power. Most importantly, the project of this book is to challenge you to think about how drug use is a part of your life. If Americans become aware of their own roles as users in these drug discourses, they are more likely to change them.

To revisit cultural thinking about drug users, notions about the desire to alter consciousness must be informed and developed. If the brain cannot distinguish between the various sources of neurochemical transcendences, as journalist Michael Pollan and others point out, then why do we?[29] Understanding how various users have incorporated this pursuit into their lifestyles requires engaging all the varieties of drug use, from quotidian to edgy, from uplifting to scary, and everything in between. The regular use of psychoactive substances occurs in all cultures. Why do so many people want to get high? Or, to put it another way: could millions of regular, controlled drug users be wrong?

CHAPTER 1

PICTURE A DRUG USER

PICTURE A DRUG USER. WHAT COMES TO MIND? YOUR MENTAL image probably depends on what psychoactive substances you consider to be "drugs." It may also depend on whether you consider yourself to be a user, or if you know drug users. Most likely, your immediate image of a drug user has been influenced by how they have been represented in US media and popular culture. Your characterization may be typical of the drug users depicted in television and film: a recreational user who struggles with drug addiction. Maybe you imagined an emaciated heroin user, an immobilized crack user, or a lesion-riddled meth user, some of the most prevalent images of drug use in US popular culture. Although caricatures of drug users have historically been part of US popular culture, those narratives have been refined in the decades of the drug war. Americans have been relentlessly bombarded with particular images about drug use through popular culture, news media, and advertising—characterizations that have become invested with a great deal of social and political power.

Are these pictures of users accurate? If the user you imagined is not based in your experience, how would you know whether it was a credible representation? What would you compare it to? Even for people with firsthand knowledge of psychoactive drug use and users, there are so many different kinds of users and situations that it is impossible to imagine a representative user. I start this book by raising the question about an imagined "drug user" because despite the countless kinds of drug users, characterizations in visual media and popular culture tend to depict extreme use—images that are more often than not inaccurate or not representative of user experience. Certainly, drug use can be normalized as well as caricatured in popular culture. For example, music and literature offer a range of exceptions to the United States's usual representative dynamic. But, for the most part, cultural images reproduce pervasive misconceptions about the use and users of psychoactive drugs, reinforcing narrowly defined narratives that have significant political implications in public policy, law enforcement, and health care.

US popular culture has consistently traded in stereotypical, marginalized images of recreational drug providers and users like the mysterious clientele of Chinese opium dens in the nineteenth century, the menace of Mexican "reefer madness" in the early twentieth century, the dropout white hippy LSD user of the 1960s, or the crack-addicted black mothers and their babies of the 1980s. Over the last forty-five years, the drug war has amplified representations of recreational use in media campaigns that denigrate certain drugs and users. In distinct contrast with those drug narratives of self-destruction, pharmaceutical drug users have been celebrated through equally targeted media campaigns in images that represent healthy, fulfilled drug users. Pharmaceutical drug narratives feature people who experience improved physical and psychological well-being due to their drug use. These narratives enjoy a relatively unexamined role in US media culture, because Americans have come to accept the authority of pharmaceutical medications as a means to health. Yet pharmaceutical drug narratives cast self-destructive recreational drug narratives into greater contrast at a time (late 1980s to 2000s) when the drug war was waged with the greatest intensity. Through this vivid dichotomy, US popular culture continues to perform a prodrug and antidrug dialogue about drugs and their roles in Americans' lives.

Where do these narrative constructs come from—and what interests do they serve? The search to answer these questions led me to think about how the representation of drug users in popular media has shaped American discourse about who uses drugs and, most importantly, why. Patterns of drug user representation during the era of the escalated drug war, from the mid-1980s to the present, engage political discourses that reach beyond drug sales or basic law enforcement. For example, the depiction of recreational drug use in popular culture news media and anti-drug campaigns covered considerable ground in this cultural war, developing from a public health concern to a matter of national security. The range of user characterizations, from self-harming to a public threat, has significant social and legal implications for users. While both antidrug and propharmaceutical narratives characterize users through the implications of their use practices, the imagined outcomes of those acts are vastly different. Drug use, these narratives tell us, offers divergent experiences and impact on others depending on both your reasons for taking drugs and the kind of drugs you choose. The predominance of images of dysfunctional drug users unable to deal with addiction, which leads to lives of crime, is offset by those of pharmaceutical users, who express effective agency in using drugs for better health and quality of life. The cultural context and social power of those narratives is worth exploring, because their ubiquity influences what Americans think about drugs and users in ways that are often unexamined. Most importantly, these narratives have been used to wage an expensive and devastating domestic war for decades.

HEARTS AND MINDS: THE CULTURAL
REPRESENTATION OF DRUG USERS

As a metaphor, the drug "war" scripts a specific cultural narrative. But what is the United States fighting for or against, exactly? How has enforcement of unsuccessful federal drug interdiction, targeting specific populations of users, endured for almost half a century? Put simply, the drug war has persisted because it has won the hearts and minds of Americans. The expression *hearts and minds* refers to a strategy to gain the consent and support of a population to wage a war against an invading army or insurgents. In the US drug war, the rhetorical approach that has been essential to the war effort was to win the hearts and minds of the American public. The key methodology in this process has been to persistently remind the public who the enemy is and the nature of its threat. Narratives that produce and recycle images of drug users in advertising, film, television, news media, and other popular forms of culture have taught American audiences about the enemy. Popular narratives have naturalized political positions about drug use expressed through criminalization and medicalization as if those ideologies are given, facilitating audience consent to particular norms about drug use. Sometimes these images are explicitly intended to instruct or deter (e.g., public service announcements or PSAs); in other contexts, their power to educate is implicit but nonetheless effective.

The rhetorical and representational strategies for winning hearts and minds over the last four decades have included humorous, banal, or hyperbolic narratives. Some images of drug use have had more cultural resonance with American audiences than others. Take an example from a drug market that is embattled, but not part of the drug war: the cigarette market. RJ Reynolds's character Joe Camel was a colossal success in winning the hearts and minds of a new generation. The cartoon figure helped shift what had become the dirty, cancer-causing image of cigarettes back to "cool," single-handedly increasing Camel's market identity among adolescent smokers from nearly zero to 32 percent.[1] Joe Camel's success in appealing to audiences expresses a key function of drug-user narratives and their contextualizing social discourses: they reinforce particular kinds of social and self-identity for drug users. The cultural knowledge produced through these characterizations acts as a kind of power, one expressed by and about those users who are identified with them. In other words, a user may identify as a smoker, but she may also be subject to the social meaning conveyed by characterizations and discourses about smokers. As smoking has become considered dangerous not just to users but also to bystanders, smokers have become "other," prohibited in many public spaces. Smoking is an effective but benign example of how social discourses about drug use practices affect users. While few people go to jail for smoking or selling cigarettes, the ability of smokers to use freely has been significantly curtailed and taxed. Such identification of specific drugs and their users as "other" has framed use of particulars drugs as a social problem. Because the drug war's discursive strategy for winning hearts and minds has been to convince the American public that it shares common enemies, recreational users and especially users of illicit drugs have become social antagonists.

Public discourses about drugs and users convey and enforce these sociopolitical positions; they establish and express the cultural norms and identifying factors to which people are all subject. Yet, one's social identity is not necessarily static or entirely binding: subjects also have agency, an ability to act.[2] For example, although a recreational marijuana user's practice may be illegal, she may reject that norm as an identifying factor and not identify as a "criminal." Subject agency is not merely a position determined by and within a discourse, but is a more dynamic political position in which subjects act within a context of cultural norms.[3] In this sense, a drug user's agency is expressed when she makes choices—whether to follow medical advice, to follow public health dictates to "just say no," or to take illicit or diverted pharmaceutical drugs. Different public drug discourses about users, such as those associated with licit versus illicit drug use, affect user agency and subjectivity in very real ways. For example, a white, suburban, middle-class prescription opiate abuser might be perceived differently by law-enforcement and health-care professionals than a white, urban, unemployed heroin abuser. Both users may have made similar decisions about using (agency), but their subjectivities might affect how an outsider perceives each user's agency or ability to make decisions.[4] The ideological partition between the drugs and users that Americans criminalize and those that they endorse amplifies many related social issues: from legal, medical, and economic inequities to the challenge of understanding that most drug users enact choice and control in their use practices. Subsequent chapters will focus on how defining drug use as either a medical necessity or an addiction has affected users across social services, criminal justice priorities, law enforcement practices, health care, and individual user experience. Understanding not just the detrimental social effects of criminalization or medicalization, but how these discourses constrain individual user agency, is critical to fully grasping the social impact of US drug politics and their narratives.

Popular narratives concentrate the symbolic power of drug consumption through a couple of extreme characterizations. There is the comically disastrous user whose episodic experimentation goes awry, such as *Taxi*'s Reverend Jim identifying cocaine as the secret ingredient in Latka's grandmother's cookie recipe, or Carlton's accidental consumption of speed in *Fresh Prince of Bel-Air*.[5] Narratively, these indiscretions gently confirm the logic of illicit drug prohibition. More frequently, however, drug narratives feature the other type: the uncontrollable and self-destructive extreme user like Bubbles, whose painful struggle with heroin addiction is threaded throughout *The Wire*. US and worldwide data show that the vast majority of users of psychoactive substances do not experience drug abuse or addiction, yet the majority of user characterizations in popular culture and media represent those extremes. (See chapter 3, figs. 3.1 and 3.2.) It is hard to overestimate the function of US media culture in forming and circulating persistent ideas about drugs and users, ideas that Americans share and reproduce. Imagine that you know nothing about the effects of alcohol. You have never known anyone who drinks or even witnessed others drinking, and you have not sampled alcoholic beverages yourself. For the first few decades of your life, you were exposed to drinkers only in television and film, in magazine ads, and through school programs. The users you have seen are severe alcoholics like *Mad Men*'s Don Draper, Tommy Gavin in *Rescue Me*, or Lucille Bluth in *Arrested Development*. If these alcohol abusers were the only examples you had of drinking, you would be likely to draw very specific conclusions about alcohol as a dangerous drug that leads to addiction. Similarly, media and popular culture focus almost exclusively on extreme representations of illicit or recreational drug use in narratives that eclipse individual agency. An illicit drug user's inability to express self-control leads us to believe that any drug use threatens individual agency and social engagement. Yet such stories frequently fit neither the self-reported experience of users themselves (including some addicts), nor the outcomes of clinical research focused on user agency.[6]

A counterpart to narratives of drug users with a distinct lack of individual agency is the cultural representation of a type of user who expresses agency that poses a serious social threat. US news media have repeatedly perpetuated grossly misleading stories about drugs and users as constituting an acute social danger. The transference of anxiety about crime, poverty, unemployment, and mental health issues onto drug users is not new; the fantastical view of drug use as the cause of these social ills goes all the way back to temperance ideology.[7] Many drugs have been featured in a pattern of "false-alarm" drug panics over the last century: alcohol, opium, cocaine, marijuana, LSD, PCP, crack, Ecstasy, methamphetamine, and bath salts. The fabricated claims of these anxious, often racist or xenophobic news stories share common elements. Sociologists Erich Goode and Nachman Ben-Yehuda write that panic narratives focus on a drug's addicting properties, its invasion into all communities, and a spike in abuse and overdose deaths. More importantly, through these drug-scare narratives a specific version of use comes to be representative for all use of that drug—as if there is a "paradigmatic experience."[8] Whether real or not, these imagined or actual worst-case episodes are retold repeatedly until Americans believe them to be the sole result of using that drug. They become archetypal narratives, standing in for many potential experiences with a particular substance.

This influence of news media and popular culture in directing viewer attention to particular issues is powerful. Stephen Siff, a historian of journalism, argues that this influence is based on two key dynamics. First, media have a greater power of persuasion when the topic is one with which audiences have no direct experience. Second, because news agencies often follow other outlets' work when generating story material, some topics persist, regardless of the issue's accuracy or prevalence.[9] These dynamics are exemplified in a drug panic like the Strawberry Quick methamphetamine hoax of 2007. A web search for "Strawberry Quick" meth yields dozens of stories about the bogus drug, including images of what are allegedly hot-pink meth crystals. This story erupted nationwide after the sheriff's department in Carson City, Nevada reported that they had seized this new substance. Major news outlets, like CBS, reported that police in other states had also found this new designer meth "that uses powdered drink mix to give the drug a pink coloring," suggesting that the sweetness of the drink mix masked the harsh taste of meth.[10] Months later, to check the media frenzy, the Partnership for a Drug Free America, the nonprofit antidrug agency that has created its own wildly misleading media narratives, took the unusual step of announcing that no such drug exists.[11] Such largely unchecked repetition of sensational misinformation explains why some drugs have an outsized public profile compared to their actual use or impact. While crack and methamphetamine have never been widely "popular," in that they have by far the smallest user base and addiction statistics compared to other illicit drugs, they have been consistently characterized as the most addictive, menacing drugs, and they are disproportionately featured in media.[12] The crack baby "epidemic" of the

1980s became one such self-fulfilling, paradigmatic media narrative. Journalists and others perpetuated the myth for years before thirty physicians publically challenged the term's legitimacy and insisted that it be eradicated.[13] This cultural tendency toward overwrought characterizations and misinformation presents a major reason to question what Americans think they know about drugs and users.

Return, for a moment, to your image of a drug user. Where did you get that image? If you grew up with these narratives, as I did, it can be difficult to think about psychoactive substances and their users outside the context of a cultural environment saturated with ideological drug discourses. While it is important to distinguish between popular culture's depictions and the actual cultural practices of drug users, it seems that American culture rarely does. Search "drug user" on the web and the images that come up from advertising, film, television, and news media will be nearly homogenous in their negative focus on illicit users: low-income, minority addicts, often with an overdose storyline.[14] Departures from the overdose storyline often employ familiar humorous or self-destructive stereotypes, which have come to be the norm for depicted drug use, and which obscure the range of possibilities and realities of altered consciousness as experienced by users of various drugs. That absence of user experience in contemporary US media and popular culture has a particular history and context, and has had a significant impact on Americans' lives and social policy.

THE DRUG WAR HAS BEEN TELEVISED: USERS IN PSAS

Although drug use has been a mainstay of American popular culture, antidrug public service announcements (PSAs) that characterize drug use in increasingly extreme narratives have become a major source of cultural production about drugs and users. During the Reagan administration's drug war, PSAs came in two styles: straight talk and scared straight. Straight talk ads educated audiences about the general consequences of drug use, encouraging adults to talk to kids about drugs. In one example, a father confronts his teenage son with a box of drugs and paraphernalia, demanding to know where he learned about them. The teenager's anguished reply suggests the dangers of hypocrisy as well as drug use: "From you, alright? I learned it by watching you!"[15] The implications were clear: using drugs is a bad idea no matter what your age. The second kind of PSA, with frightening narratives about the outcomes of drug use, began a trend of vivid tactics that would come to dominate antidrug advertising for the next three decades. The year

1988's riveting "Cocaine Rat" television spot, for example, featured a horror-movie-style soundtrack with a stark bass note striking repeatedly beneath high-pitched screeching and wildcat snarls. The dark visual was a frenetic jump-cut of a rat in close-up, frantically eating and eating until it writhes in death throes. A baritone voiceover intoned: "Only one drug is so addictive that nine out of ten laboratory rats will use it. And use it. And use it. Until dead. It's called cocaine. And it can do the same thing to you." As an intended surrogate for a human cocaine user's experience, the rat's suffering and death was compelling and horrific. The final image of the rat dead on its side called to mind extermination, with rats—and by extension, cocaine addicts—as dispensable vermin. (See figs. 1.1a and 1.1b.) While the ad seemed to feature research data, Bruce Alexander's extensive Rat Park experiments had famously demonstrated in 1981 that, if given other things to do, rats would not consume cocaine to death.[16] Regardless of its accuracy, the PSA effectively presented a compelling narrative about cocaine use as a death wish.

The anti-drug PSAs were part of a bolder drug war in the late 1980s, characterized by a highly visible national strategy. A new federal agency situated in the White House, the Office of National Drug Control Policy (ONDCP), was empowered with a mandate and the substantial means to fulfill it. The ONDCP solicited and managed media campaigns created by industry professionals. "Cocaine Rat" and other PSAs were developed by advertising and marketing professionals who worked pro bono as the nonprofit Partnership for a Drug Free America (PDFA). Its award-winning talent drove the messaging of the first decades of this renewed antidrug movement. In its first four years, the PDFA boasted $1 million a day in donated industry time and ad space. The organization did not just contribute advertising content; among its aims was to influence the news media to make drug-related deaths or diseases, especially among certain groups, more prominent in its reporting.[17] Flooding audiences with antidrug-oriented popular culture and news media was a bipartisan strategy in the 1986 election year. Over three hundred members of the House of Representatives called on the three networks and CNN to offer full coverage of this unprecedented antidrug public service campaign.[18]

Drug war messaging escalated in the late 1990s and 2000s, when drug warriors ratcheted up the effort, saturating audiences with campaigns featuring far more confrontational content across print, radio, and television, plus embedded content on popular television programs. The National Youth Anti-Drug Media Campaign outlined a five-year, national media blitz to reduce and prevent drug use among preteens and teens through $1 billion appropriated for advertising. The campaign was a major feature of the Office

FIGURE 1.1A. Still image from "Cocaine Rat" PSA, Partnership for a Drug Free America, 1988.

FIGURE 1.1B. Still image from "Cocaine Rat" PSA, Partnership for a Drug Free America, 1988.

of National Drug Control Policy Reauthorization of 1998. Although this campaign bought a great deal of prime airtime, the ONDCP also engaged television producers, inserting antidrug content in scripts for programs such as *ER*; *Beverley Hills, 90210*; *Chicago Hope*; and *The Wayans Bros.*[19] The ONDCP also disseminated prepackaged "video news releases" that featured antidrug messages presented as actual news reportage, a practice for which it was later censured by Congress.[20] The prominence of the antidrug media effort became a hallmark of the era: in 2000, President Clinton awarded the Presidential Medal of Freedom to PDFA Director Jim Burke for his organization's collaboration in the antidrug effort.

The narrative evolution of the drug user over this period, from a misguided user to a far more malevolent threat, crystallized in thirty seconds of the most watched television event in America: the 2002 Super Bowl. Just months after the September 11 attacks, the ONDCP used the halftime gallery to launch a $10 million, six-month-long national campaign directly linking casual drug use with international acts of terrorism. While edgy, unconventional Super Bowl ads had been a trend since Apple's Orwellian Macintosh commercial in 1984, the "Drugs and Terror" ads stood out even in a highly competitive, widely viewed advertising gallery.[21] The ONDCP ads featured a series of fresh-faced, thirteen-to-sixteen-year-old kids in close-up, each casually relaying his or her involvement with terrorism. One freckle-faced boy intoned: "I killed grandmas. I killed daughters. I killed firemen. I killed policemen. Technically, I didn't kill these people. I just kind of helped. Where do terrorists get their money? If you buy drugs, some of it may come from you."[22] The numbing litany of "I killed" in the television spot was softened in subsequent print ads featuring teenagers recounting benign activities, such as playing tennis or washing the car, alongside terroristic acts. "Yesterday afternoon I did my laundry, went for a run, and helped torture someone's dad." In the example in figure 1.2, the young man's expression is unyielding; his catalog of mundane first-world activities, delivered with disregard bordering on arrogance, emphasizes the violence that punctuates his list. The intensity with which the campaign's young "users" asserted "My life, my body. It's not like I was hurting anybody else" merely five months after the September 11 attacks was a distinct provocation. It played on both the ordinariness of teenage rebellion and national outrage about domestic terrorism. It also asked and answered the question: whose lives are affected by one user's insistence on getting high?

Drug use as terror carried a powerful charge in post–September 11 America: to be a drug user was to be an enemy of the state. Another PSA made a

FIGURE 1.2. "Laundry," Office of National Drug Control Policy, *Newsweek*, May 13, 2002.

more immediate connection between drugs and terrorism by showing the preparations for a terrorist bombing in a US city through a bumpy, hand-held, homemade video. "AK-47" shows the necessary gear being acquired with a price for each the item: fake ID $3000, safe house $7200, computers $1200, box cutters $2, explosives $1200, phones $100, cars $300, AK-47

$250, etc. The images of items and costs speed up impossibly fast, showing the viewpoint of someone inside a car driving on a freeway, the sound of acceleration loudly emphasizing the anticipated terrorist act. The title card, "Where do terrorists get their money?" is intercut with a close-up of bombs in the trunk, and the next title card reads: "If you buy drugs, some of it might come from you."[23] The "Drugs and Terror" campaign targeted a fearful American audience with inflammatory drug war rhetoric that matched the sense of national vulnerability and crisis. The active and imminent plot in "AK-47" is explicitly set in an American city. By setting the individual right to use drugs in conflict with the nation's fight against terrorism, the PSAs went farther than sensationalism or vilifying users. They directly pitted individual drug user agency against national security, claiming that people who asserted their right to use drugs were no different from the terrorists who endangered America.[24] Within the narrative logic of the "Drugs and Terror" ad campaign, drug use became an act of treason.

This barrage of ads ran on at least eight networks or cable channels, including NBC, ABC, and ESPN, with print ads in nearly three hundred newspapers from February through June 2002.[25] The campaign was the centerpiece of the ONDCP's strategy to meet President Bush's bold goal to reduce youth drug use by 10 percent over 2 years, and by 25 percent over 5 years.[26] The drug campaign was not directly part of antiterror policy, but the administration effectively drew the connection. At a national narcoterrorism conference in December 2001, President Bush linked international terrorism, the drug trade, and individual users: "It's so important for Americans to know that the traffic in drugs finances the work of terror, sustaining terrorists, that terrorists use drug profits to fund their cells to commit acts of murder. If you quit drugs, you join the fight against terror in America." Drug use became a proxy for the nation's broader fight: "Either you're with us, or you are with the terrorists."[27]

The "Drugs and Terror" campaign was controversial. In response to protest about the campaign's hyperbole, John Walters, the Director of the ONDCP, soft peddled this tactic: "There's a heightened awareness since September 11 that there are real enemies and harms that can be brought home. And we were careful to check all the facts."[28] This argument, which was not forthcoming with data to substantiate the alleged "facts," seemed backwards to some of the media campaign's critics, who claimed that the United States's retaliation against terrorism in Afghanistan had actually bolstered an economy of drug production and trafficking, because the Taliban's flight resulted in a significant resurgence of poppy farming.[29] Whether the

ONDCP "Drugs and Terror" campaign addressed any actual geopolitical context, its exaggerated rhetoric invoked the violence of drug production and trafficking to tap into the anger and intolerance of a freshly roused American nationalism. Playing up casual, illicit drug use as an act analogous to torture and terroristic acts of war, the television and print advertisements vilified and oversimplified drug use. The campaign also effectively shifted antidrug discourse by defining a user's choice or her agency as an act of terrorism. By tying the individual's use of illegal drugs to homeland security, drug users became the new terrorists. This narrative of national security was ironic, given the influence of the US government's global drug-war policies in inflaming narcoterrorism in drug-producing Latin American countries like Colombia, Bolivia, and Mexico.

These US media campaigns intensified the perception of drug use as a primary public threat by characterizing the drug user as an agent who endangered the nation. No such threat materialized, and Americans have continued to use illicit drugs at the same rates. One might conclude that such warnings about the individual effects or social impact of illicit drug use have not been successful deterrents—a conclusion that national studies on antidrug advertising confirm.[30] A Rand Corporation report on policy and antidrug media noted: "Everybody loves prevention; if only it worked better."[31] PSAs and other antidrug education efforts have proven to be ineffective in changing behavior. After decades of spending billions of tax dollars on media campaigns—$2 billion for youth media antidrug advertising alone between 1998 and 2002—the ONDCP cancelled its own $8 million longitudinal study of the efficacy of the ads when early results of the study confirmed their failure.[32] Although the national antidrug strategy has failed to meet its goals, antidrug PSAs continue. The PDFA, now rebranded as the Partnership for Drug-Free Kids, has gone through campaigns targeting parents ("Parents: the Anti-Drug"), exhorting youth to be "Above the Influence," and its most recent, reminding Americans about being vigilant about the drugs in their homes, the "Medicine Abuse Project."

While PSAs have not been shown to change drug-use practices, they do effectively mischaracterize drug users. As the ONDCP and PDFA have toned down their rhetoric in the last decade, other drug-warrior groups have stepped into the vacuum. Perhaps the most visible producer of antidrug media content in the last decade, The Meth Project (TMP), inundated Montana's and now seven other states' airwaves, print media, and billboards with harrowing depictions of the ravages of meth addiction.[33] Billionaire Tom Siebel, The Meth Project's creator and original financier, launched

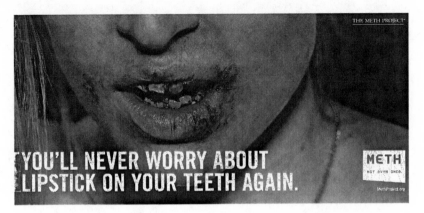

FIGURE 1.3. "Lipstick," Montana Meth Project, 2006.

a $4.5 million advertising blitz in 2006 that graphically communicated the risks of using methamphetamine. While Siebel alleges that the ads are "research based" and credible, the campaign's images perpetuate the caricatures that typify other antidrug PSAs. In their hyperbole, ads focus on narratives of desperation, such as prostituting one's teenage body for drugs: "15 bucks for sex isn't normal. But on meth it is." One ad focuses on the disfigurement of drug use, depicting the bottom half of a young woman's destroyed face, her teeth rotting and skin infected with the ironic assertion: "You'll never worry about lipstick on your teeth again." (See fig. 1.3.) This grotesque image is meant to shock and repel viewers with its association of "meth mouth"—an extreme symptom that has been commonly associated with meth use, although researchers hotly debate the accuracy of this association, pointing out that there is no empirical evidence of a causal relationship.[34] Once that correlation has been so graphically made, however, it is difficult to disassociate the supposed end from the means.

The visceral images from TMP encourage audiences to view the ravages of drug use from the perspective of an uncanny disassociation.[35] "Lipstick" focuses only on the user's destroyed mouth. Her missing eyes literalize an anonymity implied by her self-destruction. Her obscurity facilitates audience disengagement from her as a subject; she is "other." This evolution is even more extreme than the transformation of the drug user into terrorist. Sociologists Travis Linnemann and Tyler Wall write that "like spectral 'shadow people,'" meth users in the punitive social imagination appear "as images of zombie-like corporeal ruin—scarred sunken faces, blisters, and broken rotting teeth."[36] PSAs like "Lipstick" bear witness to meth's transformative power to render the user abject, described by psychoanalytic philosopher Julia Kristeva as the process by which people separate from what they are not.[37] The abject is used to draw a border between the self and what must be rejected because one cannot assimilate it into one's own experiences. Repulsion keeps viewers connected to the potential threat, in this case the lure of meth. The repudiation of the monstrous user—whether she has "meth mouth" or turns tricks in a gas station bathroom for drugs—reaffirms cultural normativity. It provokes awareness of the potential to become abject. The affirmation of an "us" delineates a "them," a horrific abjection from which the user as other might never recover. TMP's antimeth campaign reproduces images of wrecked, pathetic users for the consumption of a credulous public. Through TMP, meth has been depicted as a drug epidemic that has more in common with horror film or police procedural drama than with the social reality of methamphetamine use in the US.[38] Not surprisingly, the spectacle of drug users transforming into monstrous others is depicted in TMP's video ads by film directors such as Alejandro González Iñárritu and Darren Aronofsky, directors who are celebrated for dark, intense imagery.

The appeal to repulsion and the abject has been key to other antidrug efforts, but has taken root in antimeth media programs in ways that illustrate the imagined spectacle of methamphetamine addiction. Before and after "photos" of meth users have been promoted by police departments to illustrate the devolution of meth use. The Faces of Meth program, a photo montage created by the Multnomah County Sherriff's Office in 2004, used mug shots to demonstrate the physical changes allegedly due to methamphetamine use over time.[39] The Face2Face software program, developed by the Mendocino County Sherriff's Office in 2009, tweaks anyone's photos to create images of the supposed horrors of meth use.[40] While the Faces of Meth campaign was based on actual mug shots in the context of criminalization, the second program's entertainment value had more to do with making any person's photo momentarily monstrous than imagining oneself as a meth user. Both "Faces" campaigns engage police authority and criminalization as a framework through which to dramatize meth use in extreme, worst-case scenarios. Not surprisingly, these campaigns went viral. Journalists reporting on the Face2Face story enjoyed disfiguring their own photos early in the software's release, and later copy-cat software and Photoshop led to myriad side-by-side images of a person before and after an imagined period of meth addiction and destruction. These images still persist in K–12 education programs and on the web, despite a lack of evidence of their verity, much less that scare tactics work as a deterrent.

External reviews of TMP and other fear-based advertising have shown data that teenagers' views toward meth barely changed as a result of these PSAs.[41] Yet the immense distribution of disinformation and the denigration of users have affected how Americans imagine and talk about meth use. Extreme characterizations of users in campaigns like The Meth Project or the Face2Face photos reinforce disparaging impressions of drugs, users, and social victimization.[42] Sharing the honor for most extreme drug panic with crack cocaine, the meth scare of the last fifteen years has had as much to do with such media campaigns as it has any social crisis. While methamphetamine has been a very real blight in some communities, the proportionally small number of users in the United States suggests that antidrug propaganda has far outweighed actual meth use or abuse. Meth addicts constitute a tiny percentage (0.5 percent) of an already small percentage of all regular recreational drug users (16 percent).[43] So why has the United States endured over a decade of national media about the meth epidemic? This is an especially pertinent question because scholars of public-health campaigns repeatedly point out the lack of effectiveness of "pedagogical policing," particularly given the extraordinary amount of money that has been spent in the United States on antidrug media campaigns.[44] Despite evidence to the contrary, Americans seem committed to the notion that antidrug media and education are an important inoculation against drug use, perhaps because these are the only tactics Americans know.

Decades of grotesque, frightening, and melodramatic antidrug narratives raise other questions. Drug historian Joe Gabriel asks what effect repeated exposure to the graphic warning labels proposed for cigarettes would have on people who experience these images in their daily lives.[45] What started, ostensibly, as a public-health effort in the United States became media campaigns through which drug users have been vilified and rendered monstrous. Antidrug programs mostly teach us that drugs make users repulsive, self-destructive, and sometimes depraved. PSAs purport to show the reality and consequences of recreational drug use in instructive narratives. Seemingly, the positions represented in these ads are based in research and data. But their representation of only the most dire and statistically narrow user experiences as a totality suggests otherwise, and their representation is extremely misleading. For the most part, antidrug PSAs function as propaganda. Created at the behest of US drug-policy makers, these narratives persist in a self-fulfilling dynamic that informs US drug policy even as US drug policy creates these narratives. Users are criminalized, medicalized, and represented as subjects without agency, self-control, or the means to use in a normative or controlled practice. Trends of drug use have remained relatively static despite the continuous media presence of antidrug narratives. Yet, despite a poor return on their investment, American drug warriors show no signs of giving up this strategy—even as global reformers and policy makers argue for an end to the marginalization and stigmatization of people who use drugs.[46]

ASK YOUR DOCTOR: BETTER LIVING THROUGH CHEMISTRY

In US media and popular culture, stories about pharmaceutical drugs and their users present a very different picture: the cultural acceptance of pharmaceutical healing, self-management, and enhancement. While antidrug PSAs emphasize that recreational drug use results in addiction and self-destruction, direct-to-consumer (DTC) pharmaceutical advertisements depict a return to well-being. Most importantly, DTC ads promise control. Prescription drug use has come to be widely embraced by Americans who subscribe to the sense of agency in health-management that pharmaceutical interventions offer. What Americans consider to be "health" and the individual's role in maintaining that state have been considerably influenced by the pharmaceutical industry's impact on the treatment of various psychological disorders. Pharmaceutical drugs are welcome biotechnologies that allow users to do more than manage disease—they allow users to manage other aspects of their lives, such as attention, mood, and sleep. The emphasis on individual health choices made in collaboration with medical supervision to regulate one's body is an effective discourse of power—one to which users are subject, and, as individual agents, one in which many Americans willingly participate. Culturally, Americans support the ideology that better living through pharmaceutical chemistry brings control, comfort, and convenience to one's life.

In fact, it has become common in US television and print advertising to address what used to be Americans' most private medical concerns: depression, erectile dysfunction, or bipolar disorder. Assuring users that there is a pharmaceutical answer to every psychological or physical need, propharmaceutical DTC ads have become a major source of cultural production. The ubiquity of such narratives and pharmaceutical ads is relatively recent, the result of a federal authorization to lift the limit on DTC advertising. Prior to 1997, very few drug companies advertised directly to consumers, because the US Food and Drug Administration (FDA) required ads to include full disclosure of all side effects, which not only made for bad copy, but grossly exceeded the typical television/radio timeslot. When the FDA relaxed that regulation, it required that ads name only the major risks associated with taking a product. That change opened a floodgate of advertising: over the first four years, DTC ads increased by 40 percent, and expenditures on television ads alone nearly tripled in that same period, the era of antidrug media campaigns (1997–2001).[47] This deluge of prodrug narratives has continued, encouraging consumers to take a role in their pharmaceutical treatment. And Americans have: since 1999, at least 61 million consumers have asked about particular medications every year.[48] As pharmaceutical companies have capitalized on direct access to consumers, "Ask your doctor" has become their tagline, which epitomizes this unfettered relationship with the public. Most importantly, DTC ads have put users in the driver's seat of their drug consumption.

As has been a pharmaceutical tradition across US history, the ads of this new era of pharmaceutical marketing not only sell the promise of user agency, but do so with narratives that appeal to specific user anxieties and struggles. Although all sorts of pharmaceutical products are featured in DTC ads, the narratives for psychoactive substances like hypnotics, amphetamines, stimulants, antidepressants, and anti-anxiety drugs convey messages about everyday functionality. Ads for hypnotics appeal directly to the user's sense of lost agency. Lunesta's luminescent moth assures it will quell "your restless mind," or Ambien CR will silence the figurative rooster crowing "when morning comes in the middle of the night".[49] Takeda's popular television commercial for Rozerem, "Your Dreams Miss You," made that point with a memorable solution to work-stress sleeplessness. In the ad, an exhausted man wanders into his kitchen in the middle of the night to find his dream-friends, Abe Lincoln and a beaver, at the table. Abe welcomes him. "Hey, Sleeping Beauty! . . . we've been waiting for you. We have the chess set all ready." As the insomniac explains that he can't sleep due to work stress, Abe and the beaver tell the man they miss playing chess (presumably in his dreams). The man looks distraught and Abe replies: "It's cool. It happens to a lot of people," prompting the beaver to share the key statistic: "Absolutely, more than half of adults report experiencing some sort of insomnia at least a few nights a week." Abe tells the man, "We just want you back." The insomniac's "Thanks, guys," leads into the announcer's long litany of warnings and side effects. A title card, "Your dreams miss you" closes out the kitchen scene. (See fig. 1.4.)

The Rozerem ad plays on key contemporary cultural issues: higher stakes at work mean higher stress, the resulting insomnia, a feeling of hopelessness, and a lack of time for leisure. By taking Rozerem, the user will presumably

FIGURE 1.4. Still image from "Your Dreams Miss You" television advertisement for Rozerem, Takeda, 2006.

restore balance to his life—control over his sleep, work stress, and pleasure. While audiences had strong recall and appreciation of the ad, some pharmaceutical-industry insiders thought it was in bad taste to make light of a serious condition like chronic insomnia.[50] Most pharmaceutical ads depict the drug's "after" state of restored well-being, but this ad played on the desperation of lost control. It boldly conveyed the pharmaceutical industry's message: let us help you help yourself. The Rozerem ad typifies this narrative, which imagines a user who goes through a transformation that is the opposite of a recreational drug user's self-destruction. Through his drug use, the exhausted man will be restored from his near-abjection to a neoliberal ideal: self-regulating and able to re-engage as a focused, rested worker, for example. In ads like this one, pharmaceutical users are encouraged to reclaim that control, to exert agency over the unruly mind or body that refuses to sleep or focus at work.

Of course, Americans' confidence in pharmaceutical medications as a means to establish and sustain health is based on more than the ads themselves. Users' trust in the quality and efficacy of the drugs prescribed by their physicians resides in the medical authority associated with the physicians' expertise and the oversight of the federal regulation process. That expectation of regulation extends to the pharmaceutical industry's advertising—and has been a significant factor in the success of direct-to-consumer campaigns. Pharmaceutical users report an assumption that the quality control of DTC advertising, as well as the drugs themselves, is overseen by a patient-centered medical authority. As a result, users trust not only that prescription drugs are safe, appropriate, and necessary, but tend to believe what the ads tell them. Further, consumers assume that the federal agency that oversees drug regulation also oversees and endorses drug advertising. For example, a 1999 California survey showed that half of the respondents thought that the FDA approved all DTC ads in advance. Over a third of respondents thought that the drugs that were advertised had been deemed "completely safe," with a fifth assuming that only "extremely effective" drugs were allowed in DTC ads.[51] Yet in 2006, the Government Accountability Office (GAO) reported that the FDA, which reviews only a small fraction of DTC ads, should be doing a better job of overseeing the fifty-four thousand drug ads made each year. In 2012, Congress reauthorized the Prescription Drug User Fee Act to increase the fees added to prescription drugs in order to hire more FDA reviewers for DTC ads, though it is unclear whether the FDA reviews all DTC ads.[52]

Among its many successes, DTC advertising has significantly influenced the relationships between users and physicians. Many users subscribe to the DTC ad's invitation to assume responsibility for managing their health by requesting specific drugs of their physicians. While many consumers feel this is a positive change, feeling empowered to engage physicians about the specifics of medication and health care, physicians report mixed feelings about the trend. Almost three-quarters of primary-care physicians surveyed by the Department of Health and Human Services (DHHS) felt patients expected a prescription—and patients who asked for a medication usually received it. The Government Accountability Office estimates that about 8.5 million Americans who requested a prescription drug by name after viewing an advertisement received it. This sense of consumer agency leads to some conflict for physicians and also between physicians and patients, especially as physicians' prescribing habits are directly influenced by patient expectations. At least a quarter of physicians surveyed reported that patient interactions could become challenging when they involved requests related to DTC ads. In a survey of consumer response to DTC marketing, 40 percent of patients acknowledged that they diagnose themselves with conditions they see on television and, of those, over half receive the related drug they request. In fact, physicians admit that they prescribe medications roughly 5 percent of the time just to appease patients.[53] As pharmaceutical drug users have assumed more agency in their drug practices, DTC advertising has had significant influence on user (and doctor) behavior in ways that antidrug PSAs have not.

When DTC ads overstate their promise to restore health, their influence on users and doctors can be problematic. Just as PSAs appear to show accurate images of illicit drug users, pharmaceutical DTC ads also appear to be factual and accurate. But some pharmaceutical DTCs sell a distinctly false user narrative, listing too broad a range of potential applications and/or distracting consumers from required cautionary side effects. For example, Zoloft's famous campaign, "You just shouldn't have to feel this way anymore," focused specifically on the antidepressant's use for depression and PTSD, but also included claims about the drug's efficacy to treat symptoms of PMS, weight loss and gain, and postpartum depression, as well as its efficacy for patients suffering from depression after heart attacks. Later, the FDA found that Pfizer's research showed that Zoloft actually produced irregular heart symptoms dangerous to people with heart disease. Parent company Pfizer was issued a strict warning by the FDA about overpromising in its media campaigns.[54] While the aim of such unsubstantiated claims in DTC ads may be to capture more of an expanding but competitive market, the ever-widening circle of health complaints to be addressed means some companies are selling drugs that seem to be nearly all things for all users.

While many drugs are later found to successfully treat diseases or disorders for which they were not originally developed, it is hard for consumers to know whether any given secondary claim is legitimate or an example of the kind of deceptive mission-creep demonstrated by Pfizer or repeat offender Shire. In 2008, one of Shire's celebrity endorsers for Adderall RX, Ty Pennington, claimed that the drug *"literally changed my life*, and *gave me the confidence to achieve my goals*, like being an artist."[55] The FDA not only found no evidence to support Shire's overstatement of Adderall XR's efficacy in improving patients' confidence or diminishing their social alienation—it took issue with the ad's omission of key risk information and common adverse effects of the drug. As this example shows, often FDA regulation of DTC ads happens after the ad has aired. But sometimes the approval process itself raises questions about the appropriateness of a drug's application. Recently, Shire made headlines again with a celebrity-endorsed campaign to repurpose Vyvanse, the top-selling ADHD drug, as a binge-eating medication.[56] The FDA approved the amphetamine as a medical treatment to control binge-eating—seemingly disregarding a rich history of amphetamine abuse as a diet aid in the United States. The FDA's swift, narrow review of Vyvanse for treatment of binge-eating led to criticism, not only because the agency has repeatedly censured Shire for persistently making too-expansive claims for its drugs, but because the FDA approved Shire's claims that Vyvanse would prevent car accidents, divorce, arrests, and unemployment.[57] Because of such inconsistencies and outright fables, policy makers have questioned the role of DTC marketing, and courts are considering who is liable for issues involving drug warnings. Yet, as of 2011, the FDA was unable to directly trace deleterious effects of pharmaceutical DTC advertising, in general, on public health.[58]

DTC advertising has changed not just how Americans conceive of illness and treatment, but what they consider to need treatment. With the increase of Americans on psychoactive medications, American culture has come to expect and endorse some kinds of drug use. The commodification of mental illness through DTC marketing, psychologist Laurence Rubin argues, blurs "boundaries between discomforts of daily living and psychiatric symptomatology to the point that both can be equally and efficiently remedied through mass-marketed products (i.e., psychotropic medication).[59] Americans manage their mental and physical health through a variety of options. Yet the rise in the number of Americans on prescribed pharmaceutical psychoactive drugs, a growth that parallels deregulation of and spending on pharmaceutical DTC advertising, suggests that the pharmaceutical industry has won American hearts and minds. With over a 423 percent increase in spending on DTC ads just between 1997 and 2004 (to over $4 billion in 2004), Americans encounter DTC ads at an astonishing rate.[60] These ads have had an effect: nearly half of Americans now take at least one prescription drug medication. In 2015, the American Medical Association called for a ban on DTC advertising, citing concerns about "the negative impact of commercially-driven promotions and the role that marketing costs play in fueling escalating drug prices."[61] Should DTC ads be banned from television and print, the industry has already developed other venues: pharmaceutical companies use social media and pay bloggers to promote products directly to patient interest groups on social media.[62]

The story of pharmaceutical drug use in the United States, especially as told over the last two decades, has promised absolute user agency and health. Generations of physicians and Americans have endorsed this outcome. A user may learn through PSAs to imagine herself to be in danger of meth mouth or selling her body for sex if she uses methamphetamine, but through DTC ads she learns that she will have control of her work life if she uses a pharmaceutical amphetamine like Adderall. Or, that she will be able to control her binge eating if she uses the amphetamine Vyvanse. While there are definitely differences between a street version of an amphetamine and a pharmaceutical one, the active ingredient is the same. The stories about using that drug, however, are radically different. Those differences are ideological, and have more to do with the social politics behind product commodification, user criminalization, social class, and how people think of addiction than they have to do with the drug itself. Medical historian Jordan Goodman argues that "by stripping away the social context or by engineering it in a different frame, most of the debate on the 'drug problem' has distanced the substance from the context."[63] Interestingly, the FDA's change to marketing policy for pharmaceutical DTCs was synchronous with the 1998 laws that created extreme antidrug media campaigns. The United States seems to have intentionally created two simultaneous but distinctly different kinds of drug narratives.

Indeed, it seems that American culture is nearly blind to ways in which it has legitimized pharmaceutical drug use as opposed to illicit drug use. The fascination and even fetishization of pharmaceutical drugs in popular media and material culture reflects an ironic cultural celebration of the story of pharmaceutical health. Pills, capsules, and tablets are everywhere, especially in haute couture. In its 2007 collection, design house Chanel offered diaphanous chiffon dresses richly populated with applied pills, as well as an ornate charm bracelet dangling capsules and tablets. Damien Hirst also produced pill cufflinks, and Jeremy Scott created fabric printed with hundreds of thousands of pills and tablets for handbags and clothing. Among the cognoscenti, pills are kitsch: Betsey Johnson thought it hilariously funny to send prescription bottle invitations to her runway show in 2014.[64] The reproduction of pills and tablets as lamps, pillows, purses, candy, and other novelty items suggests that American culture has a satirical distance from and an acceptance of widespread pharmaceutical drug use. In many ways, Americans have become comfortable with celebrating pharmaceutical drug use.

DRUG USE IN POPULAR CULTURE, REDUX

The title of this chapter, "Picture a Drug User," signals my intent to trace the ways in which American culture has "pictured" drug users, including the origins and the effects of those popular narratives. The most compelling use narratives in the drug war have been visual. Drug users have been portrayed in stunningly graphic characterizations, so the majority of my analysis focuses on the ways in which the stories of drug use have been rendered in visual media. This is not to say that drugs and users are not well represented in other popular forms; they are featured abundantly in music, fiction, and visual art, among many others. Exploration of those representations would fill at least a second book. Consider, for example, American music's rich vein of drug content—most of it related to user experience. While this is not new to the era of the drug war, there is an even more telling explicitness to drug use narratives in music from the mid-1980s to the present. From the heroin punk or indie rock experience or molly-saturated (*molly* being slang for the drug Ecstasy) electronic dance music (EDM), drugs are part of the zeitgeist both for musicians and their fans. In hip-hop, for example, drugs might characterize the authenticity of an MC's experience as a user or dealer, leading to rapping about being in the distribution chain within a criminalized culture. Or, a song might simply be about the pleasures of using. Artists like Snoop Dogg have normalized and glorified use of "the chronic" (marijuana) in songs like "Let's Get Blown"; consider also Cypress Hill's "Hits from the Bong," Afroman's "Because I Got High," or Lil' Kim's "Drugs." In these songs, like The Pharcyde's "Pack the Pipe," marijuana is a means to enjoying life. Subgenres like gangsta rap focus on a romanticized urban realism, particularly the economics of inner-city drug dealing. Ice-T's "6 'N the Mornin'," Notorious B.I.G.'s "Ten Crack Commandments," or 50 Cent's "Corner Bodega" and "Ghetto Qu'ran" gave audiences a glimpse into the imagined or, in Biggie Smalls's and 50 Cent's cases, all too real street violence in the lives of "playas."[65]

While some of these narratives rehearse stereotypes, music is a popular culture form that openly represents a range of actual as well as imagined use practices. Popular music covers a complex set of relationships to various drugs; they are glorified, rejected, normalized, or accommodated. Drugs facilitate experiences: they enhance life or offer a way to understand an emotional experience. They also capture a great deal of pain and its associated drug use. Across genres, musicians speak freely about using: pleasure and partying, addiction and pain, and life maintenance. In indie, rock, metal, Americana, pop, country, and other forms, artists sing about using alcohol, marijuana, heroin, meth, crack, cocaine, MDMA, psychedelics, pharmaceuticals, and Drank (a beverage made from codeine cough syrup and soda). Some music, like neopsychedelic rock, takes its inspiration and its form from the experiences of using particular substances. Other musical forms, like EDM, have a close relationship with Ecstasy, along with psychedelics, marijuana, meth, cocaine, and alcohol as part of club use practices. While one might associate heroin, for example, with blues, rock, and indie music, it is also prevalent as content and use practice in work by artists of other forms. However, sometimes a rock anthem is just a rock anthem, a way to celebrate the very fact of using, like Queens of the Stone Age's satirical "Feel Good

Hit of the Summer" from 2000. Its lyrics, in total, consist of listing nicotine, Valium, Vicodin, marijuana, Ecstasy, alcohol, and cocaine. [66] Most of these drugs cross musical demographics freely, demonstrating that the ways in which people actually use drugs are far more multifaceted than what one sees on TV or in the movies.

Film and television have typically had less range, focusing on drug narratives that reflect the same kinds of narrow characterizations propagated by antidrug media—some of the most one-dimensional narratives American culture has about producers, users, and addiction. Through repetition of consistent narratives, television and film have helped shape a story about recreational drug use as an entirely self-destructive practice lacking rationality or agency. Stories that focus on users as a threat to the well-being of a family, community, or the nation, or those that show users as abject and destroyed, rehearse and confirm viewers' greatest fears. The prevalence of homogenous characterizations helps reinforce ideologies about particular drugs and users. Just as news media circulate stories about drugs that become paradigmatic, popular culture's representations of recreational drug users and producers are emblematic of the most frequently imagined drug users and, as such, are complicit in winning American hearts and minds in the drug war.

These stories parallel antidrug PSA messaging with narratives that depict both the violence and destruction wrought by drug production and distribution and the self-destructive impact of drugs on users. US film and television have typified these themes within a set of contexts, particularly in the era of the escalated drug war: drugs and the mob (e.g., *Goodfellas* and *King of New York*) or drugs, inner-city gangs, and the impact of urban drug economies (e.g., *New Jack City* and *Clockers*); the excesses of drug abuse (e.g., *Drugstore Cowboy* and *Less Than Zero*), and alcohol abuse (e.g., *Postcards from the Edge* and *Leaving Las Vegas*). When nonaddictive illicit drug use is represented in mainstream popular culture, it is usually somewhat normalized through humorously excessive use (e.g., the Cheech and Chong franchise, *The Big Lebowski*). Reflecting the amplification of antidrug discourse at the turn of the twenty-first century, a series of films and television programs featured extreme narratives about drug producers and users. The films *Traffic*, *Requiem for a Dream*, *Blow*, *The Salton Sea*, and *Spun* (2000–03) portray drug use through the ravages of addiction, tragedy for a user's friends and family, and lethal drug market violence. Similarly, in television programs like *The Wire* (2002–08), *Weeds* (2005–12), *Breaking Bad* (2008–13), and *Nurse Jackie* (2009–15), the violence and destruction of drug trafficking and/or drug use deleteriously impact the user, family, and community. These stories hit the nerve of American drug-war discourse in a variety of ways, but are notable in that many of them focus on white drug users and producers. While these films and television programs rehearse the same story with little that is new or compelling, it is worth examining how several of the most celebrated of them reproduce and reinforce US drug discourse about drug users, dealers, and addiction.

Steven Soderbergh and Stephen Gaghan's *Traffic*, an American revision of a British television series, represents the power dynamics of an international, illicit drug economy as a form of terrorism damaging to communities but especially to the institution of the nuclear family. Like many other drug narratives, *Traffic* depicts an insatiable desire for drugs as the root of the drug war's violence. Its three-part plot focuses on the politics of power in Mexican drug distribution, government, and law enforcement agencies, and brings that treacherous influence home to the user in the American family—in this case, the drug czar's daughter. The plot point that makes *Traffic* different from other drug narratives is that the federal official charged with waging the drug war is caught not only in an unwinnable war, but in waging it against users such as his daughter. The intimacy of this connection makes immediately apparent the irreconcilable chasm between the drug war's rhetoric and strategies and the situation of users. Drug czar Robert Wakefield discovers what most other characters—dealers, users, and American and Mexican cops and civilians—already know: that the desire for drugs is an unstoppable, deadly power for those who will exploit it. In this sense, *Traffic* leads the viewer to identify not as much with the pain of drug use and addiction, but with that pain as part of the broader disillusionment and crisis of the war zone of drug distribution. Wakefield acknowledges the blurring between a war on users and a war on the drugs themselves: "[I]f there is a war on drugs, then many of our family members are the enemy. And I don't know how you wage war on your own family."[67] In the film's oversimplified narrative arc, Wakefield is disabused of the fallacy that users are criminals. The film highlights the desire for drugs as the problem in an incisive commentary that demand is driven by hundreds of thousands of suburban white Americans. This desire empowers the supply chain that is driven and combatted by characters in the two other storylines. Unfortunately, the film fails to explore that desire. Caroline, the only main character that is a user, is silently helpless. Instantly objectified by her addiction, she is rendered other as she turns tricks for drugs, a stand-in victim for the film's simplistic drug war teleology.

Long-running television dramas *The Wire*, *Weeds*, and *Breaking Bad* kept drug narratives in US living rooms for over a decade. By engaging a more complex set of cultural dynamics that affect drug use, business, and law enforcement, David Simon's *The Wire* set itself apart from other television dramas. It reflected the drug war through its depiction of the social politics of a city in decline. For Simon, the political dynamics of an illicit drug organization mirror those of other hierarchical, dysfunctional institutions, such as the police force and city government, trade unions, public schools, and the news media. *The Wire* explored the intricacies of how all organizations, not just those of the drug trade, compromise and limit all actors. In this sense, *The Wire* is as much about Baltimore in the late 1990s and early 2000s as it is about the drug war. The drama of the Barksdale drug empire and the West Baltimore drug trade are the focus of much of the story, and many characters are involved in enforcing drug laws, distributing drugs, or struggling with addiction. In the context of Baltimore's dynamics of disenfranchisement, almost every user uses to excess, whether it is McNulty drinking or Bubbles shooting smack, and the drug trade continues unabated. Ultimately, *The Wire* continues to signal the failure not just of the drug war, but of these institutions as expressions of an American dream.

Both Jenji Kohan's *Weeds* and Vince Gilligan's *Breaking Bad* relocate drug production narratives to the middle-class suburbs, featuring white suppliers and white middle-class users in spaces that US popular culture had not yet fully associated with drug use and trade. Nancy Botwin and Walter White are absurdly unlikely drug dealers. Walter's former student and new business partner, Jesse Pinkman, even says this at the outset of *Breaking Bad*: "Some straight like you . . . he's just gonna break bad?" Walter's famous response, "I am awake," sets up the storyline: Walter, recently diagnosed with cancer, is tired of being the nice guy getting screwed over by life.[68] "Awake" seems to explain not only his willingness to risk his job, his family, and his life to cook crystal meth, but also his rise to become the incredibly brutal empire builder Heisenberg. In many ways, *Breaking Bad* (and, to a lesser extent *Weeds*) is a drug-kingpin narrative in the tradition of *Scarface* or *New Jack City* in white suburban clothing. Like Walter, Nancy enters the drug underworld because she needs immediate income—what other reason would white middle-class characters have to risk investing and trafficking in the black market? They each take to leadership and rise to the black market's challenges by addressing serious economic deficiencies and personal crises. Each transitions from a passive, ineffectual character to expressing agency in newfound control—managing the risks and rewards of lucrative drug enterprises.

Of course, involvement with a violent, unregulated market and its actors dramatically changes Walter and Nancy. The narrative arc of the kingpin, like the addict, is explicit: producing and/or distributing illicit drugs renders one monstrous. For Nancy, this transition is situational; it has more to do with the contexts in which she places herself and her family, from deep in the Mexican drug culture to jail. Walter White's transformation from a gentle chemistry teacher and family man to the ruthless killer and mastermind Heisenberg demonstrates a far more significant internalization of his new agency, one that comes at a terrible cost. When his wife says: "You're not some hardened criminal, Walt," his reply chillingly illustrates the extent of his transformation: "Who are you talking to right now? Who is it you think you see? . . . I am not in danger. I *am* the danger. A guy opens his door and gets shot and you think that's me? No. I am the one who knocks."[69] While Nancy survives loss and jail to achieve a lonely financial success, Walter's solitary death from a firefight fits the violent ending of the kingpin narrative even as it exacts the control Heisenberg prized.

The storyline about users most central to film and television is self-destroying addiction. The monstrous desire that drives drug use, imagined as monstrous addiction, forms the nucleus of *Requiem for a Dream*, Darren Aronofsky's version of Hughbert Selby Jr.'s novel.[70] The film's portrayal of drug use epitomizes addiction narratives: once a character slips impulsively into addiction, her/his original motivations for using are overwhelmed by an unstoppable desire. While addiction can proceed this way, its cinematic representation is often far more immediate and utterly out of control. *Requiem for a Dream* offers an unflinching portrayal of addiction as the result of pursuing one's dreams. The film goes deep into the depiction of the subjectivity of addiction, revealing that the heroin or amphetamine high is a proxy. It is a delusional hope that one can achieve something in life that could feel as good as the experience of being high (financial success, fame), an optimism that quickly turns on users. Both Sara Goldfarb and her son, Harry, become addicted at the same time to different drugs. Sara's empty world, populated not by her son but by infomercials, leads to her fantasy of slimming down and appearing in an infomercial. Her doctor prescribes amphetamines to accelerate her dieting results. Sara's sense of urgency and the speed high leads her to double and triple her dose, bringing on psychotic episodes in which she believes her house is alive and attacking her. Eventually, she is involuntarily committed to a psychiatric ward and undergoes repeated electroshock therapy. Harry, Harry's girlfriend, Marion, and Harry's friend Tyrone are regular heroin users who seek to escape the fruitless search for the next fix by earning bigger money—not just for drugs but to follow their life dreams. After immediate success on the way to financial security, the friends lose

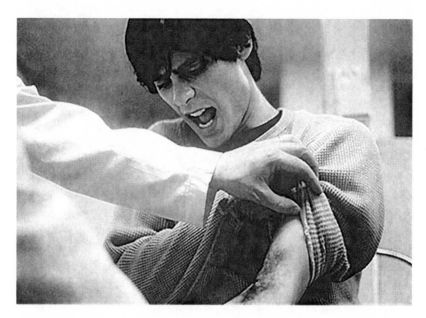

FIGURE 1.5A. Still image of Harry Goldfarb from *Requiem for a Dream*, Artisan Entertainment, 2000.

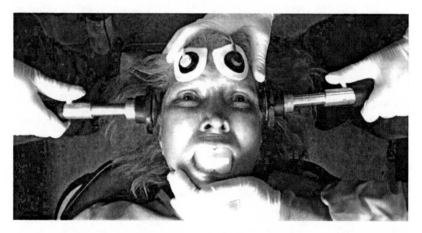

FIGURE 1.5B. Still image of Sara Goldfarb from *Requiem for a Dream*, Artisan Entertainment, 2000.

their capital and are driven apart by their need for drugs. Marion abandons her dream of designing clothes in a downward spiral of smack withdrawal, trading more and more degrading sex acts for drugs. Harry and his friend Tyrone are busted as they return from Miami with a wholesale shipment of heroin. Tyrone goes through withdrawal in the terrifying context of a racist

Southern work prison while Harry is sent to a prison hospital to have his hor-ribly gangrenous arm amputated. Each character is rendered utterly abject by seeking to feel good—and to fulfill their dreams and desire.

Aronofsky has said that the film is a monster movie in which addiction is an invisible monster in characters' minds, erasing their subjectivity.[71] Users become objectified by addiction and lack of agency, existing somewhere beyond the social order. The addiction monster is not just a threat to each character's humanity; it makes them completely other. Much like the meth PSAs, the representation of addiction in the film pathologizes users so that they are abject, no longer recognizably human.[72] The requiem is an uncanny recognition of that lost self in each character's final scene. These scenes lin-ger on Sara's visage, deranged with pain and confusion as she receives more electroconvulsive therapy, and on Harry screaming as his diseased arm is touched by a doctor prior to its amputation, stunning in comparison to the images from earlier in the film. (See fig. 1.5a and fig. 1.5b.) Addiction has rendered Sara and Harry unrecognizable and unsympathetic—victims of their monstrous desire.

Notable among the drug narratives of this era are those in which the user is not immediately rendered an addict. Television programs like Liz Brixius's *Nurse Jackie* and Sam Esmail's *Mr. Robot* explore the slippery slope of drug use as life management. In these shows, the attempt and failure to regulate one's mood, anxiety, or cognitive abilities with drugs manifest the lies that addicts tell themselves and others in addiction and, in some cases, recovery. What is most compelling about Jackie Peyton in *Nurse Jackie* and Elliot Alderson in *Mr. Robot* is the rationality and agency both characters demonstrate before they slip toward addiction. We see this in their internal monologues as each successfully manages drug use, within strict limits, and intense work lives for quite a while. Both Jackie and Elliott maintain a bubble of personal space to avoid internal pain, and try to focus outwardly by being of service in the world. Both are quite open about their emotional need for opiates. "What do normal people do when they get this sad?" Elliot asks.[73] His answer is using a strict thirty milligrams of morphine a day to numb his pain and anger—along with Suboxone to avoid withdrawal. Morphine is an essential feature of the buffer Elliott erects against the horrors of capitalism in a vapid society.

From *Nurse Jackie*'s first moments, Jackie's drug practice is framed by the history of women using pharmaceutical drugs to negotiate careers, personal lives, and social expectations, through the theme song of 1967's *Valley of the Dolls*. Like Elliot, she uses in tightly metered doses of opiates, in her case mostly OxyContin: "Sixteen grains. No more, no less. Just a little bump to

FIGURE 1.6. Still image from "Nosebleed" episode of *Nurse Jackie*, written by Paul Feig, Showtime, August 3, 2009.

get me up and running."[74] While it is stunning to see a user in scrubs snorting drugs off the ledge in the hospital bathroom, with Jackie's productivity, long hours, and laborious job, it almost makes sense.[75] (See fig. 1.6) In many ways, Jackie and Elliot are users with unusual agency: both work longs hours and excel at what they do. Elliot develops and manages code for web security, and Jackie nurses in an emergency room. With the support of drugs, both negotiate a precarious balance between pain and relief in complex, troubled lives. Only when their supply is cut off do insurmountable problems arise, with each going through a panicky withdrawal. In season one of *Mr. Robot*, Elliot comes out the other side of his morphine addiction, but loses his hold on reality. He seems to succumb to his delusions, which may have been his primary reason for self-medicating. Jackie eventually lands in rehab, but elects not to complete the program, going back to the intense regimen of her work life, instead. Overwhelmed in her first hours back to the emergency room, Jackie realizes with horror, "So, now I'm gonna feel stuff?"[76] For Elliot and Jackie, what begins as controlled drug use falls out of balance when their management strategies are compromised and their lives become too unwieldy. Although they are addicts who try (but eventually fail) to cope with their lives and emotions through drug use, Jackie and Elliott are rendered far less abject than other addicts on television and in film. Each comes back from the depths of addiction.[77]

Surprisingly, many of these shows represent the attraction and romance of drugs, as well as the downside of addiction and withdrawal. The desire to use drugs is portrayed through a stylized glorification of using before the user is rendered an addict. *Nurse Jackie* features sequences in which the viewer is lost in the light, pleasurable high with Jackie: time slows down and the world is cast in a romantic glow. In *Mr. Robot*, Elliot becomes less quirky and paranoid when high; his using allows him to shut down his inner critique of the world long enough to pass more comfortably in it. In season two, *Mr. Robot* depicts the glory of Elliot's perfect Adderall day until he takes far too much of the amphetamine. *Requiem for a Dream* presents the most stylized scenes of using as an attempt to convey the experience of using visually and aurally. The film employs a sampling technique in drug-taking montages that fetishize the ritual of getting high and seek to mimic the resulting experience. Sara's drug-taking sequences are closer to reality, most likely because she is taking drugs, amphetamines and coffee, that are both familiar to most people and easier to represent through the quick-cut editing technique. The heroin scenes fetishize desire through the ritual of getting high—a technique that is meant to remind us of its fleeting nature. We watch as Harry rips open a tiny plastic bag and heats up heroin in a spoon, followed by a microscopic view of blood cells, the filling of a syringe, drugs being ingested, the dilation of a pupil, and a sigh of satisfaction. While interesting from a filmic point of view, this depiction of heroin use is far from realistic. As the ultimate time-slowing drug, heroin is misrepresented in the mania of Aronofsky's montages, which become another form of user misinformation.

As with antidrug PSAs, these narratives seem to unflinchingly show the actual experience of addiction, with the extremity of their characterizations enhancing a sense of verity through sheer repetition. It is a familiar story. Drug and media historian Robert Stephens points out that "these visual representations shape public perceptions of addiction in meaningful ways, privileging a moralistic understanding of drug addiction that makes a complex issue visually uncomplicated by reinforcing 'common sense' ideas of moral failure and redemption."[78] Indeed, as popular texts like *Traffic*, *Nurse Jackie*, and *Requiem for a Dream* reinforce the sense that substance abuse is the path to hell's gate, they emphasize that human weakness brings on this malady. *Requiem for a Dream* interrogates the cultural story of addiction by taking its representation to extremes: the closing sound and images of the saw on Harry's gangrenous arm and Sara's wasted visage bereft of any consciousness leave us with the total devastation of addiction. But having seen the wages of addiction, what now? The narratives not only fail to offer solutions, they follow the moral logic of the drug war and US drug discourse: illegal drug use requires some kind of punishment. Sara, Harry, Jackie, Elliot, and other addicts are punished. Stephen Gaghan, screenwriter for *Traffic*, has said: "I don't think you can declare a war on a facet of human nature." Yet, the more Americans know about addiction, the more they continue to assume it is the primary outcome of recreational drug use and focus on its ravages.

Normalized drug use appears most often in television and film comedy. In these representations, no one is ever a little high or tripping just a little; users overindulge and lose control in hilarious circumstances. Here we also see pleasurable drug use. One of the few sitcoms that normalized regular drug use, David Trainer's *That '70s Show* (1998–2006), featured marijuana use as part of its retro, nostalgic experience. The notorious stoner circle, the show's device for representing the characters when high, depicts users' thoughts and conversation. The camera swings around to a close-up of each character's face, as she or he alternates between philosophical monologue, ironic stoner quips, and nonsequiturs. In a classic example, Steven Hyde starts off: "I read somewhere there are these people in India who fast, yeah. And their minds are so advanced, they can actually think themselves to death, man." Michael Kelso replies: "Oh. I wonder if I'm doing that right now. My mind's always doing things that I don't even know about." Eric Forman replies: "Man, we always think of so many brilliant things down here, but then later I can't remember any of them. I mean, they're brilliant, man!"[79] Although mostly silly (but sometimes poignant), the stoner circle featured one of the rare spaces on television where people regularly used and enjoyed drugs socially in a normalized, nondestructive context.

Matt Groening's satirical animated sitcoms, *The Simpsons* and *Futurama*, frequently expressed the ironies in our cultural antipathy toward recreational drugs. When Homer Simpson's doctor prescribes medicinal marijuana, Homer is reluctant: "But isn't marijuana, or 'dope,' illegal?" Dr. Hibbert quips: "Only for those who enjoy it." He adds: "We'll also provide you with a prescription bong." The idea that users might enjoy life through managing drug use is socially forbidden. Yet, in an episode of *Futurama*, a vending machine sells "refreshing crack" in the workplace.[80] Mike Judge and Greg Daniels's animated sitcom, *King of the Hill*, takes on the rapid rise of ADD and the powerful stimulants prescribed to children in a 1998 episode. Bobby Hill's "hyperactivity," brought on by eating several bowls of Oatmeal Cookie Crunch, to which he adds increasing doses of sugar, is diagnosed by the school nurse as ADD. Medicated on a prescription stimulant, Bobby is at first incredibly alert. The joke is that Bobby's brain is processing so fast that it gives him superhuman senses: he can hear a fly's wings or food spoiling. Sitting at the kitchen table, Bobby says: "There's some milk in the fridge that's about to go bad . . . (pause) . . . and there it goes." His older sister Luanne sighs: "I wish I had those miracle smart pills." But by that evening, Bobby has crashed: "Paying attention all day tires me out." [81] When Luanne does steal his "smart pill" and Bobby fares just as well without the highs and lows of the amphetamine, the family decides he is better off without his medication. In these comedic representations, prescribed drugs are suspect whether they are a pharmaceutical drug or medical marijuana. The commonality of this comedic treatment of drug use raises a question: why is normalized drug use represented almost entirely within comedic contexts? Another way of saying this is: why is the representation of what most drug users do, most of the time, so taboo?

Alternative representations of drug use in popular culture occur most often in literary and science fiction. As the realm of fantasy and visionary possibility, science-fiction narratives consistently feature consciousness-changing experiences that often go beyond an impact on individual consciousness. For example, in Frank Herbert's 1965 epic novel *Dune*, the drug "spice" or "mélange" is a primary commodity that prolongs life, expands consciousness, and enables the folding of space for space travel. Some contemporary narratives depict drugs that induce abilities of perception or grant access to unknown realities or dimensions. In these narratives, the user is an agent accessing higher planes of consciousness or existence. William Gibson's novel *Neuromancer* represents drugs as facilitating the user's ability to function in a virtual dimension or to avoid the pain associated with not fully inhabiting cyberspace. In other cases, that ability liberates characters, as in by Lana and Lily Wachowski's film trilogy, *The Matrix*. Neo's choice of the red pill brings about his awakening through a disruption of his neural connection to the delusion of the Matrix. Drugs can also be a weapon, as in Neal Stephenson's novel *Snow Crash*, which features an eponymous drug that functions both as a virus that infects hackers' computers in the Metaverse and a central nervous system virus in the real world.

Frequently, however, liberation or new cognitive ability is unsustainable. Neil Burger's film *Limitless* features the rapid ascent of a man who develops superhuman cognitive abilities on an unknown nootropic, NZT-48. Eddie Morra achieves a kind of "nonhigh" perfection that makes him functional in superhuman ways: "A tablet a day and what I could do with my day was limitless." [82] Yet he struggles to maintain that state without the drug. Although science fiction may imagine drugs as enhancing an individual's consciousness or cognitive ability, often the reality that is accessed is a way of avoiding a dystopic present. In this sense, drugs become a means of escape, not unlike drug use can be and often is in this world. Yet even in these narratives, the focus on the desire to feel is different from the typical addiction storyline. In US culture, pleasure in recreational use of drugs other than alcohol is generally treated with hostility or at least pity. But in some science fiction, drug use is not as black and white. While it can be about connecting with others (or the self), expressing openness about pleasure, managing the world, or seeking self-enhancement, those experiences are often multifaceted.

US popular culture and media contribute to and reinforce public drug discourses through narratives and characterizations that conceptualize drugs and user agency in dramatically different ways, depending on the substance and its legal or medical authorization. In DTC pharmaceutical advertising, the norm is a rational, controlled drug user whose life is improved with drug use. That drug narrative imagines a user who is nearly the opposite of the PSA's imagined user of recreational or illicit drugs, who is rendered monstrous and abject by her use practices, often destroying other lives as well as her own. In reproducing the extreme ideological perspectives of criminalization and medicalization, these narratives frame recreational or self-managing drug use as a social problem. Aside from moderate alcohol drinkers, American media culture seems challenged to imagine a controlled, recreational drug user who expresses intention and agency. The cultural dominance of the story of the self-destructive and socially dangerous illicit drug user central to American drug discourse had very real consequences for users when the drug war reignited in the 1980s.

VOX

Vox, voice (as in, *vox populi*: the voice of the people)

IN THESE VOX NARRATIVES, USERS OFFER EXPERIENCES THAT PUSH at the edges of cultural characterizations of "drug users." They describe a range of experiences with medical and recreational drug use for work and leisure or to manage well-being, addiction, mental illness, and life.

JIM
FEEDING MY FAMILY

In the 1970s, I was a cross-country driver working for a big trucking company. Those companies moved freight by hiring on truckers with vehicles to provide delivery. The rules were very simple: you got paid when you completed the delivery. If you had a load on your trailer and were moving, you made money. If you were at a red light, you stopped making money. Stopping to eat, sleep, or pee delayed the paycheck. Because I needed to keep moving, taking speed helped me, like other truckers, get the job done.

The only thing drivers could control was the hours we drove. There were many potential problems beyond our control: client warehouse delays for loading or unloading or winter weather that slowed travel. To make up for unavoidable lost time, we extended our workdays with speed or, in my case, a lucky introduction to Dexamyl—a time-release amphetamine with soothers for the backside. Speed was one of the tools of the trade. It was no different than my large coffee thermos or the thick leather gloves I needed for loading. Because it was an undiscussed part of the workplace, I never gave it a second thought. Those were the stakes, like the twenty-dollar buy-in at a poker game.

Over time, I learned that almost every trucker took speed, including my 67-year-old Mormon boss. On our first trip together, my boss and I drove two trucks 765 miles from Salt Lake City, Utah, to Portland, Oregon. He led the first stretch by not stopping between Salt Lake and Boise, Idaho, for six straight hours. When we did stop to fuel the trucks, we went into the truck stop for a quick cup of coffee. At the counter, he reached into his shirt pocket and pulled out two cross tops and swallowed them. I was stunned. I knew immediately what they were. He didn't say anything about it at all. It was like he was taking heart medicine. For me, it was like seeing my grandfather pop Benzedrine. Except that as a good Mormon, taking any kind of psycho-active substance was forbidden to him. And he was a very faithful Mormon family man.

In that one unspoken act, my boss made it perfectly clear that speed was the way to stay on the road and to stay on the job. That was the game: deliver the load without delay. So, you could say taking speed helped me feed my family.

MORDECAI
NORMAL

Call me the most reluctant medical cannabis patient ever. Even when it was my last option, I fought it. I was thirty-six years old, married with kids, strug-gling to control and manage a partially prolapsed colon. My doctor had tried to prescribe medical cannabis for the chronic pain. If I had listened to her and taken it six months earlier when she first recommended it, I probably would not have ended up in the hospital in full-blown medical crisis.

We had tried everything for my symptoms and pain: muscle relaxants, painkillers, and an antispasmodic that turned me into a zombie. None of it worked. I wasn't functional and I kept waking up with bleeding scratches on my face and arms due to opiate allergies. My doctor pointed out that medical cannabis has fewer side effects than any *one* of these medications I'd been taking. She argued that I needed a better management strategy or I would end up using a colostomy bag for the rest of my life.

For most people, that would have been a big enough scare to overcome any aversion to trying cannabis. But my preconceived ideas about it were shaped by the culture I grew up in. The "this is your brain on drugs" ads I watched as a kid made me believe pot would destroy all my brain cells. So I kept arguing against trying it. My doctor's observing medical student said, "Usually someone is asking for a medical card. I've never seen anyone *resist* a doctor trying to prescribe medical cannabis before." When my doctor told her it was third time we'd had this conversation, the student said to me: "It's like you're more concerned with the stigma of medical cannabis than your own health."

It was one of those slap-in-the-face moments: she was right. I was strug-gling with inadequate medicines and my condition was getting worse. I was in extreme pain, bleeding all the time, and losing entire days of work. The doctor explained that medical cannabis would relax my pelvic floor muscles, thus relieving the pressure, and that its anti-inflammatory effects would relieve the pain and inflammation that caused the bleeding. She leveled with me: "I've been your doctor now for fifteen years. I'm watching your health deteriorate, complicated by allergies to various medications. I believe that what is best for you is to get off all these other medications and to try can-nabis. If you don't like it, you can stop it."

So I left with the prescription and carried it around for almost three weeks. Although I love trying new things and taking risks, *this* scared the shit out of me. Growing up in a conservative Christian church, I had been told that cannabis would affect my core spiritualty. I was afraid it was going to somehow irreversibly change me. What if I couldn't hold down a job or became a bad father? I was also hesitant because I had my first big festival to manage at a new job. I'd been on bed rest, working from home, but had to show up in person to manage the event itself. My employment was riding on the success of the festival.

The night before the event, I was in so much pain I couldn't sleep. I watched the hours tick by, wondering how I would get through a sixteen-hour day on my feet. I got up, grabbed the rolling papers, and failed miserably at rolling my first joint. I had no experience smoking anything, so I pulled up YouTube videos on how to roll a joint. I was in incredible pain as I sifted through these stupid videos of stoned fifteen-year-olds demonstrating how to spill all your pot. Eventually, I rolled a fat, misshapen joint. It sat on the coffee table in front of me as I tried to figure out where to smoke it. Not on the porch. We have neighbors who would come out if they heard me there.

I'm not a sneaky person; I don't hide things. But there I was, walking around in the neighborhood in the wee hours, hunting for a place to smoke this joint. Standing behind a screen of bushes in a church courtyard, I dis-covered that I'm really terrible at smoking. I'd seen people smoke pot in the movies, so I tried to do what I'd seen. I took massive drags and a huge lungful of air, holding it in and coughing. I kept this up until the burn in my throat stopped me. I walked and walked, waiting for it to take effect—and felt noth-ing. So I returned home, rolled an even bigger, fatter joint, went back out to the same courtyard, and smoked it, taking huge, athletic lungfuls of cannabis.

Still, it wasn't working. I got mad at my doctor, mad that I was hiding from the cops, mad at the government that it's not legal and that I had to hide off in the dark on the street. I was distraught, still in pain. Wasting all this time trying to learn how to smoke this stupid drug, I was frustrated that it wasn't working. I gave up and went home. But the moment I walked through the door, everything looked different. It dawned on me that I was really, *really* stoned. I was also super-aware and focused, unlike when I was drunk.

I lived out every stoner stereotype I've ever seen, starting in the kitchen, where I ate a ridiculously inappropriate amount of food. Bowls of cereal. Peanut butter and jelly sandwiches. I devoured fruit and vegetables and an entire container of hummus. Then my mental state became a science project: I wanted to experience everything being stoned. I put on headphones and listened to the new Ryan Adams album. I felt like I could actually see the music, like I'd never heard music before.

By 2:30 a.m., I realized I had to get up in four hours to stage-manage fifty performers, crew members, and ushers. My not-stoned self argued with my stoned self to stop analyzing everything and to go to sleep. When I woke up and realized I was still a little high, it was strange to also feel so refreshed. I went to work and the event went off beautifully. And I felt so much better that day because I wasn't in pain. Although I was on my feet for sixteen hours, it was the first day in months that I didn't bleed.

After a week of using cannabis, it became apparent to me that I was softening around the edges in a good way. It was taking the edge off my usual compulsive behavior. It seemed like I was normalizing. I have always felt a little off because of my compulsive thinking, lying awake at night wondering if I'd turned something off or locked the door. Using cannabis was like turning off that compulsivity. Medical cannabis stabilized my feelings. I wouldn't obsess about something that someone said earlier in the day. It was such a relief to feel that I was more like other people. Ironically, using cannabis made me normal.

ELLA
TIME

Time totally controls me. Clocks, phones, and timers peep to remind me that time is passing. I cram too much into my days, and it always seems that time is in short supply. The happiest thing I can think of is a long stretch of free time.

I learned the joy of stepping out of time first when I was living and working with a community of friends in my twenties. One of my close friends was a genius of dropping time. It was the first thing he did when I met him. I was walking through the door of a party, following a friend who knew someone who knew someone. In other words, we didn't know anyone there. Juan held the door wide and welcomed us in with a big smile. He checked the wrists of everyone entering the room—an echo of the club bouncer looking for the magic stamp that said we were of age to drink. But he was looking for something else and he found it on my wrist: a watch. Juan tore a small square of masking tape from a roll and placed it gently on the face of my watch. "There, that's better," he said with a smile. *Bienvenida.*

I thought I understood his gesture, but it wasn't until later that I really got Juan's lesson. Whenever we had time off, we wandered around the city or hiked, and Juan would exult in the openness of that possibility before us. We would enjoy hashish or Ecstasy while we walked and talked. It helped us drop away from the ever-present to-do list on the other side of an afternoon away from work. That loss of the anxiety of my schedule was the first real escape from the pressures of life. It was a precious time-stopping gesture. We explored the possibilities of time and space on these excursions. Through my mental trips with Juan, I learned the most important practice of my adult life: letting go for the sake of pleasure. It wasn't a hedonistic kind of letting go, although I like that, too. He held the door open to the possibility of not being controlled by work and life pressures. Juan helped me develop the habit of stopping time to breathe in deeply and to just be. The drugs we took were necessary tools to do this, at least for me. When we hiked or hung out without those options, I would eventually worry about whatever I'd left behind. The "break" was never a real break unless I could escape the grip of time.

Life's pleasures are all around me. I love spending an afternoon in a plaza with friends, drinking wine and laughing at stories. Or the pure body high of dancing all night in a club with a great DJ and a booming sound system. But I don't *find myself* in those activities; they feel more like I'm taking a break from myself. For me the challenge is to make the time to check in with myself and to come back to a place of quiet and calm outside of the everyday world. I continue to take introspective walks with a pot brownie or some psilocybin mushrooms. A half-day spent just being, maybe hiking through nature or wandering around a museum, returns me to myself. It helps me remember that what really matters to me is timeless.

CHAPTER 2

CRIMINALIZATION

Winning the Crusade but Losing the War

> The drug war of the 1980s and 1990s was something like McCarthyism
> on steroids. . . . Almost everybody went along.
>
> —ETHAN NADELMANN, PLENARY ADDRESS,
> INTERNATIONAL DRUG POLICY REFORM CONFERENCE

THE DEEPLY PUNITIVE CRIMINALIZATION OF DRUGS AND USERS AS
it is known in the United States today developed as an ideological drug-war
narrative that crystallized through public policy in the late 1980s. Nothing
short of a cultural crusade, this movement's rhetorical and political theater
signaled the brutality of policies that have inexorably shaped how Americans think about particular drugs and users. In retrospect, the incendiary
rhetoric of that era is nearly unbelievable. The mandate to eradicate drugs
in the United States became, in practice, a mandate to eradicate certain
drug users. The consequences of the domestic war on drugs are massive and
nearly incalculable. Its infrastructure is deeply enmeshed in American social
systems—systems that continue to perpetrate significant injustices and to
inordinately affect certain populations of Americans. The imagined drug
user represented in American popular culture and media today originated
in a dogma that came straight from the White House. That user—both a fiction and a projected reality—has become reinforced through the architecture
of drug criminalization: the inequities of racial and economic profiling,
the conflicts of interest in incentivized policing, and the criminal justice
system's entrenchment of the carceral state through mandatory-minimum
and inequitable sentencing, plea bargaining, and other drug-war strategies.

US POLITICAL THEATER, 1986–1989

As part of the publicity to broaden and strengthen the drug war's reach
through the 1988 Anti-Drug Abuse Act, President and Nancy Reagan

outlined the war's domestic scale morally and militaristically. According to Nancy Reagan, "The casual user may think when he takes a line of cocaine or smokes a joint in the privacy of his nice condo, listening to his expensive stereo, that he's somehow not bothering anyone. But there is a trail of death and destruction that leads directly to his door. The casual user cannot morally escape responsibility for the action of drug traffickers and dealings. I'm saying that if you're a casual drug user you're an accomplice to murder."[1] These comments equated casual drug use with abetting murder—and not because of the potential for self-harm. For the First Lady and many of the era's drug warriors, supporting an economy by using drugs meant users were directly responsible for the violent crimes committed by suppliers to the black market. Notably, this logic did not extend to the crimes perpetuated by the US government's contemporaneous economic support of the Nicaraguan Contras, some of whom were found to be trafficking cocaine.[2]

When the Reagans officially launched their full crusade in September, they stoked the flames of the antidrug fire with speeches decrying drug use as a repudiation of "everything American." With rhetoric inspired by anticommunism, President Reagan invoked the country's divine right to freedom from drugs in a bizarre jeremiad. He called for a 50 percent reduction in drug use over three years and a "Pearl Harbor for the drug traffickers."[3] Reagan proposed measures aimed at nebulous "drug criminals," such as withholding federal funds from schools without antidrug abuse programs. The stakes of this war were imagined as absolute because, the president claimed, "drug criminals worked every day to plot a new and better way to steal our children's lives."[4] Reagan volunteered himself and his cabinet to be the first to submit to drug tests in support of his mandate to test more than a million federal employees. As the Reagans described their vision of a drug-free America, it became clear that the drug war's rhetorical and legal focus would intensify interdiction and bring the battle to users. The antidrug crusaders articulated an ideology that would become an enduring strategy, transforming the social politics of drug use in America.

As the domestic drug war became familiar to Americans, it seemed to inspire greater vigilance in those waging it. Months after being sworn in as the inaugural czar of the newly created Office of National Drug Control Policy in 1989, William Bennett established just how far he was willing to take the crusade in an exchange with a caller on *The Larry King Show*:

> Caller: My question is to Mr. Bennett. Why build prisons? Get tough like Arabia. Behead the damned drug dealers. We're just too darned soft.

William Bennett: It's actually—there's an interesting point. One of the things I think is a problem is that we are not doing enough that is morally proportional to the nature of the offense. I mean, what the caller suggests is morally plausible. Legally, it's difficult. But say . . .

Larry King: Behead?

Bennett: Yeah. Morally I don't have any problem with that.[5]

Although Bennett's national drug control strategy did not actually propose decapitation as capital punishment for drug offenders, it did focus on fear and intimidation, what he called "consequences and confrontation," in disciplining recreational users. He also intended to hold parents accountable for their children's drug offenses.[6] Later that year, the Senate came perilously close to granting various federal law enforcement agencies authorization to shoot down private planes suspected of drug running. The Senate vote was fifty-two to forty-eight, just one sign of the intensifying antidrug fervor of the era.[7]

How did public officials of the late 1980s justify such inflammatory rhetoric and the endorsement of increasingly aggressive measures to police illicit drug use and distribution? The year 1986 marked a distinct escalation in the punitive thinking about drug use and users in US politics and media, a framework that has persisted over the course of the drug war's intensification. US politicians and mainstream media acted in the social context of an antidrug panic, whipping up national anxiety into a crusade that echoed previous episodes of intolerance and xenophobia. Agitated demands for the eradication of illicit drugs like crack cocaine supplanted more tolerant social attitudes about drug use, even some decriminalization, with a neoconservative moralism. The White House found itself in what the *Los Angeles Times* called "an election-year bidding war with congressional leaders of both parties on who can capture the public confidence first when it comes to combatting drugs."[8] The exaggerations and misinformation spread rapidly by alleged experts and health officials in print and broadcast media over a few months were as alarming as their allegations about crack itself. That spring, a public theater of the absurd featured panicked warnings that crack was an epidemic like the black plague, spreading from the inner city to the suburbs and the middle class, undermining schools and industry to overtake America as the number one problem the country faced.[9] By autumn, state legislators were urged by New York City Mayor Ed Koch to impose the death penalty, and by Governor Mario Cuomo to impose a life sentence, for the sale of cocaine, heroin, or crack. Florida Representative Claude Pepper, Democrat, dryly noted that the antidrug hysteria was so elevated that a congressman could "put an amendment through to hang, draw, and quarter" drug dealers, in a political climate that would lead to drug czar Bennett's commentary about beheading drug dealers eighteen months later.[10]

Cocaine use had crested a few years before the crack panic, and was actually in decline by 1986.[11] While freebasing was not uncommon, the transformation of coke into crack made smoking the drug cheap and popular—and opened up a broader market and a new economy. Common metrics like the National Survey on Drug Use and Health (NSDUH) did not yet have a category for crack cocaine, so exaggerated declarations about the rapid surge in use were made without reference to data. Rather, the panic seemed based on crack's "downward mobility to and increased visibility in ghettos and barrios"—a social context likely to influence politicians and media producers who were anxious about young, urban users from these very demographics[12] In this same period, the sharp rise in gang activity across the United States and attendant media coverage no doubt compounded public fear of this demographic.[13] Fifteen years after the start of the drug war, and in a campaign year with little other than budget battles to inspire political discourse, the invented need to save the moral fabric of America provided rich material for both politicians and journalists. American audiences were overwhelmed with stories of the imminent danger of drugs, particularly crack. In just 9 months of 1986, there were over 260 articles about the encroaching peril of crack cocaine in 4 major daily newspapers: the *New York Times*, the *Wall Street Journal*, the *Washington Post*, and the *Los Angeles Times*, with additional substantial coverage in feature magazines like *Time*, *Life*, and *Sports Illustrated*, as well as spots on television news.[14] The readiness of the media to be recruited to join the anticocaine crusade provided the essential platform that transformed the drug war into political spectacle. A wholesale acceptance of crack as a dominant social threat and the overly simplistic way it was debated and reported framed an effective cultural discourse declaring war on individual behavioral and moral failure. This war would be won only by cleaning up the streets by throwing crack dealers and users in prison, thereby reinstating family values.

When Len Bias, a University of Maryland basketball All-American, died of a cocaine overdose in June 1986 after celebrating signing contracts with both the Boston Celtics and Reebok, there was suddenly a national face and story to the cocaine "epidemic" that appeared to demonstrate that the problem reached from the inner city into elite collegiate athletics. Congress, especially the Democrats, picked up the cause with renewed energy in the remaining pre-election months with a piece of legislation that laid the foundation for how the drug war would be waged over the next twenty-five years. Without hearings, the 1986 Anti-Drug Abuse Act re-established the mandatory minimum sentences that had been repealed by Congress in 1970, included a death penalty provision for drug lords, and withheld parole even for minor drug possession charges. In retrospect, this story presented the painful irony that Bias, an elite African American athlete and probable first-time drug user, became the defining story to focus attention on crack cocaine (which he had not used) and instigate the outsized sentencing that has disproportionately impacted African American communities. By appropriating funds for the drug war and imposing mandatory-minimum sentencing, the 1986 Anti-Drug Abuse Act intensified the detrimental effects that federal funding cuts had already inflicted on poor, urban populations. Drug offenders were sanctioned with the loss of benefits that even convicts of violent crimes retain, such as Social Security, veteran's benefits, public housing, and federal student loans. While many in Congress temporarily benefitted from appearing tough on drugs, the crack-cocaine panic helped establish laws that continue to affect the Americans who struggle the most to meet their basic needs.

Signing the law in October, President Reagan acknowledged that the drug war had broadened its scope to include drug users—whom the country would need not just to fight, but subdue and conquer. Although Reagan stated that "[t]his legislation is not intended as a means of filling our jails with drug users," the drug war's primary methods did not support the stated goal of helping users quit.[15] The 1988 law's reinstatement of mandatory prison sentences and significant broadening of law enforcement authority and resources made it clear that the drug war's most effective way to reach out to a drug user was to throw her or him in prison for a very long time. As the government aligned agencies, filled a war chest, and identified more enemies to fight in a manufactured crisis, public attention for the cause began to wane. After three years, public concern about a crack epidemic seemed to reach a saturation point in the marketplace of social problems. The crack panic marked the peak from which stated public concern about drug use started to fall at the commencement of a comprehensive, sustained domestic drug war. By September of 1989, polls showed public apprehension about illicit drugs at a high of 64 percent, falling to 34 percent a couple of months later and bottoming out at 8–12 percent in the next few years.[16] Some critics characterized the panic as a public-relations exercise a mere month after the passage of the 1986 Anti-Drug Abuse Act. New York Democratic Congressional representative Charles Schumer admitted that the rush to act left us with "policies . . . aimed at looking good rather than solving the problem."[17]

By the end of the decade, the public platform of the crack panic had come and gone. But the federal government's relatively unopposed expansion of legal authority had become formidable. In a pattern that would be repeated again in the late 1990s, politicians legislated drug users as a substantial social threat, a characterization reinforced by broad media attention and rigorous law enforcement activity in a specious domestic war on drug use.

FROM INTERDICTION TO WAR AS SOCIAL POLICY

Social fear about drug use and trafficking has been part of US public discourse for well over a century. Anxiety about opium use in the late 1890s evolved into a practice of profiling users that flourished during alcohol prohibition and was enhanced during the war on drugs. Legislation designed to regulate drug distribution and use originated in the early twentieth century, and was a work in progress for decades. Although the Harrison Narcotics Tax Act of 1914 set out to regulate opiates through taxation and licensure of all who trafficked in opium (from producers and distributors to importers and patent manufacturers), and the Anti-Heroin Act in 1924 prohibited that drug entirely, it took several other efforts to create the Food and Drug Administration in 1938, and to establish prison sentences for drug offenses via the Boggs Act of 1952 and the Narcotics Control Act of 1956. Yet drug interdiction and law enforcement developed a far more influential scope in the 1970s, when the Nixon administration successfully lobbied Congress for a national anti-drug policy at the state and federal level. The Comprehensive Drug Abuse Prevention and Control Act of 1970 was an omnibus reform law, combining various efforts in an authoritative system for drug oversight. It significantly changed the rules around drug manufacture, dispensing, and distribution, as well as penalties for possession or use through a ranked schedule of psychoactive drugs. President Nixon's declaration of a "war on drugs" in 1971 and his subsequent creation of the Drug Enforcement Administration through executive order in 1973 established the governmental authority, enforcement agency, and massive funding to wage a domestic war—although the scope and impact of that war would escalate dramatically over the next two decades.

In retrospect, it is difficult not to view this seminal policy through the lens of the twenty-first-century drug war. The 1970 Comprehensive Drug Abuse Prevention and Control Act set the foundation for the current exceptionally punitive drug war. It outlined the structure and enforcement guidelines for controlling psychoactive substances, established the foundation of current US drug-control policy, and invented a drug schedule that codified psychoactive substances according to levels of value and harm for purposes of controlling their distribution and possession. Title 2 of this law, the Controlled Substances Act, provided the legal basis to criminalize drug use, increased police surveillance and drug busts, and overtly targeted the countercultural left and African American users. Yet it also provided funding resources for community-based treatment, as well as addiction research. Importantly it repealed mandatory-minimum sentencing—a severe practice that would later be reinstated during the crack panic. Drug historian David Courtwright argues that the 1970 law was designed to rationalize and liberalize aspects of our drug policy, not to "operate in such an inflexible way, or serve such punitive ends. . . . [T]he severe character of the much-amended [CSA] was a concomitant of an evolving, politicized drug policy."[18] Over time, the Controlled Substances Act's policies have been revised to reflect the increasingly strident political views of drug-prohibition advocates in a dramatic expansion of the drug war. The evolution of drug interdiction policy has provided cumulative federal authority and resources to wage a cultural war that has had far-reaching sociopolitical effects over the last four decades.

When the Reagan administration escalated drug interdiction toward contemporary levels of funding and oversight, it set a course for what has become the United States's largest mobilization of domestic law-enforcement and criminal-justice resources. As a policy mandate authorized by the Anti-Drug Abuse Act of 1988, the war on drugs took on the absolute goal of "a drug-free America." It also located responsibility for waging an aggressive war on drugs in a newly formed agency responsible for the oversight of all aspects of drug control strategy: the Office of National Drug Control Policy (ONDCP), with a director referred to as a "czar" (elevated to a cabinet position under Presidents Bill Clinton and George H. W. Bush). More importantly, the law authorized the ONDCP "to set priorities, implement a national strategy, and certify Federal drug-control budgets . . . to seek to reduce . . . the number of users, and decreas[e] drug availability."[19] Full control over budgeting, strategy, and command of a multi-agency drug war came under the aegis of the drug czar. Working with the military, as well as intelligence, federal, and state and local law enforcement agencies, the ONDCP put combat troops in the air and on the ground. Search and seizure of drug-dealer and drug-user property was further streamlined to bypass court hearings, and became an unofficial source of revenue. The deputizing of national forestry officials and other remote agents allowed for access to marijuana farmers, and enhanced coordination at the federal and local levels led to ongoing on-the-ground raids of users and dealers in rural as well as urban areas. Penalties were amplified: a life sentence for a third federal drug offense, plus the death penalty, was finally instituted at the federal level for drug felons who killed someone (either accidentally or deliberately). By the late 1980s, the federal government had the authority, funding, and manpower to wage a full-scale domestic war, and it did so, often with extraordinary force, in places like New York City and rural Northern California, but also in cities like Buffalo, Tucson, and Kansas City. Forty of the nation's forty-three largest cities saw significant growth in drug arrests from 1980 to 2003, of which six saw more than a 500 percent increase during that period.[20]

The development of anti-drug legislation over the three decades after the Controlled Substances Act significantly refined the punishment of users as the locus of the social drug problem. The 1988 Anti-Drug Abuse Act, in name and in content, raised the profile of and penalty for drug use and abuse, and included sanctions designed to increase pressure on drug users. Implemented by newly elected President George H. Bush in 1989, the law included the explicit strategy of enforcing user accountability. All Americans were encouraged to "make it clear to [users] that using drugs will lead inevitably to a range of civil and criminal penalties, from loss of professional license to court-ordered drug treatment, as well as social sanctions from family, school, and community."[21] The breadth of this law and the expectation that the war on drugs would become enmeshed in all aspects of American life shaped what anthropologist and legal scholar William Garriott calls the broader sphere of "narcopolitics." Among the various dynamics included in that sphere of power: "the election of officials, the administration of justice, the practice of law enforcement, the shaping of legal consciousness, the process of law making and the formation of public policy (both foreign and domestic), the allocation of social services, the use of military force, the interpretation of law, and the behavior of the judiciary."[22] The influence of narcopolitics on the functions of US governance and social services has embedded sanctions and punitive treatment of users across public life. With the normalization of the drug war's logic, the criminalization of users has become not just acceptable but the purpose of the drug war across federal, state, and local governance functions. The outcomes of war as social policy have devastated and decimated particular US communities, especially African American communities, and radically reshaped law enforcement and criminal justice, entrenching social control—as opposed to social welfare— as the logic behind public drug policy.[23]

After the tough-on-crime electioneering of the 1988 presidential campaign, which resulted in more raids and increased arrests and prosecution, the drug war saw a second major era of reinforcement and growth ten years later. The big business of the anti-drug effort led to laws that significantly expanded the ONDCP's scope. While the 1988 Anti-Drug Abuse Act increased the budget by 40 percent to about $6.4 billion, over the next decade the ONDCP budget increased almost threefold to $18 billion. Citing "the drug crisis facing the United States [as] a top national security threat," the 1998 ONDCP Reauthorization Act required that the office develop a *long-term* national strategy for combating illegal drug use and distribution.[24] A decade after calling for a drug-free America, the ONDCP found that the war on drugs would not be won but, rather, had become an unending crusade tied to many other US interests. It became a mainstay and revenue source in state and federal law enforcement, a key issue in foreign policy and, seemingly, an eternal source of crime.

The perpetual nature of US drug interdiction and its attendant narco-politics has, over time, rendered the concept of a domestic war virtually routine. But waging a domestic war to enforce policy is an unusual form of governance. While the "war on drugs" may, in part, function as a rhetorical flourish to signify a tough stance on a social issue (as in the "war on poverty"), it has also employed the kind of conflict, aggressive rules of engagement, and uncompromising objectives that typify actual warfare. Most importantly, the declaration of war authorized the identification and engagement of an enemy. Through increasingly punitive and well-funded prohibition campaigns, presidents, Congress, and government agencies have proclaimed and enforced policies to eradicate not just the presence of illegal drugs but, in the face of continued use, to eliminate users, as well. "War," as it has been waged in domestic drug interdiction, justifies severe sanctions. David Simon, journalist and television director, articulated the latitude implied in this act: "Once you're at war, you have an enemy. Once you have an enemy, you can do what you want."[25] The drug war has progressed from articulating drug use as a choice to specifically identifying users with terrorism—the most politically treacherous depiction possible. In a country that has, for the last decade, also been engaged in a war on terrorism, that characterization puts drugs and their users on a dangerous and high profile front line.

This prominent, politically charged context for drug use contrasts with the minimal legal infraction in most drug arrests. The original mission of drug prohibition—to eradicate drug supply and demand—belies what, in practice, the drug war has most often policed. In the US criminal justice system, possession of a controlled substance is one of two main offenses; possession with intent to sell or distribute is the other. Possession serves as a proxy for the actual act of *using* the drug. The law functions as a conceit, conflating the potential for harm (drug possession) with a harmful act (drug use). This distinction is significant first because it disassociates the stated concern from what is actually policed. It raises a second issue, as well: the definition of a crime and the related justification for punishment depend on an assumed harm to another person or her property. But who, exactly, is harmed or violated when one uses a controlled substance? The answer to that question is often unarticulated and based on assumptions. In a typical drug offense, no one is identified as a victim or having been harmed. Yet the suppositions about drug use may include that a drug user somehow commits social crimes (through theft and/or using social benefits without contributing to the economic good), and that a user hurts those around her, as well as herself, physically and emotionally. Possession is also used as an indicator of the likelihood for future criminal acts.[26] Law scholar Michelle Alexander points out that drug law enforcement differs from other types of law enforcement because the activity it polices—buying and taking drugs—is not only consensual but popular.[27] In any year, more than one in ten Americans violate drug laws. Thus, typically, the people involved in obtaining and using drugs do not want to report it as a crime. Framing of drug use as an ambiguous social offense is misleading because it is a victimless crime, albeit one that the United States has prosecuted with more prejudice than any other. The assumption that drug use creates social harm has become a given. Americans have confirmed that cultural assumption obliquely, extrapolating from the harms of extreme use to conclude that all illicit drug use is damaging. As a war on users, the drug war engages a vast ground of ideological assertions and unquestioned beliefs about drugs and users, assumptions that have driven criminalization. The unexamined nature of the drug war's "enemy" continues to be America's most grave policy oversight in this endless war.

THE CONSEQUENCES OF WAR

America's forty-five-year domestic war has desensitized Americans to its methods and their consequences. The longer it continues, the more the drug war reinforces its self-fulfilling logic. Ongoing arrests and prosecutions suggest the necessity of the war's vigilance, and Americans become accustomed to those increased measures. As more offenders come through the criminal justice system, perceived need begets more funding, which puts more police power on the ground to find more perpetrators. Increased arrests and convictions appear to exemplify the extent of the problem, and

Congress allocates more funding for the drug war. This seemingly incessant cycle has not only obscured critiques and evaluations of the war's efficacy, it has masked the drug war's deleterious effects. From aggressive policing, which leads to severe sentences and long incarceration for people committing low-level drug offenses, to the lives destroyed by the violence of black-market economies and distribution, the drug war has devastated individuals, families, and their communities. It has also consumed well over $1 trillion of the nation's resources. Like every war, it has been costly by every measure. While two-thirds of Americans would like to end the prosecution of drug users, the crusade continues.[28]

To understand why, it is important to recognize that warriors have wielded the drug war as a political tool with discourse and actions that convey a fundamentalist ideology. Based on the belief that drug use and users are immoral, this fundamentalism conceptualizes users not just as individuals living outside of conservative values, but as a direct threat to social and moral stability. As a result, the primary article of faith for drug warriors in this crusade is "zero tolerance" of drug use.[29] The presumed amorality of users justifies the war's severe methods of targeting them for elimination. In many ways, the legal apparatus of the drug war is not designed to limit drug use but, rather, to dramatize zero tolerance as a doctrine. By reinforcing a cultural anxiety about the alleged need to police drugs through the numbing repetition of the arrest and prosecution of users, the drug war performs a destructive drama through which zero tolerance became a cultural norm.[30] The drug war promises to reinstate an imagined moral and social order through the battle against particular kinds of drugs and users. The ideological stakes of this social spectacle explain why, despite its lack of success in changing drug-use practices, the crusade has continued to be waged primarily on nonwhite, lower socioeconomic populations for decades.

The methods used to exact zero tolerance have significantly influenced US social institutions and agencies with detrimental, long-term consequences for all Americans. The drug war has been highly successful in establishing and developing the infrastructure and war chest needed for increased law-enforcement and criminal-justice capacity at the federal, state, county, and local levels. Aggressive funding of police agencies and grant programs for other law-enforcement bodies over the last few decades has created and filled needs at all levels of government.[31] This infrastructure and its related resources provide a strong rationale to continue to wage war: county law enforcement and criminal justice systems now depend on that antidrug economy. In addition to the economic impact, the drug war has changed the way that business is done at all levels of law enforcement and the criminal justice system, as well as affecting how convicted offenders engage with related systems such as social services and education. Among the most effective strategies designed to police and prosecute users are asset seizure, arrest, plea bargaining, mandatory-minimum sentencing, coercion to identify others, drug courts' mandated treatment, and the state surveillance of users. The institutionalization of such drug-war measures is part of what law and policy scholar Toby Seddon calls a "lexicon of force."[32] The jargon used to describe egregious drug-war practices such as no-knock warrants and mandatory-minimum sentencing disassociates these practices from their impact and intimidation. Many Americans have become inured, accepting the practices in our lexicon of force as the cost of the antidrug crusade. (See fig. 2.1.) Thus, the comprehensive and compelling nature of domestic narcopolitics has many intended and perhaps some unintended consequences that may not be recognizable as artifacts of the drug war.

One of the foundations of the drug-war economy has been incentivized policing, expressed through both the funding of drug law enforcement through funds granted for demonstrated outcomes and the seizing of civil assets for profit. With funding of law enforcement tied to effectiveness goals or quotas, arrests for drug possession provide an uncomplicated, abundant funding source. The funds that provide the economic engine of the drug war are distributed both through regular budgets and supplemental federal grants, such as earmarks in bills like the 2010 federal stimulus package, which included nearly $4 billion in additional funding for law enforcement. The competitive nature of these drug-war activity grants means law-enforcement agencies have strong incentive to demonstrate impressive drug arrest statistics and to spend more of their time in this kind of policing. For example, California's Shasta County Sheriff spent $340,000 annually on rural patrols for marijuana farms because it made the department eligible for close to $500,000 a year in federal antidrug funds—money that saved jobs and provided equipment necessary for all operations. Sheriff Tom Bosenko freely acknowledged that his department had more critical priorities, but could not function without the grant.[33] This cycle of demonstrating success to acquire necessary funding leads to practices that pursue what are widely acknowledged to be far from first-priority concerns at the street level of policing. But demonstrated activity in antidrug law enforcement fulfills grant expectations, and the grants provide for other policing needs.

Asset forfeiture, or the spoils of war, has become a substantial resource for police agencies that increase their drug arrests. The Comprehensive Crime

FIGURE 2.1. Drug surveillance notice, San Francisco, California, 2016. Photo by LisaRuth Elliot, 2016.

Control Act in 1984 transformed less-used forfeiture practices by moving control of forfeited assets from a general federal fund to specific funds in the Department of Justice and the Department of the Treasury.[34] These monies, allocated proportionally through "equitable sharing," are now returned to law-enforcement agencies for everything from purchasing equipment to paying informants or building prisons. This strong financial motive for increased antidrug law enforcement and asset forfeiture has grown as states have made deep budget cuts. The result is higher arrest rates, more home invasions, and a massive spike in property seizure over the last thirty years. Because civil-asset forfeiture law requires no due process—no charges or conviction prior to the seizing of property—the burden of proof is on the accused to disprove charges. Proving innocence in court is not only costly, it is a challenging, inverse legal process. As a result, most civil-asset seizures go uncontested. Even the property of people who are merely suspected of drug offenses can be seized. Vehicles, homes, real estate, and other major assets become police property, are auctioned off, and are returned as revenue for departments around the country. The result is a dramatic spike in forfeiture figures, from $93.7 million in 1986 to over $4.5 billion in 2014—a *4667% increase.* A lack of transparency and excessive use of this practice cuts across city, state, and federal agencies. In a recent report, the Institute of Justice assessed thirty-five states with a grade of D-plus or worse when it came to evaluating the government's demonstrated standard of proof for an asset owner's guilt.[35] The prerogative to shift the financial burden of the drug war onto offenders emboldened the state of Illinois to go even further, with court-imposed restitution and fines imposed on convicted drug offenders. Considered reimbursement for investigation, response, and other costs of enforcing drug laws, these fines tax offenders with subsidizing police activity. Illinois Governor Pat Quinn asserts that the law ensures "that those [who] commit crime pay the tab."[36] This unusual cost mandate sets a powerful precedent, assuring that part of the financial burden of the drug war is imposed on those with the least ability to oppose it.

Counterparts to militarized policing and the targeting of specific drug users include the criminal justice system's coercive strategies to control and sanction offenders: the overuse of the plea bargain in drug offenses, mandatory-minimum sentencing, drug-court-mandated treatment, state surveillance and drug testing, and the restriction of resources through the felony drug ban. The criminal justice system is stacked against defendants of drug crimes. Due to mandatory-minimum sentencing, defendants in most criminal drug cases are persuaded to plead guilty to a lesser charge to avoid more severe sentences. This pressure to plead guilty and the circumvention of a public hearing put drug defendants at a distinct disadvantage. Prosecutors often use that leverage to convict offenders of secondary crimes using drug laws, because those charges ensure a conviction, as opposed to charges for another, primary offense. Prosecutors may also choose to cite past convictions to multiply a drug defendant's sentence, or to charge a defendant with extra crimes to persuade her or him to turn witness against another defendant.[37] As some states have tried to reform drug laws to rein in excessive drug arrests, followed by outsized sentencing and incarceration, judges and prosecutors have pushed back, because they have come to rely on the ability to do business through the plea-bargain process.

In addition to shaping a substantial antidrug economy and dominating law-enforcement and criminal-justice practices, the drug war has reconstructed social space, mapping it to track and control illegal substances and their users. This geopolitics of surveillance has affected both urban and rural areas in the United States through drug-free zones (DFZ), originally designed to create a buffer around children by imposing harsh penalties for drug sales near schools. (See fig 2.2.) This designation of public space means that it can matter where one gets caught for a drug offense. Infractions in DFZs tend to incur harsher sentences, often doubling the maximum penalty for the original offense. While intended to sanction drug sales, even drug

FIGURE 2.2. Drug Free
Zone sign, Tacoma,
Washington, 2016. Photo
by Ingrid Walker.

possession in a DFZ will incur serious charges. In many states and cities, DFZs have been extended beyond schools to include parks, public housing, and public transit areas, or may even encompass the entire city.[38] Thus, while these laws were meant punish drug sales to children, DFZs have been extended such that they primarily affect interactions among adults. State by state, the geopolitics of drug laws result in widely varied penalties for drug possession and trafficking. For instance, depending on location, possessing a small quantity of marijuana, the most commonly used psychoactive illicit drug, could mean a one-hundred to five-thousand-dollar fine, and a sentence from six months to a lifetime. If a user carries a medical-marijuana card, however, she might legally possess and use a small amount of marijuana in many states. In a handful of states, she would be free to possess and use marijuana in limited quantities. The patchwork of laws and severe sanctions in particular DFZ areas results in drastically varied penalties that unduly impact users in particular areas, like urban public housing and transit zones.

The exercise of excessive police force and prosecutorial power in the pursuit of zero tolerance has been most visible in the extraordinary numbers of Americans arrested and incarcerated for low-level drug offenses. The Department of Justice reports that arrests for drug possession alone rose by 80 percent between 1990 and 2010. The increase in arrests for pos-session contrasted sharply with a 30 percent decline in arrests for drug sale or manufacture. In 2014, over 1.7 million Americans were arrested for drug violations.[39] The social concentration of drug arrests through the profiling and targeting of specific populations—especially poor African Americans, Latinos, and immigrants—has decimated entire communities. African Americans and Latinos make up 75 percent of people imprisoned for drug offenses, *although the majority of drug users and dealers are white*. In fact, while African Americans use drugs in similar proportion to whites, they are nine times more likely than whites to serve prison time for drug crimes.[40] This substantial disparity in drug arrests reflects policy and practice deci-sions, not per-population rates of drug use.[41] The overt profiling of young men of color for stop-and-frisk policing has become such a common practice that the threshold for "probable cause" has ceased to be a real measure. Buy-and-bust or sting operations that target users are common, exemplifying the police focus on arrests, versus building a more difficult case against dealers. For immigrants, drug possession—even if the person has a green card—more often than not has led to deportation. Further, the violence with which the drug war has been executed in certain communities exemplifies the mili-tarization of law enforcement in the drug war. The sharp rise in no-knock drug raids, in which armed SWAT teams burst into homes to serve warrants for drug arrests, increased by more than 1000 percent from the start of the Nixon drug war to 2001.[42] These invasive tactics have literalized the militari-zation of "war" in minority and poor communities across the United States.

The ultimate expression of the drug war's dominance, however, has been the expansion of the carceral state through a prison industry that has prof-ited from mass incarceration. Looking at prison data, one might assume that drug use has become a greater social threat. However, while conviction of drug offenders has undergone a decades-long escalation, drug-use sta-tistics remain relatively unchanged. Although the rationale for the buildup of the effort's war chest has been the eradication of illegal drug production and distribution, the war has primarily focused on low-level drug offenses by users. A snapshot of 2014 illustrates the sheer magnitude of the drug war's effects at the ground level. In 2014, the number of arrests for drug violations represented almost three times that for all violent crimes, with an incarceration rate for those crimes of more than four times the rate for all violent crimes.[43] Figure 2.3 depicts how heavily the drug war relies on drug possession to drive its arrests. Four out of five drug arrests (83.1 percent) in 2014 were for drug possession, which means that only 16.9 percent of

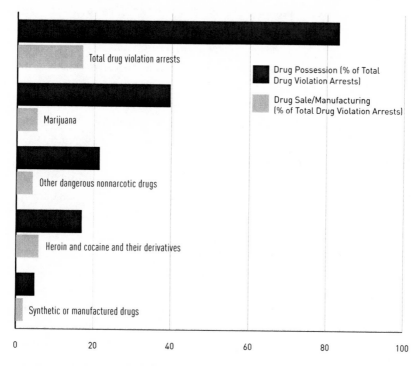

FIGURE 2.3. FBI arrests for drug violations, 2014. Data from FBI Uniform Crime Reporting, Arrest Tables, 2014.

all drug arrests were for intent to sell or manufacture illicit drugs. Of the 1.56 million total drug arrests made that year, nearly 40 percent were for marijuana possession. Overall, drug convictions have eclipsed other areas of criminal justice in stunning proportion. From 1989 to 2009, more people were incarcerated for drug offenses than for all violent crimes combined.[44] The criminal justice system clearly prosecutes low-level drug violations more successfully than other crimes. As a result, the number of drug offenders in federal prison skyrocketed by 900 percent from 1980 to 2015.[45] By 2014, drug offenders were half of the total federal prison population (50 percent of men; 59 percent of women) and 16 percent of the state prison population.[46] Judges have severely curtailed probation as a sentencing option for drug offenders. In 1980, 26 percent of drug offenders were offered probation. By 2014, that figure had dropped to just 6 percent, so that in recent years, nearly all drug offenders have been sent to prison.[47] The amount of time served by drug offenders ballooned by 153 percent between 1988 and 2012, especially compared to growth in the time served for property and violent offenders: 39 percent and 44 percent, respectively.[48] Even the data, over-whelming as they are, cannot fully convey the influence of an industry that has seen staggering growth to unprecedented levels.

The punitive effects of the criminal justice system's conviction of drug users last long after sentences have been served. Drug laws at federal and state levels restrict voting rights as well as services and benefits for those convicted of drug crimes—in effect prolonging their sentences indefinitely. Some of the people most in need of welfare support and public housing are denied access. Financial aid for college, granted even to felons convicted of violent crimes, is denied to those convicted of the most minimal drug offense. In some states, a felony drug conviction means a lifetime ban from access to food stamps. Affecting over half a million convicted drug offend-ers, these practices ensure that users (like all convicts) have few options with which to re-enter society in a functional manner post-conviction. Even efforts to reform the criminal justice system's practice of imprisoning users who suffer from substance abuse have, ironically, led to another equally coercive means of state control over drug offenders: drug court. Designed to offer defendants with drug problems treatment rather than imprisonment, drug courts mandate stringent measures. For example, most drug courts see use as abuse and mandate treatment whether or not an offender has a drug-abuse problem. Being compelled to go through a rehabilitation program if you are a controlled user who was simply caught possessing drugs is not only a waste of considerable resources, it is a distinct punishment. Other forms of drug-court-mandated treatment include: work-oriented discipline (job training, GED completion), surveillance (through regular onsite drug testing and other checks, sometimes persisting for years), and anti-drug counseling. If these sanctions are not successfully completed by, for example, finding a job, judges have the discretion to impose a more severe sentence than the offense originally warranted.

Forty-five years and over a $1 trillion later, drug criminalization has effectively instituted an opaque drug war with severe authority over many Americans' lives, but has yielded little in terms of its goals. The challenge of comprehending the effects of overzealous policing, prosecution, and incar-ceration is staggering. Spawning law enforcement and criminal justice sys-tems that have over-performed, the drug war has overcrowded prisons past a breaking point, with offenders serving unjustifiably long sentences with no legal recourse. The combination of social apathy, a relatively unchecked criminal-justice system, and a high-cost corrections industry have led to inhumane prison overpopulation. The situation is so dire that in 2011, the US

Supreme Court ordered California to reduce its prison population by almost a quarter of its entire prison population, or thirty-thousand inmates, because prison conditions violated the Eighth Amendment's ban on cruel and unusual punishment.[49] This is the inhumane but predictable consequence of decades of what has, in effect, been a war of incarceration. If nothing else, the overcrowding of prisons would be the most likely reason for scaling back the drug war's voracious appetite for prosecution and imprisonment.

Declaring a war created a funding mandate and put enormous numbers of people in prison, but it has not assured outcomes by ending or even effectively diminishing drug use. Figure 2.4 shows longitudinal trends in psychoactive drug use from 2002 to 2014 for some of the drugs most targeted by the drug war. Use percentages for heroin and methamphetamine, as well as for OxyContin and other painkillers, are nearly static across the decade, diverging less than 2 percent per drug per age group, with the exception of non-OxyContin pain relievers, a very broad category. Overall drug use remains relatively stable in every category. In 2009, NSDUH data show that 14.6 percent of the US population used illicit drugs; in 2014, it was 16.7 percent of the US population (not represented in fig. 2.4). If you look at the data for heroin, methamphetamine, OxyContin, and other pain relievers for those years, it becomes apparent that the meth epidemic was based on very small use percentages, and thus even smaller addiction percentages. (Unfortunately, the NSDUH does not offer longitudinal drug use data without breaking it out by age group, so the table reflects the NSDUH's categories. Also, crack has not been a consistent category across this time period, and thus there is not data to support its representation in this figure.) Figure 2.5 shows a breakout of all illicit drug use for 2014, showing figures that also have not deviated much over time. (See chapter 3, "Recognizing Users: Where Are All the Addicts?")

While availability may influence use figures slightly, it is clear that people continue to use what they want to use regardless of criminalization. People use drugs and, proportionally, suffer less addiction than the drug war would have Americans believe. With more Americans using drugs recreationally despite forty-five years of anti-drug efforts, the policy goal of a "drug-free America" is not only unrealizable, it seems to miss the point altogether. While billions of dollars have been spent to deter drug use, Americans continue their drug use practices.

Criminalization's silencing of users may be the most detrimental consequence of the war on drugs. Drug policies have been created and enforced with little to no input from those most affected by them. Not only has the

SUBSTANCE (AGE RANGE)	2002	2003	2004	2005	2006	2007	2008	2009	2010	2011	2012	2013	2014
Heroin (12–17)	0.2	0.1	0.2	0.1	0.1	0.1	0.2	0.1	0.1	0.2	0.1	0.1	0.1
Heroin (18–25)	0.4	0.3	0.4	0.5	0.4	0.4	0.5	0.5	0.6	0.7	0.8	0.7	0.8
Heroin (26+)	0.1	0.1	0.1	0.1	0.2	0.1	0.1	0.2	0.2	0.2	0.2	0.2	0.3
Methamphet-amine (12–17)	1	0.7	0.7	0.7	0.7	0.5	0.4	0.4	0.4	0.4	0.3	0.3	0.4
Methamphet-amine (18–25)	2	1.9	1.9	1.8	1.7	1.2	0.8	0.9	0.8	0.7	1	0.9	1
Methamphet-amine (26+)	0.5	0.5	0.6	0.5	0.6	0.4	0.3	0.4	0.3	0.4	0.4	0.4	0.4
Pain Relievers (12–17)	7.6	7.7	7.4	6.9	7.2	6.7	6.5	6.6	6.3	5.9	5.3	4.6	4.7
Pain Relievers (18–25)	11.4	12	11.9	12.4	12.5	12.2	12	12	11.1	9.8	10.1	8.8	7.8
Pain Relievers (26+)	3.1	3.3	3	3.3	3.6	3.6	3.3	3.5	3.6	3.2	3.8	3.4	3.1
OxyContin (12–17)	—	—	0.8	0.7	0.8	0.9	0.9	0.9	1	0.9	0.7	0.6	0.7
OxyContin (18–25)	—	—	1.7	1.7	1.8	1.7	1.8	2.3	2.2	1.8	1.6	1.4	1.2
OxyContin (26+)	—	—	0.2	0.3	0.3	0.3	0.3	0.4	0.5	0.4	0.4	0.4	0.3

FIGURE 2.4. Examples of drug use as percent (%) of the US population, 2002–14. Data from the NSDUH, Substance Abuse and Mental Health Services Administration, 2015.

silence perpetuated costly social policy and devastated so many lives, but it has promoted misconceptions about substance using and users that affect all Americans. It is hard to know what the actual outcomes of drug use are for various users—socially, politically, and medically—because so much of the public discourse has justified the war and its view of all drug use as criminal. Not only are users unlikely to be forthcoming about their practices in such a climate, but potentially useful information is, as a result, suppressed. For example, methamphetamine use has declined. Is that because meth production has been limited by efforts to control the sale of its constituent elements? Has the flood of readily available prescription amphetamines also affected this trend? Because those questions are not being asked, researchers have no way to know what use practices are important to people and why, or how use practices affect us individually and as a community.

With little information about drugs and users outside of pharmacological research, limited psychological research, and sociological studies restricted

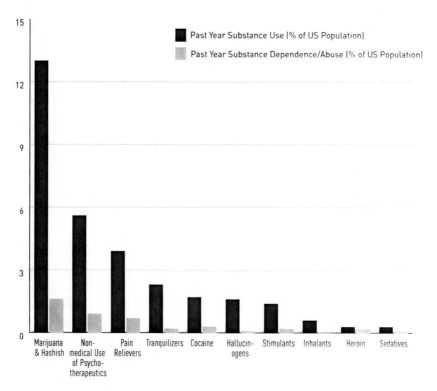

FIGURE 2.5. Illicit drug use and abuse, 2014. Data from the NSDUH, Substance Abuse and Mental Health Services Administration, 2015.

in their access to non-problematic users, the drug war has operated far and wide with virtually no assessment or informed revision. What is missing is an evidence-based review of data on the causes and effects of drug use, interdiction, harm reduction, etc. While Congress mandated the ONDCP to provide data-driven evaluation of its programs and claims, it has yet to do so, instead reporting its data to highlight political issues. In any given year, the report may highlight data about a particular drug (such as methamphetamine or OxyContin) to direct attention to a drug use issue that may be topical, culturally, but may not be statistically significant. By focusing on that substance in its executive report, the NSDUH puts emphasis on the use of that drug whether or not that added attention signals a significant change in use practices. Then, barriers to research of illicit drugs, from federal regulation to risk-adverse institutional review boards, make it unnecessarily hard to do the relevant research. Too often, how Americans understand what influences substance use has been predicated on unsubstantiated interpretations of discrete bits of scientific data. For example, the classification (scheduling) of illicit substances is formally based on potential for harm, known pharmacological effects, potential for and history of abuse, recognized medical use, and potential for risk to public health. However, the drug schedule was not the product of research and data about those criteria. Thus, the schedule's ratings for several substances that have been at the heart of the drug war, such as marijuana and LSD, seem to be the product of ignorance and, perhaps, fear about their effects. For example, marijuana, LSD, and Ecstasy (MDMA) are listed along with heroin as Schedule I—the category of the most dangerous drugs and the toughest legal penalties. Cocaine, methamphetamine, and oxycodone, however, are in Schedule II. The DEA declined to reschedule marijuana in 2016, despite its wide use and medical application. Because punishments for use, possession, and distribution of these drugs are based on this classification, recalibration based on a broader dataset about use and harm, such as the United Kingdom's revision of its drug schedules, would be helpful. The United States needs research to produce different, better, and more diverse data about drugs and their users, which is a nearly impossible task in a climate of criminalization. Drug users do not want to be public about their use, and for good reason.

THE POLITICS OF USING: REFORM EFFORTS

In contrast with the monolithic ideological hold of the drug war, various drug reform efforts have demonstrated other possibilities for thinking about drugs and their users. Throughout the drug war, the Drug Policy Alliance (DPA) has sustained efforts to reform policies such as New York's draconian Rockefeller sentencing laws, California's three-strike sentencing laws, and the federal-level disparity between crack and cocaine penalties. The DPA has also worked to effect harm-reduction policies and practices that limit the negative consequences of drug use and promote therapeutic alternatives to incarceration. These legislative and media efforts at the federal and local levels have helped establish drug use as a realistic and valid choice. The effects of this evolution are apparent in the first Global Commission on Drug Policy report, released in June 2011. It marked the fiftieth anniversary of the UN's Single Convention on Narcotic Drugs with a worldwide evaluation modeled on the 2009 Latin American Commission on Drugs and Democracy.[50] The heavily researched and coordinated report made a set of recommendations that fundamentally confront drug-control policy and practice in countries such as the United States, which have championed the drug war. Following the lead of organizations and nations that have addressed illicit drug use as a human-rights issue, the GCDP took a progressive position on drug use, policy, and interdiction in pointed criticism of drug policies worldwide. The report made a persuasive call for depoliticized, knowledgeable discourse and action to displace the ideological imperialism that has driven drug policy. Among its compelling findings was the GCDP's recommendation to reverse the "criminalization, marginalization, and stigmatization of people who use drugs but who do no harm to others," and its challenge to, rather than reinforcement of, misconceptions about drug markets, users, and addiction. Further, the GCDP acknowledged the vested interests of various groups and decision makers in maintaining a law-enforcement focus, specifically distinguishing the United States as the key player in repressive drug policy and enforcement. While the Obama administration has expressed the futility of a drug war, the United States was explicitly charged by the GCDP to reform its punitive practices and to lead such reform internationally. Unfortunately, the ONDCP's official position in terms of reducing the ideological and aggressive aspects of its policy implementation have been in conflict with its actions on the ground, which continue to pressure and raid businesses in states that have legalized marijuana sale for medical purposes, for example.

More informed debate about drug policy and drug use requires us to understand drugs and users more fully. Through the terms of the drug war, drug use is understood solely as abuse, with every user defined as an addict and/or criminal, and all illicit substances understood as substantial social threats. These are both accurate and inaccurate ways of seeing drug use in that they are but part of a larger, far more complex reality. Perhaps one of the most critical aspects of the GCDP's report is its assertion that of the estimated 250 million drug users around the world, less than 10 percent are addicts. That is a drastically different view of users than that promoted by US drug-war discourse and by medical discourse, although one supported by US data. Clearly, many users practice controlled use and are misconstrued by the systems and ideology with which the United States perceives and engages them. The GCDP maintains that "the majority of people who use drugs do not fit the stereotype of the 'amoral and pitiful addict,'" and calls for a challenge to rather than reinforcement of common misperceptions about drug markets, users, and dependence.[51]

The most effective drug-reform efforts in the United States have come on the ground level of the drug war, from people seeking to reduce the drug war's harms. Those people most tasked with waging the drug war have been among the earliest to articulate its problems and work for drug-law reform.

Law enforcement professionals and others on the front line trying to deal with the deleterious effects of a one-approach drug war have organized officially as well as unofficially, and have made ending prohibition a major cause. Law Enforcement Against Prohibition (LEAP), a nonprofit group founded by police officers, seeks to reduce the harmful consequences of the war on drugs, and to end drug prohibition through education of the public and policy makers. Legalization, from LEAP's perspective, would mean ending the monopoly that the black market has had over drugs and users through the institution of drug regulation and a controlled market. In its education campaigns, LEAP points out that prohibition actually creates many of the social issues that the drug war purports to solve. Executive director and former police officer Neill Franklin notes that a two-pronged approach—ending criminalization and reforming the medical approach to users—would result in a dramatic decline in problematic drug use. With police enforcement making low-level drug law enforcement the least of its priorities, a regulated market with better products, and less ideological and more accurate informed public drug education, the United States would develop a more reasonable health approach to drug use.[52]

Some city and county law-enforcement agencies are working on alternatives to arrest and incarceration by partnering with social services to divert substance abusers from engagement with the criminal justice system directly to other resources. These pre-arraignment programs connect nonviolent low-level drug offenders with treatment programs and other services. Seattle's Law Enforcement Assisted Diversion (LEAD) project diverts eligible individuals to services instead of arrest to reduce the impact of the criminalization system on drug users. Still in its early years, LEAD succeeded in connecting uncontrolled substance users with the support they need rather than engaging users in a pattern of criminal recidivism. An evaluation of the pilot program demonstrated that users in LEAD were 58 percent less likely than a control group that went through typical criminal justice processes to be rearrested.[53] Law-enforcement agencies in over a dozen states have developed similar programs for diversion or intervention, endeavors that have limited the effect of recidivism.[54] However, like drug court, these programs are designed for substance abusers only, and there is currently not room for all who might benefit from what the program offers. For users who are not substance abusers, but who are caught in possession of illicit or controlled drugs, these programs are not a solution. Some in the judiciary have publicly critiqued disproportionate sentencing, such as retired Supreme Court Justice John Paul Stevens and Federal Court Judge Nancy Gertner, who has become an activist to seek clemency for those sentenced by judges like her under mandatory drug laws.[55] Other kinds of harm reduction efforts also advocate to limit harm to uncontrolled drug users through efforts such as needle exchanges, the availability of drugs like the opioid antagonist naloxone to emergency responders, and advocating for safe injection and use sites with medical oversight. Generally, harm reduction targets the extreme end of the drug-use spectrum, focusing on users with substance-abuse issues. In this sense, controlled users—most users most of the time—are invisible to even those social systems focused on drug users.

While drug-legalization proponents have made progress by focusing on social-justice issues related to prohibition, other reformers have made inroads into drug law by appealing to economics. Drug prohibition, like alcohol prohibition, intensified an enormous black market with terrible consequences in the United States, and particularly in other drug-producing countries. Interdiction amplified the many hazards in the production, distribution, and use cycle of an unregulated, uncontrolled market. As a result, the illegality of drugs has inflated drug prices substantially. With more than 60 percent of US marijuana users reporting that their biggest concern when purchasing marijuana is buying it from a legal source, a primary argument for legalizing and regulating drugs would be to benefit from that market's revenue.[56] Estimates project that drug legalization would save approximately $40 billion a year on government law-enforcement costs alone.[57] Marijuana legalization in Colorado and Washington has been lucrative, generating sales that far exceeded expectations: in 2014, Colorado saw over $700 million in sales, and Washington saw nearly $145 million.[58] Both states are estimated to reach $1 billion in marijuana sales in the next few years, with one market-research agency predicting twenty times that in total annual marijuana sales by 2020.[59] With such a strong demonstrated demand for legal drug sales, regulated markets ensure state revenue while avoiding the perils of black-market commerce, such as uncontrolled dosage and content, violent enforcement, and the risks of arrest and conviction under drug laws.

Beyond tax revenue and savings in domestic law-enforcement and criminal-justice budgets, a broader argument can be made about the impact of drug legalization on the poorer countries who produce them. The drug trade most adversely affects the poor in many ways in the United States and abroad, but particularly as gangs in drug-producing countries work through systems where those exposed to the greatest violence make the least profit. Economist Allison Schrager notes that drug legalization shifts the power dynamics of production, affecting everyone (not just drug producers) in those countries. Farmers in developing countries who grow drug crops would face global competition and either grow other crops or develop a competitive advantage in the cultivation of drug crops. The legal enforceability of contracts, property rights, and labor rights, as well as tax revenues in drug production, would benefit even those unaffiliated with the trade.[60]

Other experiments demonstrate that users benefit from some kind of market regulation— even consumer rankings, readily available anonymous medical advice, and other harm-reduction measures. The short-lived online and anonymous Silk Road was, for some drug users and reformers, an unprecedented, user-forward drug marketplace. Some harm reductionists, epidemiologists, physicians, and criminologists have suggested that this model may offer a very different kind of market that both limits the violence and harms of a black market and allows for better information sharing among consumers.[61] The Silk Road was an online, user-rated market not unlike eBay, offering diversity of choice, a range of sellers, and users sharing collective knowledge of vendors and products. Many of the dangers associated with street transactions were reduced in this context. In addition to user ratings about quality and dosage that acted as a kind of quality-control system, the indirect nature of the transactions offered stronger protections for users. Most importantly, however, the Silk Road featured a volunteer harm-reduction discussion thread staffed by "Dr. X," Dr. Fernando Caudevilla, who offered information and advice to users. Dr. Caudevilla points out that deep-web marketplaces offer a particularly powerful form of harm reduction for users, because of the user-controlled system and the open channel of communication protected by the anonymity of online identities. Users were emboldened to pursue and engage specific health information about drug use when they did not have to directly face a health-care provider. Dr. Caudevilla collected data about user interactions via detailed conversations about the effects and interactions of drugs. For example, questions might be from a type-1-diabetes patient asking about MDMA's effect on blood sugar. Dr. Caudevilla was also able to interact with drug users about issues that might not be related to drug use. When a heroin user thought his pain and fevers were related to withdrawal, Dr. Caudevilla encouraged him to get tested, and the user learned he had leukemia. The ability to embed professional advice about health care and drug use was one of the Silk Road's key benefits for users.

The drug war has brought the United States to a social and economic tipping point. Addressing the calamitous effects of this domestic war requires not just radically re-imagining drug use, but rethinking and revising the vast political empire and economic engine built on this ideology. The drug war's systems will not be easily dismantled, because much power and funding is at stake. Even if Americans could imagine a future without the drug war, it is an unlikely scenario without a major revision of how and what we think about drugs and their users. Revising assumptions and beliefs about drugs and users after forty-five years of the ideological and political dominance of a particular view will require more than information and alternative per-spectives. It will require understanding how many other factors influence drug use. With more and more states legalizing medical and recreational marijuana markets, the most-used drug after alcohol and nicotine has become more available. Such reforms make it easy to imagine the United States is moving past the draconian era of the drug war. But Americans are far from escaping the influences of drug-war discourse and policy—not only in terms of issues related to the substantial infrastructure surrounding drug criminalization, but also in terms of the ways in which medicalization has shaped US perceptions of drug users. Perhaps the most essential element of an informed and evidence-based discussion of drug-control policy and drug use is the understanding that users come in many forms. There are different kinds of users with a variety of reasons for using—choosing from a universe of substances used to manage moods and experiences. Although controlled, recreational use of drugs is as much a reality and far more prevalent than addiction, most Americans would not know it. The question is why? Aside from the characterizations of popular culture and criminalization, why are the use patterns of most drug recreational users invisible in the United States? The answer has to do with the other dominant cultural drug dis-course: medicalization.

VOX

JASON
THE LITTLE ENGINE THAT COULD

I am an alcohol and drug scholar. I am also a drug-court graduate. Until quite recently, the prevailing consensus among my fellow scholars held drug courts in high esteem as an alternative to incarceration. As someone who transgressed the boundaries of intoxication and public safety, I struggle to square this academic view with what I observed on the ground. Most scholars—those without firsthand experience—speak of drug courts that stand in stark contrast to my lived experience.

Scholars are now catching up to what many drug court "graduates" and flunkies have long known: drug courts reinforce the coercive nature of the justice system. They ensnare addicts and social users alike—problematizing and criminalizing their personal choices to use intoxicants. Drug courts are also big business for municipalities, the drug treatment centers aligned with specific courts, and in many cases, the prison-industrial complex. In addition to finding new ways to coerce and punish, drug courts reaffirm the race-based and class-based biases of the criminal justice system. I am lucky to have been born white, middle class, and from a suburban district. If this were not the case, people would identify me today first and foremost as a felon instead of a nonthreatening, trustworthy, gainfully employed professor.

In my early twenties, I got drunk and I got stopped. Despite passing a sobriety field test, my Breathalyzer blow read 0.16. I was arrested in the suburb where I had grown up, and spent the evening in a small, safe cell. I spent the evening actively shaming myself, replaying those moments where I had clearly made poor decisions. I worried about both my immediate and long-term future. Would I be a felon? Should I be a felon? The moment the lights of the squad car flooded my rearview mirror remains etched in my mind's eye. Even now, the sight of police lights makes my heart rate jump in much the same way as it did that night.

The following morning—a Sunday and St. Patrick's Day—the Irish American judge was in no mood to be bothered by drunks and drug users. Rather than release me on my own recognizance per usual, the self-styled law-and-order judge had me transported to the county holding center. The holding center was a legitimate jail with a horrible record of abuse and poor sanitation. Being of some means, I was able to call my parents to bail me out. For the three other people arrested and transported with me, this was not an option. They, like others, were simply driving through the suburbs, but, because they could not make bail, they would not be treated as I would be in drug court.

My best friend was a local attorney and pointed me to the right lawyer. When my legal representation explained to his golfing buddy—the judge—that I was a young doctoral student, a local resident, and a "good" kid, my DUI charges vanished. All that was left was a parking ticket and drug court. I will always wonder, and dread, how my life might be different had I been punished with the scarlet letter of felony status. I carry the knowledge of why I escaped that punishment. Still, though, drug court was a unique form of punishment all its own.

In my relief at avoiding a felony, I made the mistake of being honest with the drug counselor in my pre-court screening interview. I admitted to regular social drinking, often drinking to get drunk, and to smoking marijuana before bed to quiet my mind. Despite being arrested for an alcohol-related charge, the counselor decided in our ten-minute discussion that I was addicted to alcohol and marijuana. This triggered forty mandated sessions of both group and individual drug and alcohol counseling. There is no doubt that I abused alcohol in these years, but I was definitely not an addict. A year without alcohol and marijuana struck me simply as an unnecessary inconvenience. But I learned to accept my diagnosis publicly. Participants that argued with counselors over whether or not they were addicted were frequently met with considerable resistance. I made peace with this by agreeing with counselors that addiction is, functionally, a broad spectrum, although we disagreed over my place on that spectrum.

For all drug-court participants, weekly attendance at town court and a calendar year of drug testing were required. Any choice to use that went beyond the scope of my original transgression was now controlled and subject to punishment. Violating these new boundaries would mean a felony offense. Despite my strict adherence to swearing off alcohol and marijuana, public urine tests left me unnerved. I could not pee on command, particularly with officers standing in my personal space to deter foul play. The longer I took, the more court officers suspected my guilt. Sometimes, even I found myself feeling guilty. What if I could not get myself to go? I worried that this would lead to a tacit assumption of guilt, and jail time until I produced urine for a negative test.

Thankfully I had good health insurance and the flexible work schedule of a graduate student. The two- and three-hour afternoon appointments were manageable for me. Most working adults would not have that same flexibility: mandated appointments meant the potential for of lost wages, then perhaps lost employment, and the constant, looming threat of punishment. People that lived elsewhere had to rely on underdeveloped and often unreliable public transportation. If participants were two minutes late due to a bus that was behind schedule or the mile-long walk from the bus stop, they were jailed until the following week's session. I watched with naiveté, then frustration and discomfort, as this happened week after week. It left me feeling simultaneously enraged with the system and guilty for avoiding the injustice meted out to some drug-court participants. Withholding my objections for two and three hours felt like an epic struggle upon my powers of self-control. Afterward, I would often sleep for hours, exhausted by the effort.

The tardy were not the only ones to land behind bars. Those that tested dirty were remanded to jail for a week or longer, depending on a variety of variables. The judge reasoned that if you were honest and admitted to use before a failed test, he might be compassionate. This no-strike policy for drug use fundamentally misunderstood how addiction works. Addiction involves compulsive use despite adverse consequences. The punishment stick did not work. Addicts and many social users were not inclined to preemptively turn themselves in. Most tried to beat the test. Those that did not pass were punished and treated with explicit disdain in open court.

I learned that this temperamental judge and his drug court were held up as a national and even international model as an alternative to punishment. How could this be? Why were other states and, for that matter, Australians taking his lead? I bore witness to a variety of problematic practices. Disparate treatment of local residents and outsiders remained the most consistent element to drug court. The judge routinely showed up significantly late for court on purpose, despite explicit expectations for drug-court participants to be on time. By his own admission, this was because our time had become less valuable. In fact, it was not our time at all. It was his time, the court's time, to do with as he pleased.

All participants were treated with varying degrees of disrespect and contempt. "Graduates," though, the special few who had been good soldiers, received a heartfelt gift from the judge. Each of us received *The Little Engine That Could*, a testament to the powers of determination, overcoming adversity, and the patronizing worldview of the judge himself. To complete the drug court's spectacle of coercion, "graduates" were forced to stand before the court and their fellow participants to offer words of wisdom. Had my freedom of speech been truly free, the open court might have heard a few choice words.

Years later I am able to make more sense of the experience. Drug courts are simply a new version of control and punishment. The driving impulse fueling this "alternative" to incarceration is the constant threat of punitive measures. The drug court had monetized, medicalized, and criminalized both intoxication and addiction without taking the time to understand either experience. Often, the court and the judge conflated addiction and intoxication. This hardly imbued the court with a spirit of trust, cooperation, or therapeutic progress.

My experience did, however, reaffirm what I already guiltily knew. Individual experiences, in drug court and the justice system more broadly, vary widely based on socioeconomic status and access to social capital. My prior history with the judge illustrates this well. I had worked as a bartender at a local bar and grill where the judge was a "regular." We were instructed to put twelve of his beers of choice on ice when he arrived to effectively "keep them coming." The judge routinely finished at least half of his personal stock quickly, then proceeded to drive home. Each week in drug court, the judge appeared to have forgotten me, as well as his hypocrisy. I did not forget.

MARCUS
REFLECTIONS OF A PHILOSOPHER-COP ON THE DRUG WAR

When I embarked upon my police career in 1990, I wholeheartedly and idealistically embraced the "War on Drugs." I took it for granted that using the criminal justice system as the primary means for tackling the crisis of drug addiction was a sensible thing to do. I believed that by fighting the drug war, I would be helping people.

It is no exaggeration to say that during a typical patrol shift, the majority of the calls for service that I handled related either directly or indirectly to drugs and drug addiction. Beyond the overdoses or direct instances of drug use and dealing, the situations were innumerable. Domestic violence? One or both parties were nearly always drunk. Car prowls, burglaries, identity theft, and other property crimes? Most of the people I arrested for these offenses had addictions to one or more drugs. In violent crimes such as shootings, robberies, and homicides, both victims and suspects frequently had close ties to drug dealing or drug use. With noncriminal death investigations, I witnessed premature mortality brought on by decades of heavy tobacco use. When I was not responding to incidents like these, my self-initiated activities such as traffic stops were driven by the relentless search for drugs and drug offenders.

My earliest felony drug case came just a few weeks after I graduated from the police academy: I stopped a car for speeding, arrested the driver for having a suspended license, and found marijuana, an electronic scale, and cash when I searched the car. The arrest left me enthused and energized. I had caught a drug dealer! A few months later, I received a notice from the prosecutor's office advising me that they were declining to file felony charges in lieu of misdemeanor possession of marijuana. Even though it was pretty apparent that the defendant was selling marijuana, the amount in his possession when I searched his car was below the forty-gram minimum. This case and many others were my introduction to case declination, plea bargaining, and other realities of an overburdened criminal justice system.

I kept responding to drug-related calls. As a patrol officer, most of the people I found were "small fish"—people with addictions selling drugs to support their own habits, or the retail suppliers one level up in the distribution chain. Street cops rarely stumble on major drug caches by themselves. However, I vicariously partook in the larger hauls by providing uniformed-patrol support to the interagency drug task force in my patrol area when they served search warrants or conducted "buy-bust" operations. My early experiences at swooping in to help arrest a suspected drug dealer delivered a heart-pounding, hand-trembling adrenaline high, though one that tempered with time and experience. After my first several years of patrol work, I reflected on the utter strangeness and futility of drug enforcement.

I had an epiphany following my participation in a buy-bust operation that culminated in the arrest at gunpoint of an alleged crack-cocaine dealer in the parking lot of a busy movie theater. The lot was choked with cars and people heading to matinee performances. Fortunately no one was hurt; however, I found myself asking what larger social gain was to be won by having nearly ten cops and undercover detectives arrest someone over a hundred-dollar crack deal, let alone doing so in a setting where the risk to innocent bystanders was clearly not worth the benefit. It wasn't merely that the location and timing of the arrest could have been better planned: this incident captured and magnified my growing frustration at the futility of arresting the same people over and again, whether for using drugs, dealing drugs, or both.

The tide of drug arrests, convictions, and incarcerations was unrelenting, but the tides of addiction and supply and demand proved even more so. I was struck by the fatalism of the people I arrested: many of them were completely blasé as they racked up more convictions and prison time, and even as their addictions intensified, sometimes to the point of death. In some cases, I witnessed addiction and drug dealing cross generations. I vividly remember one father who introduced his son to meth on his thirteenth birthday, and a woman who used her twelve-year-old son to carry drugs. In another case, a teenager returned home to find his mother dead of a heroin overdose just months after she'd been released from prison. He was already struggling with heroin addiction himself. These countless intimate situations led me to question the wisdom of the war on drugs that my colleagues and I were fighting shift after shift.

This is why, during the second half of my career, I became directly and vocally involved in drug-policy reform. I advocated for changes such as decriminalization of marijuana and a shift of police resources away from low-level drug cases to gun-violence reduction. I recommended greater discretion for street-level officers to channel people with addictions to health care, and for the kind of closer collaboration among social services, public health institutions, and law enforcement that might make this possible. Many of my colleagues were amused, others quietly agreed with me, plenty reacted more skeptically or critically, and a few were completely vicious.

Fast forward to 2013: I retired from police service three years ago, and now teach at a large public university. A reporter recently asked me if I felt vindicated that the kinds of legal and policy reforms for which I advocated over a decade ago are becoming street-level reality. I told him that while I saw cause for optimism in the widespread realization that a myopic, enforcement-only approach to drug addiction is unfair and ineffective, I am troubled by some new trends, especially the potential consequences of the legalization of marijuana in Washington and Colorado. When law and policy change, the people who feel the impact first are those who live in the margins of society. While I welcome efforts at stemming the suffering of the poor and the dispossessed caused by poorly wrought laws and policies, I am deeply saddened by the rapid, disproportionate proliferation of marijuana stores in the same communities that for too long have been the front lines of the drug war. Legal marijuana offers no viable path to economic empowerment for neighborhoods crying out for jobs, long-term stability, and development. One more regressive sin tax that will only add to the burdens of the poor is hardly a step on the path to greater equality. If the well-intentioned elites who have pushed for marijuana legalization become willing to have the stores primarily located in affluent, leafy suburbs and upscale neighborhoods, I will be surprised and pleased in equal measure.

CHAPTER 3

MEDICALIZATION

Defining Drug Use

> To posit the existence of a single, compendious substance called
> "drugs" is also to get away with the fiction that taking them is an
> eccentric pursuit found only in a deviant, dysfunctional subculture.
>
> —STUART WALTON, *OUT OF IT*

THINK BACK TO THE LAST TIME YOU HAD AN INFECTION. IT MAY have been viral, in which case you probably rested more to let your immune system fight it. Or, if it was bacterial, you may have seen a physician for prescription medication. If you were unsure, your doctor may have posed questions or ordered tests to determine which type of infection it was. Chances are that you followed the doctor's recommendation because, in the United States as in many countries, healthcare is something outsourced to professionals. From birth to death, socialization into a medical model of self-understanding shapes many aspects of Americans' lives. People are taught to understand their physiological and psychological selves within a medical framework. That framework determines that physiological or psychological concerns often require medical oversight, as if it the need for intervention is inherent in our biological form and function. In this context, health is iatric—a medical state of being sustained by professional support, monitoring, and treatment. The term for this framework is "medicalization"; it describes both the extension of medical authority and practice across greater areas of human life, and the understanding of human existence through an epidemiological approach to health.[1] Medicalization provides an epistemology—a context for knowing oneself—as an organic being within a culture of knowledge and authority vested in medical institutions, practices, and cultural norms. As a social evolution that has radically influenced how people see themselves both as individuals and members of a public body, medicalization is one of the most influential cultural transformations of the second half of the twentieth century.[2] Through its expressions in health care and pharmacology, medicalization has been an especially dominant force in shaping cultural norms about drugs—especially how Americans conceptualize, discuss, regulate, research, and consume them. Because most people inhabit the culture of medicalization so completely, it can be difficult to perceive its influence in shaping expectations about drug use and addiction as anything but objective fact. That definitional power—the rhetorical construction of users through the lens of medicalization—has had significant implications for drug users of all kinds.

US health care generally defines drug use from two divergent perspectives. First, it regards the use of prescribed, licit drugs as medically necessary and a primary tool in medical practice. Whether an analgesic, statin, NSAID, stimulant, or antidepressant, the use of approved drugs is not only sanctioned, it is often strongly promoted. The growth of the pharmaceutical industry has greatly influenced the use of drugs as part of a treatment plan or, increasingly, as the sole treatment in lieu of making difficult lifestyle changes. Pharmaceutical industry lobbying has been a driver in that evolution by working two fronts: influencing physicians and providers with incentives for prescribing particular drugs, and targeting the public as the primary audience for direct-to-consumer marketing. Growth in advertising volume and scope has facilitated a transition in cultural expectations and practice from physician-directed drug prescription to drugs-on-demand as a consumer right. Americans' acceptance of the promise of pharmaceutical drugs as the means to better health has been demonstrated by the last half-century's unprecedented escalation of prescription drug consumption. With 60 percent of Americans taking at least one pharmaceutical drug under a doctor's care, and over 20 percent of Americans using a prescription drug specifically for a mental health condition, pharmaceutical drug use has become a widely practiced cultural norm.[3]

Conversely, the discourse of medicalization has classified elective drug use—whether nonprescribed therapeutic or "recreational"—as unsafe and problematic. Unmanaged drug use includes pharmaceutical drug diversion—when users take a pharmaceutical drug for recreational use or medical repurposing without medical oversight. It also includes the use of illicit drugs. This disposition toward medically unmanaged drug use makes sense within the logic of medicalization. The prevailing assumption is that drug use outside the jurisdiction of medical oversight is harmful, which it can be. But it may also be that health-care providers predominantly interact with illicit drug users when drug use has become extreme and/or addictive. Unproblematic or controlled elective drug use is likely to be invisible to health-care professionals for a variety of reasons, not the least of which is that users of licit and illicit drugs tend to conceal or underreport their use to doctors and other medical professionals.[4] So, health-care professionals understandably focus on the physical and psychosocial risks that come with excessive drug use, which, in turn, results in the conflation of recreational drug use with "addiction" in health care.[5] This unease with elective drug use extends, in particular, to recreational drug use and the desire to be intoxicated. Recreational, diverted use of certain drugs, such as painkillers or amphetamines, is often seen as an indication of patient distress—an unhealthy process of self-medication that circumvents professional health care. Even the use of medical marijuana (which in its very name invokes the consent-authority of medicalization) can be understood by heath care providers to be abuse or addiction. This double standard regarding managed as opposed to unmanaged use of drugs reflects the logic of drug regulation, development, prescription, and promotion over the last century. Concern about the particular drug used can be as much about deeper social politics (ethnic and economic differences, or the destabilization of a medical framework, for example) as it is about the drug, itself.

Unmanaged drug use that is recreational or therapeutic has been stigmatized and pathologized through both the criminal-justice and health-care systems. While the social authority of criminalization is quite recognizable as a cultural force that has defined users, the social authority of medicalization may not be as apparent. Among the dynamics of medicalization, the social privileging of medical models and approaches to understand human behavior deeply affect the perception of drug use. Medical professionals have the authority to oversee and regulate our physical and mental health—an authority that shapes and, sometimes, even compels individual choices. So, it may not be apparent that the distinction between medically authorized and recreational drug use is a social construct with its own history, politics, and effects. Because health care has focused on illicit drug use almost exclusively as abuse or addiction, while at the same time promoting and expanding the use of pharmaceutical or licit drugs, American culture has contradictory discourses and cultural norms about illicit and licit, managed or unmanaged drug use. Some psychoactive substances, such as alcohol, have come through a cultural process of education and awareness about user abuse. They are less stringently regulated and understood to be substances that may cause problems, but are used in a controlled fashion by most users. Users of recreational drugs, on the other hand, are imagined to be in danger of self-destruction and incapable of using in a controlled fashion. The cultural paradigm for thinking about illicit drugs and health in particular has informed distinctions that are, in application, less about the drugs and drug use than they may seem. Considering how the discourse of medicalization enables or constrains individual drug user agency is critical to understanding the social impact of divergent drug politics in the United States.

The medicalization of drug and users in the United States has a long, complex history that has been well established by scholars who have documented the social context and politics of illicit and licit drug use, medical oversight and treatment of users, development of the pharmaceutical industry, and addiction research and treatment.[6] This chapter looks *across* such foundational research and various professional discourse communities to connect medical definitions of addiction with cultural norms, narratives, and practices that have become reified over the last four decades. The contexts of criminalization and medicalization that frame drugs and users have consequences far beyond the control and use of illicit drugs. Medicalization's epidemiological framework of drug use extends beyond medial professions, health care, and scientific research to policy makers, the media, and business. In the spirit of humanities scholar David Lenson's call for a "stronger anti-disciplinary attitude" in approaching drugs and their cultural meaning, I seek to highlight how some of key assumptions founded in medicalization have shaped cultural and scholarly thinking about drugs and their users. Specifically, I trace how the polarization of medical definitions of drug use as either a medical necessity or as abuse (addiction) affects users by defining their practices in a problematic binary context—mischaracterizing and silencing many users about their drug-use practices in the process.

Medicalization is expressed through many dynamics, among them: the articulation of social and personal issues as medical concerns, individual submission to medical authority, and a social deference to medical models and approaches to understanding human behavior. Primary among the outcomes of medicalization for drug users is an implicit assumption that most or all voluntary users who take psychoactive drugs without physician prescription and oversight are potential abusers or addicts. This perception is deeply embedded in health care and more broadly in American culture. *Addiction* has come to be a prominent and broad term, a signifier of cultural as well as biological pathologies, but it is frequently a misnomer or is misapplied. Although it is the colloquial term most broadly used to signify drug dependence, *addiction* is not an actual medical diagnosis (see next section, "Defining Addiction"). Momentarily unchecked drug use can be misinterpreted as addiction. It has also come to be a widely accepted custom to assume a user of specific drugs—heroin, for example—is addicted. Such assumptions reinforce and constrain user identity to a particular set of behaviors, limiting awareness of alternative modes of using. Professional and disciplinary discourses that conceive of recreational drug use as abuse and, often, addiction, reinforce this limited identity within the medical model. This is visible in some disciplinary language in medical practice and research, but especially in how research, treatment, and recovery are represented in data and public media. Through an exploration of shifting terminology drawn from diagnostic and treatment discourses, as well as from research, data sources, and the social contexts that have shaped medical representations of using, this chapter examines the dominance of addiction as a sociomedical paradigm that describes and constrains the way drug use and user agency are understood in US drug discourse.

To be explicit: addiction is a very real and extremely challenging issue. For a group of psychoactive drug users and the people in their lives, it is an affliction with terrible consequences. However, we must recognize that the medical profession, rehabilitation industries, policy makers, and other influential social actors have represented addiction to be far more prevalent than it actually is—a distortion that informs and reinforces the cultural politics of drugs, from public policy to research to treatment programs. The emphasis on addiction in social and political discourse exaggerates its risk and thus erases whole majorities of users who do not suffer addiction. Although figures vary by research context, substances studied, and overall study focus, researchers corroborate that both nationally and globally, no more than 10 percent of users are addicted to illicit drugs.[7] (More addiction statistics later in this chapter.) The inflation of Americans' perception of addiction has been informed by particular inputs to public drug discourse. The overstatement of addiction further prevents accurate understanding and assessment of psychoactive drug use and contributes to conflicted cultural norms: even as addiction to illicit drugs has become an intensive focus of health care, the production, prescription, use, misuse, and abuse of pharmaceutical drugs has grown to unparalleled levels.[8] Interest in identifying the cause of addiction has driven a race to develop biomedical technologies to identify the biology of addiction, which may further encourage exploration of pharmaceutical solutions. The focus on treatment and recovery dwarfs harm reduction and other ways of engaging users, including any acknowledgement of the prevailing experience of normalized, controlled drug use. This tendency to focus almost exclusively on addiction perpetuates the cultural narrative of addiction as the end point of unmanaged drug use. The assumption that users who take drugs outside the context of medical care will become addicted has strong currency and broad impact.

One factor contributing to this assumption is that some highs are more socially acceptable than others within a sociomedical context. Cultural tolerance of use practices varies by psychoactive drug and user demographic, and has been mutable over time. Drugs that have been approved for public consumption with or without the prescription of a doctor enjoy a protected status in American culture, whether used moderately or excessively. Alcohol and nicotine, for example, have gone through various trends and prohibitions, but continue to be legal, widely used, and regarded as acceptable for moderate or controlled use.[9] Similarly, use of pharmaceutical drugs, including the use of prescription opiates and stimulants, is a common practice, just as opium, cocaine, and marijuana were used legally a hundred years ago. This particular cultural norm stands in strong contrast to the prohibition of illicit drugs with similar constituent elements and psychoactive properties. In other words, it is socially permissible to use OxyContin but not heroin. Many people take Adderall, but are prohibited from taking methamphetamine. Because those pharmaceutical opiates and amphetamines are legally approved, distributed, and permitted if prescribed by a physician, they are socially endorsed. In many cases, the question is not which drugs or states of consciousness are permitted but, rather, whether the way one gets there is medically sanctioned within a context of differential drug prohibition.

The social and medical approval of drugs understood to have medical merit and the condemnation of drugs deemed to be addictive are not distinctions based entirely on research. Rather, our attitudes are the consequence of medicalization in the development of health-care professionalization and markets, and social and regulatory politics of pharmacology. A persistent yet fluid cultural boundary between what drug historian Nancy Campbell calls "problem-solving pharmaceutical drugs and problem-causing illicit drugs" has developed in an increasingly professionalized pharmatherapeutical market. With the aid of narcotics laws, that pharmaceutical market distinguished itself from drugs that were branded as addictive and immoral, such as opium and heroin. In this way, drug cultural norms are dynamic; classifications shift with social relevance. For example, once forbidden to women, smoking was a sign of independence for early female adopters. By the middle of the twentieth century, it became an equally enjoyed ubiquitous

American custom. Half a century later, smoking has been banned in most public places as a public health hazard, yet cigarettes are widely available. Currently, Americans have determined that cigarettes are problem-causing and highly addictive, yet nicotine gum, patches, inhalers, and e-cigarettes are considered to be problem-solving drugs for smokers who struggle to quit. Thus, characterizations of addiction over the last century have varied in cultural meaning, at times more focused on the user rather than the drug, or perceiving addiction as either a moral failing, a crime, or a disease, depending on the drug and its social representation.[10] Cultural understanding and acceptance of drugs' functions—and, particularly, what is deemed to be drug use or abuse—has been and continues to be a moving target.

In the last four decades, the pharmacological evolution has contributed significantly to these attitudes. Pharmacology has shaped what is considered "healthy" through the industry's influence on the description and treatment of psychiatric and physiological maladies. A well-cultivated trust of problem-solving pharmaceutical drugs influences how medical professionals advise patients to establish and sustain health. In a drug-taking culture, we now expect diagnosis to be followed by medication, whether practitioner- or self-prescribed. The medicalization of the use of particular drugs has come to be widely embraced and internalized by Americans and American institutions, becoming normalized as a solution or resource. Any stigma previously associated with taking antidepressants or medications for anxiety or attention issues has been diminished as more disorders are treated with drugs. The emphasis on individual health and medical supervision to regulate our bodies has become an effective discourse of social power that Americans internalize and practice–what philosopher Michel Foucault theorized as "technologies of the self."[11] Americans perform these discourses in earnest, participating by self-diagnosing and self-prescribing remedies, sharing nutritional information and diets, supporting lifestyle changes, and considering all of these impacts "health." This intentional involvement in our health is a collective action in which people are mobilized through discourses of medicalization to participate in and shape their diagnoses.[12] The narratives of health performed and deployed have a particular logic and politics in terms of managing drug-use practices. They express the particular hegemony of medical authority, depending on whether use practices are licit, managed or illicit, unmanaged drug use. Users negotiate media reports that a glass of wine or two is actually good for you, or that the endocannabinoids in marijuana replicate those that occur naturally in one's brain chemistry, to adopt narratives of health that justify user choices. In its broad reach, medicalization engages consumers, insurers, journalists, families, schools, employers, and other social institutions in narratives and practices of health.

Within medicalization's culturally pervasive context, the ways in which drug use is defined are multidimensional and not necessarily consistent. One significant issue is that the cultural line between problem-solving and problem-creating drugs oversimplifies the varieties of user experiences. In an era of widespread psychotropic prescription treatment for mood disorders, for example, interpreting "unmanaged" drug use to change one's mood or psychological experience as addiction ignores a broader and more nuanced psychological ground of drug use. What are the phenomenological possibilities for altered consciousness along a spectrum of drug use? And how would one plot the points between taking a drug to feel less bad (to treat depression, for example) and taking a drug to feel good? In surfacing the underlying logic expressed in current distinctions between use and abuse, one might ask: in a medical model, what are those distinctions based on? And what are the implications of those distinctions, for all kinds of users?

DEFINING ADDICTION: DRUG USE, ABUSE, AND DEPENDENCE

Addiction has never been a fixed concept or an agreed-upon state of being in US health care and research. As a framework for classifying drug use, addiction is understood as anything from extreme, regular, or episodic use to consumption that is socially or physically debilitating. *Addiction*, as a label, explains irrational or otherwise inexplicable behavior. Often it is tied to desire through a behavior, a compulsion that leads to the loss of control. Contemporary definitions and descriptions vary: addiction is a brain disease, a psychological or physical need, a socially constructed state, or perhaps not a fixed state of being at all. What is classified as *addiction* matters because, among other things, the definitions signify cultural assumptions about individual user agency and particularly addiction's end point—whether addiction is a chronic or variable condition and whether it is informed by biological, psychological, and/or social circumstances. From its classification as a multidimensional set of behaviors to its more deterministic classification as a brain disease or a lifetime identity, addiction is often seen as a fixed, controlling state. Yet user experience and research suggest that drug use that has been characterized as addiction is far more variable than some of our leading definitions would suggest. Even within the context of constructing addiction as a somewhat deterministic state, disciplines central to addiction research and diagnosis, such as psychiatry and neuroscience, vary in their terminology, definitions, and understanding of addiction's etiology or cause. Consequently, professionals working with users can operate from quite different assumptions.[13]

This section identifies some of the key concepts inherent in the construction of addiction through principal diagnostic terminology. My intention is not to attempt to represent complex institutions and professions but, rather, to consider how their language and discourses construct drug use and users. While I did not set out to do an analysis of diagnostic definitions, in researching and writing about medical perspectives, I became aware that there were influential distinctions underlying this language. The changing definitions of addiction across time and professional discourse groups suggest the challenges in understanding a state of being that is far from constant or singular. A note about terminology: for the sake of clarity and consistency, I use the word *addiction* to refer to what has been understood to be a biological or psychological drug-dependent state, as acknowledged by different terminology within these disciplines and institutions across time—although most have moved away from that specific term.[14] While drug use is frequently conflated with addiction, drug use is sometimes distinguished from addiction through classifications such as dependence. Many of the key organizations and institutions involved in addiction diagnosis, treatment, and research employ language that frequently overlaps and/or signifies slightly different referents. These include: the American Psychiatric Association (APA), the American Medical Association (AMA), the World Health Organization (WHO), the American Society of Addiction Medicine (ASAM), and the relevant National Institutes of Health (NIH): the National Institute on Alcohol Abuse and Alcoholism (NIAAA), the National Institute on Drug Abuse (NIDA), and the Substance Abuse and Mental Health Services Administration (SAMHSA). This discussion is technical to demonstrate some of the ways in which shifts in terminology and definitions convey an evolution in our conceptualization of addiction. Implicit in this terminology are assumptions about the nature of drug use, user agency and experience, and human biology, assumptions that have strong implications in the construction of addiction as a diagnosis and a principal user identity.

Addiction originally served conceptually as a nonmedical and nonpejorative referent to denote a strong habit or tendency. In the United States, the contemporary cultural understanding of addiction characterizes individual conduct through discourses of morality, the autonomous subject, and medical rationality.[15] This is rooted in the temperance discourse of the late eighteenth and early nineteenth centuries, in which inebriation and addiction became a lens for identifying and framing social issues related to drug use and user agency. In this context, addiction was articulated as a moral issue of individual self-control. Addiction was further elaborated as a disease of the will in the postprohibition twentieth century through Alcoholics Anonymous's focus on the pathology of the drinker. The medicalization of addiction evolved through addiction treatment communities as a disease model, a metaphor disconnected from medical research but following the logic of epidemiological infectious disease.[16] This model of addiction as a process of degeneration into pathology endures. The current "brain disease" model defines addiction as the result of drug use's disruption and change of the brain's structure, resulting in a chronic, relapsing disease that affects behaviors and outlook. Alternative definitions of addiction rooted in the behavioral sciences conceive of the user as a culturally contextualized agent in what might be seen as a continuum of harm. Those definitions often see the individual to be capable of behavioral change, as opposed to subject to degenerative pathology. Contemporary perceptions of addiction continue to associate its origins with the terms established in these same cultural trajectories of biological risk, environment, and individual control.[17]

How to register the point at which drug use becomes problematic, dangerous, or truly harmful is unclear. Trends in diagnostic language suggest just how inexact definitions of addiction have been and continue to be. In the United States, a cultural understanding of addiction has been expressed through recovery movements and political movements, but most dominantly through the dual discourses of psychological and physical medicine, as expressed in diagnosis and treatment as well as research. While a variety of addiction models have influenced treatment, diagnostic language in psychiatry and medicine have predominantly followed the concept of addiction as a disease, even as their criteria are largely based on behavior. By the middle of the twentieth century, the World Health Organization and the American Psychological Association had each established language for their respective diagnostic texts, focusing on a user's increased drug tolerance and withdrawal symptoms. These organizations span medicine from the perspectives of physiological and psychological care. Their diagnostic manuals define disorders and diseases in those professions; for the WHO, the *International Classification of Diseases* (ICD-10); for the APA, the *Diagnostic and Statistical Manual of Mental Disorders* (DSM-5).[18]

Early diagnostic definitions of drug addiction focused on "drug dependence." The WHO's two initial categories, addiction and habituation, delineated the effects of particular addictive drugs as opposed to those drugs that were merely likely to be physically habit-forming—a distinction that acknowledged differentiation among drugs and their effects on users—notably, that not all drug use leads to addiction. Similarly, in early incarnations of the APA's DSM, *drug addiction* specified users who were dependent on drugs other than "medically indicated drugs taken in proportion to the medical need."[19] In 1980, the WHO and the APA both adopted the terminology and conceptual reframing of addiction as a "drug dependence syndrome" based on the recommendation of an international working group sponsored by the WHO and the Alcohol, Drug Abuse, and Mental Health Administration (ADAMHA), the Substance Abuse and Mental Health Services Administration's predecessor. This change reflected an inclusion of both psychological and physiological dependence factors in a cluster or "polythetic syndrome" definition (no single criterion was required as long as three of a list of potential symptoms were present within a year). While this version preserved the complexity of various aspects of individual user experience, "drug dependence syndrome" obscured the potential to understand drug use within the context of normalized and/or habituated drug use.

In 1994, the DSM's fourth revision further emphasized a continuum of abuse in which drug dependence was the extreme end point in a range of drug use, from mildly abusive states of use to full drug dependence. In 2013, the fifth and current DSM revision further combined abuse and dependence into a single category of maladaptive use, "drug use disorder," with a continuum of mild to severe drug use—taking into account four areas of concern: impaired control, social impairment, risky use, and pharmacological criteria (i.e., tolerance and withdrawal).[20] This version attempted to disrupt the correlation between dependence and addiction, while noting that substance abuse is often the opposite of the "mild" end of the use spectrum. In a 2003 report, the WHO emphasized a distinction between "drug dependence" and "drug abuse," noting that some critical medical treatments require the continued use of dependency-producing drugs (e.g., opiates), indicating that the use of those drugs is an essential aspect of medical treatment and appropriate.[21] In other words, a physician may oversee drug dependence (addiction) as a necessary part of treatment. The ICD-10 uses the term "harmful use" to signal the mental and physical consequences of problematic drug use.

These transitions from "addiction" and "drug dependence" to a more inclusive diagnostic category, "drug use disorder," signal key conceptual shifts. *Disorder* now refers to either (or both) a behavioral syndrome or a physiological dependence on a drug. The 1980 international working group suggested "neuroadapation" to signify the latter and to allow for a distinction between behavioral and biological dependence, but that recommendation was not adopted. "Disorder" also distances diagnostic language from the social stigma of addiction and the previous implication of a disease of one's will, bringing the diagnostic language into line with other maladies. Finally, as a polythetic diagnosis, drug-use disorder potentially offers nuance in understanding addiction as an interrelated cluster of physiological and psychological symptoms that exist in varying degree without any particular bright line between drug dependence and nondependent, recurrent drug use.[22] In other words, at the diagnostic level, users' engagement (or not) of their social contexts, behaviors, psychological health, and physical health are considered as part of a composite picture in determining the impact and dysfunction of their drug use.

The evolution of diagnostic categories codifies medical understanding of addiction such that even as the DSM and ICD have attempted to represent the vast range of problematic user behaviors and experiences, the assumption is that addictive drug use is somewhat static and chronic. Further, the diagnostic focus is part of a broader trend: although treatment tends to focus on *behaviors* related to drug use, those behaviors tend to be understood by researchers as symptoms that signal a *biological disease* rather than expressing user experiences and conditions in social contexts.[23] The WHO now frames addiction within a "bio-behavioral" view of dependence—based on the biological and psychological aspects of individual learning that create habitual use or dependence—but its language frames addiction as a *biological* process. Similarly, the AMA and its Committee on Alcoholism and Addiction have historically sidestepped the social aspects of drug abuse to approach addiction as a protracted biological illness. This position is shared by the US National Institutes of Health related to drug use and abuse (NIAAA, NIDA, and SAMHSA), which frame "dependence" as a chronic brain disease, and increasingly emphasize biology rather than a variable set of behaviors.[24] In some ways, the issues surrounding addiction research and its presentation have to do with conveying a complex set of etiological and symptomatic factors in layman's language. While the WHO cautions that the "challenge for the neuroscience community in the field of drug dependence is to explain drug dependence in biological terms without depicting people with drug dependence as automatons under the control of receptors in their brains," it nevertheless emphasizes the biological determinism of drug use and obscures psychosocial factors.[25]

This tension within an overt shift toward a stronger biological emphasis in addiction diagnosis and research implies an inability to distinguish physiological experience from psychological experience. A history of separating the biological from psychological in addiction has bred indeterminacy that is itself one of the key drivers of addiction debates and discourse.[26] Diagnostic terminology reflects this inextricability and expresses ideological differences about addiction's causes and its expected outcomes. How does one separate biological basis from the embodied subjective experience of the user situated in a particular cultural context? Substance dependence and addiction are largely identified psychologically through their effects— an urge that drives compulsive actions.[27] Translation issues regarding the description of the biology of addiction through user behavior and emotions surfaced in the controversy over the APA's most recent revision of the DSM. Concerns raised about the APA's revised diagnostic framework reflect psychiatry's focus on biology at the expense of what some practitioners argue are the psychosocial basis of substance-use disorders. In an open letter to the APA, a group of psychologists and psychiatrists expressed a need for a more comprehensive conception of the distress that "addiction" might signal, putting it on a spectrum with normal experience that takes into account factors such as unemployment, trauma, and poverty.[28] Diagnostic criteria related to social factors a user may suffer, such as "legal difficulties," have been cut or limited in favor of seemingly physiological criteria, such as "craving."[29] Some psychologists argue that the DSM-5 overmedicalizes personal and social problems as symptoms of an illness or medical condition by contending that compulsive behaviors involving activities like gambling or sex reflect a problem that should receive psychological intervention.[30]

Even when psychological aspects of using are acknowledged in these official diagnostic tools, as in the DSM-5's lists of symptoms, little room is left for the recognition of individual agency and the changeability of drug use relative to the weight given to the biological nature of "dependence." The revised classification, "drug use disorder," with its attendant levels of severity, seemingly outlines a continuum of use. Yet the conflation of abuse and dependence into one category eliminates a previous distinction between problem users who are not addicted because they moderate drug use and addicts who cannot moderate their use. This consolidation inadvertently supports the assumption that all substance-dependent users are chronic, lifetime addicts. Sociologist and drug scholar Craig Reinarman argues that, in the evolution of the addiction-as-disease model, "[w]hat are taken as empirical indicators of an underlying disease of addiction consist of a broad range of behaviors that are interpreted as 'symptoms' only under some circumstances. They can be aggregated to fit under the heading of 'addiction' only by means of some degree of epistemic force."[31] While the effects of physiological symptoms and the new severity scale may make it seem that drug-use disorder diagnoses are more "objective," they still rely on the interpretation of the evaluator and the user to identify and determine a symptom like "craving." Stanton Peele, a psychologist and addiction researcher, points out that biological evidence does not indicate that a given individual is addicted because "[w]e cannot detect addiction in the absence of its defining behaviors."[32]

The APA and WHO diagnostic categories have profound effects. At the least, the newer drug use disorder's lower threshold for diagnosis is expected to create a dramatic increase in dependence (addiction) diagnoses, with the largest increase expected at the lower end of the use spectrum, what some psychologists and psychiatrists call "unhealthy users" rather than severe abusers of psychoactive drugs. Diagnostic tools that cast addiction as chronic, versus potentially changeable, perceive users as uniform in their use patterns and outcomes, framing them within a lifelong condition. Although this is not new to addiction discourse, the brain-disease model's increased emphasis on "identifiable" biological origins moves research and treatment toward pharmaceutical solutions that could have serious impact if addiction continues to be seen as a static, chronic condition requiring management. Time will tell if the substance-abuse disorder changes in the DSM-5 will contribute to more of a biological focus in treatment, particularly a pharmaceutical response to addiction. Increasingly, a focus on biological origins signals a privileging of neuroscience as the best way to explain human behavior—but we have yet to use these technologies to find an addiction treatment.

The slippery slope of defining and identifying addiction demonstrates how various professional classifications collapse the varieties of human behavior and experience with psychoactive drugs into seemingly discrete, static categories. Practitioners are isolated in epistemic communities where, as Nancy Campbell points out, they "trade in relatively narrow and coherent structures of belief that enable and constrain the lexicons, techniques, technologies, and practices that are considered legitimate ways to speak authoritatively about drugs in a given domain."[33] Those frameworks become tacit and binding even as they purport to clarify elements of human experience. Medical discourse proposes to "unmask" addiction, as sociologist Helen Keane argues, through its pursuit of rational and objective knowledge about users and drugs—a process that promises liberation from addiction.[34] It seems that the process of unmasking requires a deterministic construction of substance use and user, ways of thinking that are established and reinforced within those epistemic communities of practice. While potentially liberating addicts from their dependencies or use practices, addiction discourses frame them within particular static identities that tie users to that practice (past or present). The medicalization of users seems to be moving researchers and treatment communities away from seeing users as agents in their own use practices.

ADDICTION RESEARCH AND TREATMENT:
IDEOLOGIES OF PRACTICE AND USER AGENCY

The dominant addiction theory in public discourse of the last decade, the "brain disease" model, represents one extreme of the effects of medicalization in addiction discourse. Nora Volkow, psychiatrist and director of the National Institute on Drug Abuse since 2003, has visibly advanced previous director Alan Leshner's project of characterizing addiction as a "hijacked brain," promoting the model not just in neurological research and public policy, but also in the arena of public opinion. This model explains addiction as a chronic brain disease, summarized in the reductionist thinking that addiction is all about dopamine.[35] Researchers and clinicians working with the brain-disease model consider addiction to be a chronic, relapsing illness, like asthma and diabetes. Not surprisingly, this model envisions a future of medical, perhaps pharmaceutical, intervention as disease management, a biochemical solution to a biochemical dysfunction. One treatment currently in development is an addiction vaccine that would promote production of antibodies in the immune system of a user to limit the narcotics' effect.[36] The strategy of blocking a drug with another drug (an immunologic) as addiction rehabilitation manifests medicalization's logic of controlling the body and disorder pharmaceutically—a logic expressed, for example, in methadone treatment. Although the science in the neurological mapping of the brain is complex, its current expression to the public as an addiction theory tends to be oversimplifying and deterministic. As Volkow and a co-author have written, "Addiction can be viewed as a pathology in how importance is attached to stimuli that predict drug availability and how the brain regulates (chooses) behavioral output in response to those stimuli."[37] The notion that the brain "chooses" behavior reflects the brain/mind division: in neuroscience, there is less attention to the thinking organism embodying the choosing brain.

That disconnection between the brain's biochemical impulse and the user as agent signals a gap between theory and practice in addiction research. The brain-disease model largely ignores decades of therapeutic practice and a body of research that demonstrates addicts successfully addressing and/or resolving substance abuse or dependence. It conveys the impression that the user's behavior is a direct and unmediated product of her brain chemistry, regardless of her socially situated condition. Although awareness of these issues may get mention, such as the WHO's caution to avoid "a lack of attention towards remediable social causes and social policy options for reducing the prevalence of substance dependence, including drug control policies," it often is overshadowed by the seeming objectivity of neurological data.[38] Drug czar Gil Kerlikowske (ONDCP) promoted the brain-disease view as the cornerstone of the Obama administration's drug policy: "Drug policy reform should be rooted in neuroscience—not political science."[39] Policy makers may appreciate the seemingly straightforward approach of neurobiology, but how it contributes to public health by treating and addressing addiction is unclear. Neuroscientist Carl Hart asserts that "[w]e are nowhere near being able to distinguish the brain of a drug addict from that of a non-drug addict" in the way that we can recognize diseases like Alzheimer's or Parkinson's.[40]

Despite its disassociation from addiction treatment, brain science enjoys a persuasive role in American visual-media culture's representation of addiction research. Offering a window into the unknown, brain imaging has resulted in high visibility for an evolving science, a superficial validation that addiction is a physiological process. Researchers have found that photos from brain imaging are influential in mainstream-media stories about addiction, both by directly persuading readers and because these images inform biomedical researchers, policymakers, and other stakeholders (drug producers), who in turn shape perceptions of drug users. Because MRI brain images seem to illustrate how our brains work, viewers often mistake the implicit for the explicit, making a direct correlation between the parts of the brain lit up in a particular neurological function and a verifiable cause of addiction. These colorful images are better thought of as what drug historian Timothy Hickman calls visual metaphors or "figures of sight" because they represent a hypothesis about brain response based on complex statistical computing.[41] The capacity of brain images to illustrate a suggestive narrative affects not just the uninitiated, but those who work in these research fields, as well. Neuropsychologist Dorothy Bishop writes that the allure of brain imaging has resulted in clear biases among researchers, editors, and academic reviewers. In her review of a series of studies, Bishop found consistent methodological flaws in those with neuroimaging. This was attended by a tendency among the editors and reviewers "to overlook weaknesses in research design and analysis if a study involves images of brains or brain activity."[42] These images carry substantial cultural weight in signifying a perspective that people *are* their biology. The essentialism of this approach implies that if our biology is deterministic, and addiction is a biological disease, then users cannot help but express that logical outcome of their brain function.

In treatment, however, the user is expected to be something more than the sum of her biology. Many treatment models require that a user identify as an addict and/or as a recovering addict—an identity that, in some contexts, is understood as lifelong. For recovery culture, the requirement to become accountable about one's addiction and live the identity of a reformed addict is an end in itself. But recovery from addiction can imply various states of being. Addiction therapies propose a wider set of possibilities. In recovery, a user might transition from the liminal state of "addict" or "recovering addict" to "recovered addict" or even to a non-addiction-related identity. While *recovery* is often considered to mean "drug free," the characterization or definition of that end state depends on the methodology used to get there. Some therapies find addiction to be a chronic condition requiring some sort of regular maintenance to recover. Drug maintenance therapies, for example, that replace opiates with methadone or buprenorphine target the user's body as the site of the pathology. In this context, the addict becomes obligated to that new drug, as well as its clinical administration and oversight, as the means of control, in exchange with giving up the challenges of using the previous drug. From the standpoint of treatment providers, therapy drugs like "buprenorphine [are] offered as a prosthetic device—a technology for maintaining homeostasis," but from the standpoint of user agency, they also represent a hegemonic relationship and, in many cases, an alternative that creates another set of addiction risks and problems.[43] Some countries have hybrid drug-replacement and harm-reduction programs, offering heroin addicts heroin-assisted treatment such as daily maintenance shots in a clinical setting, or giving alcoholics limited beer in exchange for work. Models such as Alcoholics Anonymous, on the other hand, require a non-drug-oriented maintenance and oversight, in which addicts perform the "work" of the twelve steps in a daily program for abstinence. In these models, the user is an addict; whether she is liberated from that state depends on how one interprets lifelong maintenance of that identity as a fundamental part of the self.

While drug maintenance and twelve-step treatment models sustain the essentialism of addiction as a chronic disease and/or identity, other models offer the potential for the addict to recover by creating a nonaddicted identity. Of the methodologies most commonly employed in addiction treatment, psychotherapy most contrasts the brain disease-model's construction of the addict as a permanent condition and identity. Psychotherapy engages the addict in a process of self-examination, focusing on what psychologist Mike Page terms "how the mind works, not where the brain works."[44] This model can be ambiguous and individualized, identifying invisible and visible causes (emotions, reactions, behavior), and seeks to partner with the addict to change behaviors and thinking rather than treating a disease. Cognitive-behavioral therapy, one of the most prevalent psychotherapy models, emphasizes the user's experiences, associations, perceptions, and behaviors related to drug abuse. In this framework, addiction is considered to be a mode of learning: associations get made, then reinforced, and become a primary focus. Therapists work with users over time to understand contexts and alter patterns of thinking and behavior that have led to addiction. By identifying thoughts as a way to influence behavior, cognitive-behavioral therapy ascribes a significant level of agency to the user.

The expectation that users are capable of intentional change suggests that addiction may be far from a brain disease, but, rather, that it has to do with how we actively respond to stimuli. Psychologist Gene Heyman stresses understanding addiction as a "behavior of choice" situated within specific social and personal contexts.[45] This moment of choice, what philosopher Owen Flanagan calls "the zone of control" for addicts, is a threshold researchers are finding to be a critical point of agency.[46] Results based on studies, and treatments related to user agency and choice, may be less culturally discernible than brain imaging, but they demonstrate a greater efficacy in helping users resolve addictive drug use. In experiments that provide users with an option to choose money or a dose of their drug of choice, addicts have demonstrated the ability to deliberately avoid using if it is in their economic interest and/or if the costs of using become too severe. Research in contingency management, a behavior-modification therapy, focuses on providing addicts with the rewards for making alternative choices and reinforcing those choices through repetition. Some researchers believe that engaging the element of desire is what creates an addiction and is also what can help a user refashion that experience into something else.[47] The National Institute on Alcohol Abuse and Alcoholism's major study, the National Epidemiologic Survey on Alcohol and Related Conditions (NESARC), found that over 70 percent of all people with alcohol addiction overcame it. Further, it found that of those who overcame addiction, 75 percent did it on their own, without programs like Alcoholics Anonymous, and without any rehab or treatment program.[48] According to these researchers, the variability of individual circumstance, social context, momentary options, and the cost/

benefit of using suggest that differences in how addicts use or do not use drugs are multifaceted and unlikely to be accurately encapsulated in a rigid category or determined solely by biology. Even for addicts, the effects of drugs vary depending on the individual's set and the setting.[49]

Looking across various addiction models, theories, and treatments, it is evident that addiction is dynamic and may be irreducible to any single category: cultural, psychological, or biological. The challenge of articulating a comprehensive definition of a "bio-psychosocial disorder" is less about distinguishing between psychological and physical drug dependence than accurately articulating the complexity of this relationship as a constellation of factors experienced by unique individuals within various social contexts. A key consequence of addiction discourse is a glaring deficit of research into why users who become addicted engage in extreme drug use. Public health historian Caroline Acker argues that as a social problem, addiction is most prevalent in geographic areas with "multiple dimensions of structural disadvantage." Seeing addiction as a disease, Acker argues, "casts it as a pathology of individuals and shifts attention away from powerful social influences on drug use."[50] Howard Kushner, a medical historian, argues for a "cultural biology of addiction" as the most comprehensive ground for understanding the vagaries and patterns of addiction. Addicts have multiple triggers and pathways that are both organic and cultural, and any successful model must take into account how addictions are "informed and 'enabled' by an interaction of culture and biology."[51] Recognizing the material significance of drugs should not mean that their cultural significance is discounted. This concept of cultural biology, or an awareness of socially constructed and biological determinants, attempts to bridge a "naïve dualism" that distinguishes psychology as categorically distinct from biology.[52] A cultural biology model that recenters the user as a socially situated agent capable of intentional action might express the multifaceted dynamics of addiction. Too frequently, these models privilege biology or addiction behavior and, for the most part, do not engage meaningfully with the social conditions in which we use. Even when behavioral psychologists address cultural issues, the focus is on individual behavior as opposed to the broader social context. Some recovery models do help individuals acknowledge the contextual factors in their use practices, but often at the cost of constraining users within an identity as an addict.

Naming a human experience or practice has strong consequences: it establishes and enforces expectations about the referent. Diagnostic and cultural definitions of addiction compel users, in some way, to adopt and enact an addict identity. The cultural assumption that addiction is the most likely result of psychoactive drug use leaves little room for other possibilities or resistance to that characterization. Some addicts themselves raise the issue that recovery programs and the brain-disease model reinforce a permanent identity that encumbers further social development.[53] It is easy to see why the addict identity—regardless of the individual addict's circumstances—might be problematic: once a user is considered an addict, she inhabits what frequently is perceived as a relatively static identity that, in some cases, allots her minimal agency to address her own condition. Depending on how a given addiction model constructs addiction and user agency, progress in treatment can only go so far toward reaching a state of nonaddiction. Addicts must engage with external assessments that may or may not be accurate to their experience, from the inception of a diagnosis—in which protestations that one is not addicted are often interpreted as part of the addict's self-delusion—to the points along the way in which recovering addicts are believed to have an inability to manage normative use. As a defining identity, "recovering addict" functions as a perpetually unattainable state.[54] Many addicts do not conceive of themselves as helplessly in the grip of a chronic disease because they acquire skills, strategies, and self-knowledge in moving through addiction such that it is not a "recovery" to a prior state so much as it is a further development of self.[55] The cultural emphasis in recovery of addiction as a lifetime identity is particularly troubling as recovery is becoming part of earlier life experiences, such as recovery-based high schools and college dormitories, or even in drug-court-mandated boarding programs for young users. What are the effects of identifying a still-maturing teenager as an addict? How does it affect psychosocial development? Will students be able to evolve away from that identity, and would that evolution be desirable?

If inherent in the term *addict* there are multiple expectations or assumptions (an outcome of drug use, a diagnostic category, a personal identity), how do we talk about *addiction*—or even *drug-use disorder*—without enacting the polarizing power dynamics of that term? Cultural norms about addiction are expressed at the individual level. Philosophers Anna Alexander and Mark Roberts write that we see addiction as "a socially deviant, unacceptable behavior that must, in virtually all respects, be feared, ferreted out, and contained. And the addict, as the subject of his or her addiction, tends to become largely vilified and eclipsed."[56] The medicalization of addiction promotes the individualization of social problems because we seek to change the "victim" instead of society.[57] From the construction of a set of criteria to the application of the diagnosis, the medical narrative often casts an addict's identity in a discourse over which she has little input or control. Anthropologist Todd Myers argues that for the health-care provider, the addict becomes "a category of thought that is negotiated within medicine and therapeutics, inside and outside the clinic." Addicts must deal with this medicalization of the self as they confront "an over-determined picture of a dependency-free future."[58] Ideologically, some contemporary addiction models and recovery programs inscribe radically different notions of the self from those typical to psychological therapies or harm reduction. In these models, practitioners and users will be more likely to attribute problems to neurochemical imbalances than to conceive of having any agency, much less control, over their drug use.[59] That perspective is articulated clearly by Volkow: "a person that's addicted to drugs cannot properly execute their free will. They cannot stop taking the drug even though they may consciously want to do that."[60] For brain science, an addict's brain—and thus the addict—is not sufficient to function on its own as a healthy organ (or person). The brain-disease solution would be a sequel to other contexts in which the subject cannot achieve normative selfhood without medical intervention or enhancement.

Among the primary implications of framing the user as an addict, then, is the potential alienation of the self as the object of medical authority. Gender studies scholar Eve Kosofsky Sedgwick traces the politics of this process for the addict: "[F]rom being the *subject* of her own perceptual manipulations or indeed experimentations, she is installed as a proper *object* of compulsory institutional disciplines, legal and medical, which without actually being able to do anything to 'help' her, nonetheless presume to know her better than she can know herself—and, indeed, offer everyone in her culture who is *not* herself the opportunity of enjoying the same flattering presumption."[61] In this vein, some scholars and researchers point out that a user's drug "dependence" may result more from the "prohibitive power of family, the state, and the corporation" as described through a discourse of addiction. The term "drug abuser" invokes the perception that individuals are at fault for their addiction.[62] This sociopolitical "use disorder" identity becomes adopted as part of a user's subjectivity and experience of using.[63] In this sense, the diagnostic and clinical language of addiction discourses construct a wider, more culturally pervasive narrative, what psychopharmacologist Richard DeGrandpre calls a "placebo text": an unwritten script that frames cultural expectations about a given drug, including the phenomenological experience for the user and the expectations of health-care professionals about that drug's effects on users.[64] Despite their different approaches and perceived causes, many addiction discourses share an essential commonality: they fashion an addict without agency, and construct addiction as the logical outcome of the use of most psychoactive drugs. But is that an accurate assumption?

RECOGNIZING USERS: WHERE ARE ALL THE ADDICTS?

For all the attention and resources committed to addiction research, care, and recovery, one would logically assume that the United States is experiencing an escalation in addiction. Yet, the reality is that addiction is far less of a risk or factor than addiction discourses suggest. Although the figures vary by source, both global and national data from the WHO and NIH show that addiction is suffered by a minority of users of all psychoactive drugs—with the exception of cigarette smokers. The National Survey on Drug Use and Health data show a static, small number of substance addicts in the United States, even though the APA has recently broadened its diagnostic categories to include "non-substance addictions" or behavioral disorders such as gambling, which may increase the number of reported "addicts" substantially.[65] Only 2.7 percent of illicit drug users surveyed in 2014 were substance abusers or substance dependent, a figure that has remained steady for the last decade and longer. (See fig. 3.1.) In fact, both illicit drug and alcohol abuse or dependence have slightly decreased over the last twelve years, with alcohol abuse at 6.4 percent in 2014. The NSDUH does not offer aggregate statistics of all abusers of all drugs, but taking these two categories together, less the 1 percent of users that the NSDUH reports are people who abuse both alcohol and illicit drugs, a collective figure for substance abuse would be 8.1 percent of users. That is not a number to be ignored, but it demonstrates a critical point: the majority of drug users do not suffer abuse or dependence—what, by any definition, we think of as addiction.

Where are all the addicts? For Americans age twelve and older, the NSDUH estimates that in the past year, 66.6 percent used alcohol, 30.6 percent used tobacco, and 16.7 percent used illicit drugs. (See fig. 3.2.) The NSDUH estimates that 6.4 percent of those who used alcohol abused it in the past year, whereas only 2.7 percent abused illicit drugs. Looking at the breakdown of the data by various substances, it is significant that the users of the drug most used after alcohol and cigarettes, marijuana, report only a 1.6 percent abuse rate for the 13.0 percent of illicit drug users who used marijuana. Interestingly, the NSDUH does not report the number of users who report abusing tobacco products. However, we know that nicotine addiction rates are higher than those for any other drug. Neuroscientist David Linden writes that 80 percent of all people who try smoking cigarettes

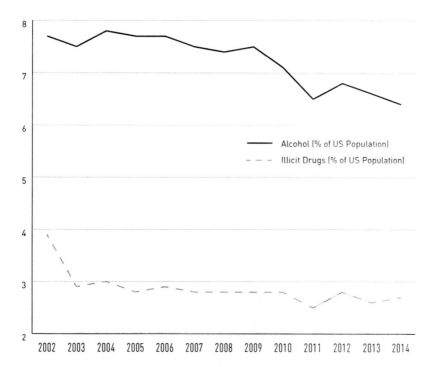

FIGURE 3.1. Drug and alcohol abuse rates, 2002–14. Data from the NSDUH, Substance Abuse and Mental Health Services Administration, 2015.

become dependent, yet the term *addict* is rarely applied to smokers in public discourse.[66] The NSDUH notes that 55.2 percent of smokers smoked in the past month and, of them, 40.3 percent used daily, smoking one or more packs a day, which, given the data on difficulty quitting smoking, suggests a prevalence and quantity that would indicate a use pattern like other drug abuse or drug dependence.[67]

To put the question another way: why are there not more addicts? Over 97 percent of Americans who use an addictive drug other than alcohol do not become addicted to it. For drinkers, the percentage is nearly the same: over 92 percent do not become addicted to alcohol. In other words, *only 3 percent of those who use illicit drugs become addicts, and only 7 percent of alcohol users become addicted.*[68] Those are significant numbers, percentages that are almost hard to believe. While any number of addicts is too many, these figures are radically divergent from the cultural discourse about the dangers of drug use and addiction. To begin to answer the question, there are fewer addicts than we expect for a variety of reasons. Addiction discourse

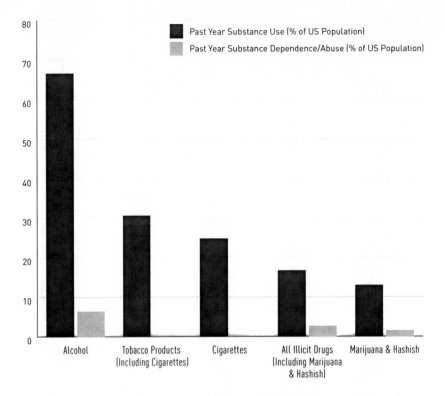

FIGURE 3.2. Drug use and abuse rates, 2014. Data from the NSDUH, Substance Abuse and Mental Health Services Administration, 2015.

constructs user identity as part of what American culture scholar Eoin Cannon calls "an imaginary democracy of sufferers."[69] The general cultural discourse about psychoactive drug use presumes that users' biological, psychological, and phenomenological experiences of these drugs are the same and have but one end point: addiction. But research across fields shows us that users adapt differently to the same drugs, and that users' circumstances and context influence use.[70] More to the point, the overestimation of addicts is based on observations of a distinct subpopulation more likely to be seen in clinical settings. Health-care professionals extrapolate from extreme cases to create what Hart calls a "caricature of addiction."[71] The director of the NIAAA's Division of Treatment and Recovery Research, psychiatrist Mark Willenbring, acknowledges that the context and expectations for addiction research have directly influenced an overgeneralization about psychoactive drug use and addiction. "[R]esearchers have studied the patients seen in hospitals and clinics most intensively. This can greatly skew understanding of a disorder, especially in the alcohol field, where most people neither seek nor receive treatment and those who seek it do so well into the course of disease."[72] By looking primarily at extreme use, research has delimited the field of inquiry and thus the ability to learn about what makes a minority of users drug-dependent in the context of a majority who are not.

Because the focus on drug use has largely been on addiction—an extreme but variable point at the end of the user spectrum—and professional and social discourses have conflated use with abuse, Americans have misrepresented and generally failed to acknowledge other kinds of drug use. Users who do not fit the profile of addiction but are "other" (users whose use practices may be medically unmanaged, casual, recreational, infrequent, or controlled) can be invisible to health-care professionals and researchers—especially users with financial and social resources and fewer of the risk factors that lead them to medical treatment.[73] The reasons why most users do not become addicted are complex and specific to each user and situation. One group rarely acknowledged by researchers and healthcare professionals is the significant number of people who discontinue excessive drug use without treatment.[74] Those users, who may have episodes of abuse or dependence, but self-resolve their drug dependence, experience what researchers call "natural recovery." Some of these users have strong social safety nets to help them avoid addiction. Others simply stop using on their own. Some find compelling external incentives to overcome addiction. Controlled or nonproblematic users of psychoactive drugs are not often discussed in drug discourse. We rarely hear about episodic drug abusers or controlled drug users because they do not fit our cultural or institutional narratives, and thus do not register within our systems to track excessive and problematic drug use. Given the strong belief that elective drug use results in addiction, it is understandable that controlled users are silent.

When it comes to more comprehensively understanding practices of drug use, it is difficult to determine what drug use is cultural and what is simply a preference, what is user-controlled, and what is psychological and/ or physical drug dependence. In the debate about whether some substances have more of an addictive liability than others, it is clear that, whether or not a substance is stronger (say, fentanyl versus heroin), it may not be more addictive. The cluster of factors involved in the use of a drug most likely affect addictive potential. Such factors include availability, use frequency, reason for use (self-medication for a psychological problem as opposed to general recreation and leisure), methods of administration, and other broader life factors such as whether one has a job and regular income, immediate family, etc. In addition, the relative availability of drugs, alcohol, and tobacco and the social norms about their use also impact user practice. Nicotine is widely available to users eighteen years of age and older. Its use rates have dropped in recent years due to social efforts to limit smoking in public places and to encourage nicotine users to stop smoking. However, teen smoking is on the rise, and other nicotine-delivery devices, such as electronic cigarettes, are growing in use among smokers. While the NSDUH shows that the use of street drugs like heroin and methamphetamine has seen modest decreases and increases somewhat relative to the availability of these drugs, the repurposing of pharmaceutical opiates and stimulants has increased. Furthermore, in social context, user practices are multidimensional. An example of this is the contemporary norm of working long, productive hours, a practice which creates an imperative to sleep on demand. This expectation has led to powerful stimulants and sleep medications to which users can become dependent. Which is the greater danger: a reliance on (or even addiction to) stimulants and sleep medications, or the cultural expectation that we live and work in such a way as to exceed the capacity of our circadian rhythms—and thus necessitate such interventions?

RETHINKING USER AGENCY: WHO'S USING?

Framing most practices of psychoactive drug use as addiction has inadvertently co-opted the potential for more nuanced understanding of drugs and their users. It has also dictated cultural responses to using, from policy, to funding for research and law enforcement, to an emphasis on recovery. Addiction stands as a cultural metonym for psychoactive drug use that takes place outside the scope of medical authority or oversight. This misconception not only limits the perceived field of drug use, it erases agency by imagining that users cannot or do not control their practice—because they are thought to be compelled by either a brain disorder or an uncontrollable behavioral compulsion. Such direction of attention and resources away from the broader spectrum of psychoactive drug use also prevents discussions and research about how and why people use, including the acknowledgement of enjoyment as a key element of the altered states of intoxication or mild indulgence.

All discourses that cast psychoactive drug users as passive, substance-dependent agents misconstrue users in one significant way: often, this is not how users view themselves while using. Nor is it how they recount their experiences later, even after they cease using.[75] Even some harm-reduction discourse, often seen as pro-user, assumes that illicit drug use leads to harm and downplays the fact that millions of users get pleasure from drug use. Addiction discourse, especially in the medical and public health domains, has often masked the social contexts related to drug use. Using drugs, medical anthropologist Kim Sue writes, might be seen as "an epistemological stance towards the world."[76] Some scholars argue that extreme use and/or addiction, albeit risky, can be seen as a form of life experimentation.[77] The drug-induced experience of opening one's mind to intellectual, psychological, and social connections, or letting go in a temporary lack of control, is what many users of particular drugs describe as a reason they use.

Human agency is complex: it is multifaceted, responsive to context, and dynamic. Subjectivity is expressed through and against the cultural frameworks that shape and constitute us. In this sense, it is useful to think of user agency like any other composite of identities and choices people make about consumption, experiences, and lifestyle in any given moment. Hart, Heyman, neuroscientist Marc Lewis, and other researchers who study addict agency have found a reliable ability in users—even those who are substance dependent—to make choices that do not serve substance dependence. That moment in which using is a controlled choice can be and, the data show, is actually the norm for the majority of users. Illicit or other psychoactive drug use is no different from the use of licit, socialized psychoactive drugs. In some ways, use of illicit or repurposed psychoactive drugs is as (or more) controlled than some "social drinking" of alcohol. If someone takes a hallucinogen or MDMA a few times a year, for example, is that user's agency any more or less controlled than someone who gets intoxicated on holidays? If she smokes a little marijuana daily, is that any different than having a glass of wine or two with dinner? Or, if she uses Adderall or crystal methamphetamine on occasion to focus at work or to stay out late partying, is that any different than consuming several energy drinks or cups of coffee to do the same? Answers to these questions are often based on an ostensibly medical rationale that one drug does less harm than another—which is more of an assumption than a medical finding. We have not studied the use of these drugs in ways that compare apples to apples.

Building on Kim's notion of drug use and even addiction as an epistemological stance toward the world, one might conceive of the varieties of drug use as expressing not just individual desire or need, but also a strategy of individualized well-being within a cultural imperative to medicalize the self. For some users at some times, drug use is a path to health and well-being. For others, it is a lifestyle practice that does not have a medical association.

Still, for others, using may at times be a means of self-expression and exploration. Drug use is a way to engage cultural rituals: whether a toast celebrating the culmination of a project, a smoke on a work break, or a pill to study for finals. People's use practices are expressions of individual agency and desire. Discourses of addiction and medicalization constitute frameworks that do not begin to adequately encompass the many practices of using in the United States. Much of Americans' drug use is off the radar, not only because some of it is illegal, but also because culturally normalized behavior such as drinking alcohol is not recognized as psychoactive drug use. What Americans think about using depends greatly on who is using what drugs.[78]

One legacy of our various addiction discourses is that addiction has come to be a broadly used cultural idiom. Aside from its clinical diagnostic use, *addiction* functions as a vernacular term that normalizes a state of excess. The broad application of *addict* to various activities and choices that are unlikely to meet any professional standards for dependence further confuses the word's meaning. What does one mean by the generalized use of the word *addiction* to describe immoderate or problematic compulsive behavior? When used outside the context of substance-dependence, *addiction* often describes overindulgence in a disingenuous or remorseless way, ironically or even proudly proclaiming one's compulsions: "I'm addicted to these cookies." Do we really mean we have substance dependence? Or is the ability to use that term so loosely a tacit indication that the speaker knows she is *not* an addict? The effects of this trend are both subtle and substantial. It suggests that most people are addicted to something. Or, it could mean that people fail to recognize addiction as a serious condition. It might mean that while Americans grasp the severe impact of addiction, they have given up any expectation of self-control or individual agency. In an ironic twist, *addiction* can imply a socially acceptable way of excusing poor self-control.

While the majority of Americans are not addicts, most are psychoactive drug users. Psychoactive drugs in regular use are so ritualized and standardized that people may not consider their consumption to be drug use. Strong interest in uncontrolled use of addictive drugs has all but eclipsed notice and discussion of elective or controlled unmanaged use. Rather than conceiving of controlled use as a norm, the addiction/recovery industry's medicalization of using casts abstinence—the absence of use—as a norm for many drugs. This skews the view of drug use with cultural inconsistencies: using alcohol is acceptable; smoking is not. Using caffeine is acceptable; using amphetamines is not. From the perspective of users of whatever drugs, it is possible to understand that experience not as a pejorative identity but as a social reality with various cultural and political ramifications. Even individual users have a variety of practices: periods of use, sporadic use, and continuous controlled or uncontrolled use of both licit and illicit psychoactive drugs. What is missing in the cultural conversation about using is an honest dialogue about all using as a spectrum, with normative, controlled use on one end and addiction or uncontrollable use on the other. Thinking of use beyond addiction raises questions because scientific or sociopolitical trends or tolerance for particular drugs come and go. Neuroscience enjoys a current vogue that seems unassailable, obscuring economic, historical, political, and other ways of understanding experience. But minute shifts are taking place as harm reduction, decriminalization, and other successful social means of engaging users evolve.

Conceptual frameworks that have been constructed through language shape how American culture conceives of drugs, users, abuse, treatment, and medical authority. These definitions are cultural—and culture has the potential to change. The cumulative effect of cultural shifts enacted at the level of communities of treatment and practice—reframing how we describe, discuss, and engage drug use and addiction—might mean that a user would understand herself and her use differently. If addiction is greatly overrepresented in American drug discourse, what might be learned from drug users if the majority who do not suffer "drug use disorder" are recognized? How might Americans begin to understand user agency? Beyond recovery communities or treatment of abuse, broadly reconceptualizing *using* has the potential to change how people conceive of ourselves and our bodies. In a very real way, it might radically change people's sense of who they are. Perhaps Americans are not the depressed, diseased sum of their nutritional inputs. Perhaps they are far more in charge of their selves and, as part of that agency, seek various experiences, some of which are found through the pursuit of pleasure in the use of psychoactive drugs.

VOX

LUCIUS
NOT WHAT YOU THINK

I am an addict. I've dealt with addiction since I was an adolescent, and it's plagued me most of my adult life. I struggled with three different substances—meth, alcohol, and tobacco—over thirty years. Now I am clean and I choose not to use anymore.

My life is not what you think: I no longer crave those drugs. What I struggle with is the desire to overuse something, anything that will push me beyond the edge. Pushing myself past that boundary is a high like no other. I constantly check to see if something I am enjoying is affecting me in a negative way. Now that I exercise and eat right, I have to make sure that I don't overdo those things. Am I working out too much? Is twice a day too much? I ask myself: is this addiction? I know it's better than drinking a case of beer and chewing a can of Copenhagen in one night. It's also better than snorting meth lines the size of coke rails just to feel normal.

Each of my addictions took a different approach to resolve. They all had a unique hook into my brain, but whether they were socially acceptable also really affected my ability to stop using. Alcohol is in stores, on TV, in magazines, on the Internet, on my Facebook feed, everywhere. I tried for years to reign in my drinking. I simply couldn't. My drinking only accelerated. It was hard just to come to terms with the fact that I had a problem. I finally checked myself into rehab for almost three weeks and had friends remove all drinking-related paraphernalia from my home. Aversion therapy was my way of getting clean: I received electric shock therapy to reprogram my brain to have a negative response to alcohol. When I got out, I created social barriers: I cut off all friends that drank from my life. I became a hermit inside my own home, because leaving it would expose me to the poison that could kill me.

There isn't good support for people who want to overcome illicit drug use because, in the eyes of society, you are a criminal. You have broken the law to use those drugs. So, to quit amphetamines, I removed myself from the situation and the subculture, which broke my link to accessing meth. That made meth the easiest substance for me to stop using. After leaving that scene, all it took was a week or so of self-care and I was done. No withdrawals, no serious rehab, nothing. If anything, I missed some of the people, but that was it.

When I mention that I was a tobacco user, most people just shrug their shoulders. It's no big deal. But nicotine was by far the hardest drug to quit. I tried maybe twenty to fifty times to stop. The hook is different with nicotine. The temptation is always there. The chance of relapse is so much higher. Monitored ways to quit using nicotine, like residential treatment, just aren't available. It has been a year since I last used it. I hope this time I kicked it.

As a parent and a professional, I find it both easy and hard to talk about addiction. I can talk openly about my alcohol problem because it's socially acceptable. One day, in my son's high-school class, they were discussing substance abuse. The teacher asked if anyone had firsthand experience. No one raised their hand or said anything. He finally did and said "My dad went to rehab." I was very proud when he told me that. I was very open with my kids when I decided to seek help for my drinking problem. In contrast to being open about alcoholism, though, I can't talk openly about my meth use. My kids have no idea their dad was "a dirty meth user." That is what we see in our mind's eye when we hear that someone used meth. I can't talk about it to most people because they have a preconceived notion of what I may have been, or what I may be.

Addiction, for me, is a disease. It's like having ADHD or OCD. Just like those things, it's genetic. My dad and all my grandparents died as the result of their addictions. I don't want to. I think somewhere deep inside of me that history is a driving force to stay clean. It has been lonely not having those family members in my life. I don't want my kids to have to go through that.

NADINE

LIKE A STORM

Depression comes to me like a storm, briefly outlining my world in silver. In that moment, I am painfully and completely alive and it is beautiful. Then meaningless grief engulfs me and the stone lodges in my chest, heavier than gravity. I look at the world through inverted binoculars. It is hard to move or think or even breathe. I've suffered from periods of depression my whole life. I started taking medication in college, when doctors dispensed Prozac like aspirin. At some point, a doctor put me on Paxil with the promise that it would change my brain chemistry. That sounded good to me. After many years without feeling the depression, I decided my brain chemistry was suitably repaired and I could wean myself off the drug. I was wrong.

Paxil withdrawal produced a different sort of depression. I became horribly permeable. Random words imposed themselves on me: *sleestak sleestak sleestak*. I didn't even know what a *sleestak* was until I looked it up, but no matter, there it was: *sleestak sleestak sleestak*, over and over. I stopped riding the subway because the faces of strangers broke my heart. If I sat down, I froze, unable to move. While frozen, I wanted to smash my head against the countertop. I knew I had to crush either the left side of my left hand or the left side of my left foot and I was filled with guilty sorrow for my helpless little fingers and toes. Sometimes, it took days to get unstuck, and when a doctor said I should go to the emergency room, I had to tell her that I could not move.

My increasingly desperate doctors tried to find a cocktail that would mitigate the Paxil withdrawal, but in the end, I went back to my original dose and had to add two more antidepressants to become human again. Paxil, it seems, wove itself into my brain structure, and pulling it out crumbled my psyche.

During those months, I tried my own DIY treatments, ranging from meditation to self-injury. I drank a lot. I tried marijuana for the first time in twenty years and it kindly reminded me that my brain could feel delight, but the effects did not last. I slept too much. I listened to relaxation CDs. I stabbed myself in the thigh with a sterile syringe and dragged the point until it threatened to break. Physically, I felt nothing. Mentally, I felt everything. It was too much.

Finally, I tried opiates. They worked. With opiates, I felt normal again. Ten milligrams of an opiate drew a sweet softness around me, sedating my vigilant brain so I could remember what it felt like to be human. Nothing hurt anymore. I looked at each fear and regret without any attachment, without any suffering. My grasping ego let go and I just *was*. I can't say opiates made me happy, but they made me OK and that felt like a miracle. Each time I used, I tried to burn that normalcy into my brain so I could eventually find my way back without any drugs.

In time, I stopped dreaming of smashing my head against the countertop. I wriggled my fingers and toes with gratitude. I stood up. I looked back at the faces of strangers. Once I felt better, I walked away from the opiates as easy as you please.

Here's what I want you to know: a prescription drug undid my mind, and the illegal use of another one gave me my mind back. Drug packaging informs me that all medications have risks and benefits, and my doctor has decided that the benefits outweigh the risks. Paxil inscribed itself permanently into my brain chemistry, rendering me an addict. I think about the risks and benefits of tinkering with my brain chemistry differently now. My little stash of opiates is tucked away in a safe place just in case, but now that I feel better, I have no desire to use them. They are medicine, after all, and I am finally no longer sick.

JOSÉ

THE CURE

Think of methadone as an agency consolidating your bills into manageable payments, but with even more difficult escape clauses than the drug you are taking it to get away from. Methadone is many, many times more addictive than heroin: the withdrawal period is eleven to fifteen days (compared to the five for heroin). During the 1960s, the Black Panthers burned down many methadone clinics in a war against a treatment they considered worse than the drug that was and still is wrecking so many cities. On the plus side, with methadone, you get a controlled dosage with no surprises. So many weekends, when a much-stronger-than-usual-batch of heroin would hit the streets, a half-dozen people would bite it. So you avoid that terror known only to someone unlucky enough to have a toxic reaction to the shit they cut the heroin with, or the unclean spoon you cooked the dope in, or the fiber of cotton that snuck in, and within fifteen minutes your temperature shoots up to 104, and you're vomiting and convulsing. In this case, you either (a) die, (b) do another shot to hopefully counteract the effects of the first, or (c) get your first experience with paramedics who think you're below the level of scum and don't give a shit whether or not you die. They inject you with Narcan, a real motherfucker of a drug that hits your brain within seconds like a sledgehammer, kicks all the heroin out of the opiate receptors, and sends your body into total and instant withdrawal. But even worse than all of this is the required counseling you are required to attend while on methadone. The only thing comparable to the tortuous boredom of hanging out with a whining smackhead whose chin keeps dropping to his chest is an ex-smackhead who thinks you want to hear every insipid detail of his formative drug experiences. I am equally suspicious of the people offering the Ibogaine cure: how can you trust the good intentions of someone selling for three thousand or twenty thousand dollars a cure that costs them less than twenty dollars?

BRITTANY
ASK YOUR DOCTOR

When I was diagnosed with epilepsy at age twenty-nine, I was put on an antiseizure medication called Lamictal. I was in a fog about my surprising diagnosis and put all my faith in my doctor to help me manage my illness. He didn't give me much information about the medication, and I didn't question his decision or do a lot of research. If I had, I would have discovered this: Lamictal may cause your mental health to change in unexpected ways. In clinical studies, about one in five hundred people who took anti-epileptics such as Lamictal became suicidal during treatment. Some of these people developed suicidal thoughts and behavior as early as one week into the study. The symptoms read like a worst-case scenario: you may develop panic attacks; agitation or restlessness; new or worsening irritability, anxiety, or depression; acting on dangerous impulses; difficulty falling or staying asleep; aggressive, angry, or violent behavior; mania; talking or thinking about wanting to hurt yourself or end your life; withdrawing from friends and family; preoccupation with death and dying; giving away prized possessions.

A few weeks after I began taking the medication, I started having most of those symptoms. I was incredibly sensitive to comments people made to me, I would cry constantly—and I mean constantly—and when asked why I was crying, I didn't have an answer. I would rock back and forth on the bathroom floor at night and just sob, thankful that I could hide and cry while no one was watching. I couldn't sleep. I constantly thought all this sadness made my life not worth living. Then one day, I thought about jumping off the balcony, and I knew: "Houston, we have a problem." I was no longer in control of my thoughts or feelings or, really, my own being, except for a few moments in a day. It was a loss of control I had never experienced before. I considered stopping taking the Lamictal, but I was terrified of the consequences. My seizures happened while I slept, and there was a very real possibility that I would stop breathing.

Over this period of months, I lived with someone who observed how the medication was affecting me. His father was a doctor, so he got me in to see a physician at Mercy Hospital. The new doctor switched my medication immediately. When I had urged my original doctor to change my medication, he repeatedly told me that the symptoms I was having were a normal psychological reaction to the diagnosis, not the medication. In other words, my doctor completely ignored my concerns. Physicians can't predict all the effects that a drug can have on a patient. But I truly believe that if my doctor would have paid any attention to what I was reporting, all this could have been avoided. It was 2001; there was plenty of information available to him. He just wasn't interested in hearing my complaints. A few years later, my new physician called me at work to tell me that my previous doctor had been fired. And to think, I trusted that doctor with my life.

CHAPTER 4

WHY WE USE

The Pleasure and the Eros of Drugs

> What kind of journey is desire that its direction is so deceptive?
> —JUDITH BUTLER, *SUBJECTS OF DESIRE*

THE FIRST TIME YOU EXPERIENCED ALTERED CONSCIOUSNESS, when you noticed that you were perceiving the world a different way, what did it feel like? Was it an experience of uncertainty or excitement? Maybe you associated that set of sensations with enjoyment, anxiety, or confusion. For some, that pleasure may have been discovered in childhood with the euphoria of intentionally getting dizzy or riding a first caffeine buzz; for others, being intoxicated may have been a welcome relief from teenage angst when trying alcohol or marijuana for the first time.[1] The initial sensation may have been comforting and chances are, some version of altered consciousness through psychoactive drug use has become a customary part of your life. Whether it was introduced by your community of friends and family or was a forbidden pleasure, altered consciousness is a shared human experience. The use of psychoactive drugs—or pursuits that produce similar results—is social and often ritualized. Although Americans sometimes struggle with and even ban certain use practices of pleasure, they celebrate and instill the practice of others. For many people, some form of psychoactive drug use is part of the behaviors learned from family and social systems, which they continue to practice. In the United States, nonacquaintance with any psychoactive drug by the time one is an adult is an exception to the norm.[2]

Why do people choose to alter consciousness through psychoactive drug use or activity? The answer, in part if not entirely, is that they find it pleasurable. There is a distinct desire in the pleasure that informs various use practices, from the tantalizing smell of morning coffee to the bitter tang of a cold beer on a hot day. The anticipation and satisfaction of a particular pleasure is the basis of its sensual appeal. Yet, despite a cultural predilection for indulgence and intoxication, expression about pleasure itself is often conflicted in the United States. Although some practices and discourses of pleasure, such as wine connoisseurship, have become central to acts of consumption, the intoxicating pleasure of indulgence is not often the focus of that discourse. Rather, oenophiles write and talk about a very controlled, experiential enjoyment of wine that disassociates part of the drug's appeal (taste and smell) from its intoxicating effects. While Americans practice and capitalize on the thrills and excitement of pleasure, there can be a social reluctance to discuss pleasure for pleasure's sake when it comes to certain psychoactive drugs and, especially, intoxication.

Some pleasurable psychoactive drugs have become so acculturated that their gratifications are commonplace or even unnoticeable. The habitual consumption of coffee, tea, chocolate, alcohol, and tobacco is central to and even expected in the United States.[3] At the same time, the pleasure found in using many other drugs in the United States can be coded as deviant: criminal and/or compulsive. Many psychoactive drugs, particularly illicit drugs, have been subsumed almost entirely into narratives of maladaptation or addiction—narratives that specifically correlate use with a motivation to self-medicate (for psychic or physical pain), a lack of individual control, or extensive hedonism. But all drugs have variable functions for users. Drug historian David Courtwright and others have noted that historically, "alcohol and other drugs played multiple, often positive social roles—as markers of identity, occasions of conviviality, talismans of faith—that had little to do with addiction."[4] Indeed, the end point of most psychoactive drug use is for pleasure or to enhance mood, whether through a glass of wine, a cup of coffee, a cigarette, energy drinks, or prescription stimulants. Frequently, these drugs fit comfortably within the social norms of many Americans' day-to-day experience as practices of controlled use, practices through which people have integrated altering consciousness—and pleasure—into their lives.

Controlled or normalized use does not mean that people use these drugs without noticeable effect. Although there are many possible experiences that result from taking psychoactive drugs, intoxication is potentially the most significant experience and reward. Intoxication expresses a spectrum more than an endpoint: experiences of intoxication incorporate various changes in perception, cognition, affect, and behavior. Social responses to these states also express a broad range of experience. Some intoxications or highs are fairly tolerated as expressions of individual consciousness. They can function as a temporary means to transgress boundaries or cultural norms. But the permission to let go and get tipsy or wasted still hangs in balance with the imperative for social order. Not surprisingly, when public policy and research discourses focus on intoxication, they tend to focus their gaze where public health or social order is impacted: at the extremes of use. This disproportionate emphasis on the negative effects of various use practices unfortunately elides the role of pleasure as well as the user agency in those pursuits. Although US discourses of medicalization and criminalization have diminished the legitimacy of psychoactive pleasure, the choice and desire to get high have to be examined apart from these cultural paradigms. To understand the choice to alter consciousness through psychoactive drug practice differently, one must set aside preconceptions that drug use is pathological, irrational, and demonstrates a lack of user agency or control. If most controlled or normative drug use is an expression of some form of pleasure seeking, then users plot a vast terrain of experience and agency. As the primary motivation in the choice to alter consciousness, the desire for pleasure is essential to understanding the practices of all drug users. This chapter seeks to reconfigure "drug use" by considering the desire to alter consciousness and the pleasures expressed therein as a rational, controlled behavior at the heart of American culture.

Psychoactive drug use practices create a range of rewarding sensations and experiences that users seek *to feel good*. This is not to oversimplify the complexity and range of psychoactive use practices so much as it is to focus on the use practices people less frequently acknowledge and examine. The experience of a particular drug can be quite variable among users—and even for the same user across different incidents of use. Further, the experience of a drug is certainly affected by much more than rational choice and agency. Set and setting deeply influence a use experience, despite the user's original intent and freedom to choose it. For example, many users find that ketamine can provoke a bold, immediate high, a disassociation from self, and/or hallucinations. But researchers note that for severely depressed patients, the feeling is different, as if something plaguing the user had been removed.[5] While there are many potential experiences with the use of any psychoactive drug, among them are the reliable pleasures normative users seek in their use practices for a variety of reasons. For example, I consume marijuana or hallucinogens like mushrooms or LSD on occasion as a welcome break from the constant pressures of work. These drugs help me let go of my inner taskmaster, and promote a different way of feeling and thinking. All of those are pleasures that involve the sensations from the actual psychoactive drug itself, as well as the feelings of respite and/or social activity that I enjoy. The psychological and bodily experience or phenomenology of drug use is complex and invites study of the nuanced, motivating aspects of user pleasure—whether mild stimulation or more captivating intoxications.

To contemplate what cultural historian Stuart Walton calls "the whole field of experience of intoxication," I include a wide range of use practices in this discussion.[6] Use practices that alter consciousness so we experience different pleasurable states include practices and drugs of many sorts: from spiritual practices (i.e., meditation, prayer, fasting, and charismatic activities) to secular practices that alter consciousness (i.e., ultramarathoning), and use practices involving different psychoactive drugs—from stimulants to sedatives, anxiolytics to opioids, and marijuana to hallucinogens.[7] While this definition of *using* may be too inclusive for some readers, consider suspending disbelief to entertain the possibility of consciousness-changing use practices and drugs as a spectrum of options. If people identify, recognize, and legitimize the desire to pursue pleasure as a rational act, they find themselves looking at their own and others' use practices differently—often through an alignment with those practices that they already understand and accept. What does drug use or use practice mean for various people, and what does it represent? What can people learn from their use practices about drug use as a common behavior that expresses individual agency in the pursuit of pleasure? This analysis will explore drug use and use practices in this context, as a form of embodied subjectivity through which users express self-knowledge and identity.

PLEASURE AND THE QUESTION OF USER AGENCY:
WHO IS IN CONTROL WHEN YOU LOSE CONTROL?

While Americans' actions exhibit the intoxicating or sublime pleasure of psychoactive drug use, the driver of US drug discourse has been the question of personal and social control of such impulses. Use practices involving more transparent drugs that improve functionality, drugs like caffeine that do not obviously interfere with one's ability to perform, are widely socially acceptable. Such drugs seem to involve a minimal shift in consciousness and so their pleasure is practical in nature and often helps maintain self-control. Consider the American workplace's institutionalization of coffee breaks (and, formerly, cigarette breaks) and, now that break time has become less common, the availability of coffee and other caffeinated drinks onsite. Alert workers are more focused, productive workers. Although the functionality of these stimulants brings pleasure to users, that pleasure itself is usually not censured in the way it can be with drugs associated with more noticeable psychoactive changes. While its sensory effect is the key attraction of any drug that favorably changes one's experience or mood, social acceptance of these more powerful experiences of unrestrained pleasure has a fraught social history. In a country where the temperance movement and drug prohibition have framed such states as personally and socially dangerous, American actions and discourses are conflicted. Pleasure, especially that found in illicit drugs or use practices, but also that found in any sought-after expression of intoxication, can be suspect largely because it represents a loosening of control. Literary scholar Marcus Boon points out that, historically, "Drugs themselves were pictured as seductresses," illustrating the power we ascribe to drugs, whether real or imagined.[8] This fundamental issue—who is in control when you "lose control" through intoxication?—informs a social ambivalence about the pleasure sought through psychoactive drug use.

For users of particular drugs, the question of self-control and discourses of excess may have less social significance. In such cases, pleasures that can be interpreted within other cultural discourses are less answerable to charges of self-indulgence. For example, if spending an evening in a bar with friends, the user may be regarded within the context of consumerism, quite capable of making rational choices about the products and behavior that suit the situation.[9] Similarly, the craftsman culture around wine, beer, and cider have made drinking alcohol a destination activity: the entire point is pleasurable indulgence while consuming the product in a context of expert enjoyment. Or, such pleasurable excesses can be more acceptable if they are thought to be good for your health. (I think here of the dozens of distance runners I know, including myself, who have run themselves into debilitating injury by adding more and more mileage.) Yet even if a user is perceived as capable of rational agency, the drug itself may become the locus of irrational risk. The lack of regulation of street drugs, for example, results in an overdose risk, one that has involved a rise in heroin deaths both by longtime heroin users and former prescription opiate users who are encountering fentanyl or other extremely strong drugs in their "heroin." While altering consciousness with socially accepted drugs such as alcohol clearly expresses a recognized and legitimate individual agency, use practices at the margins of mainstream culture are not always understood as sensible expressions of user agency. Drug use that is not standardized within cultural practice—such as the diversion of prescription stimulants or use of street drugs—tends to be stigmatized as uncontrolled use. Not all pleasures, pleasure seekers, and users share the same cultural authority—this varies by social, economic, and material conditions, as well as by use practices and drugs. In the contexts of criminalization and medicalization, the variation in degree of acceptability among pleasures is an expression of social power.[10]

Because Americans expect some level of intoxication to be the principal expression of any "high," this sort of pleasure seeking is understood as antithetical to the actions of a rational subject. In this context, sociologist Angus Bancroft writes, intoxication becomes deviant, "a threat to individual autonomy, the self-willing, self-activating, and self-making personhood at the heart of liberal philosophy. . . . walled off from day-to-day life, surrounded by strict moral regulations and conceived of as a space of abandonment, where necessary repressions are briefly suspended."[11] Here, the subject is defined through her ability or failure to meet social norms by controlling her desire. Users who reject such social interventions between desire and action—either by temporarily suspending social repressions or by abandoning them entirely—express an autonomy that threatens social order. Even within the discursive context of self- and social control, there is a fundamental connection between pleasure and user rationality, because pain and pleasure are constituted as a spectrum of rational calculation.[12] Still, as medical anthropologist Cameron Duff and other researchers point out, this ends-oriented behavior model frames illicit drug users through "a grim calculus of perceived risks and benefits" in which "[p]leasure is conceived of as a 'good' . . . only in those instances where putative benefits outweigh any real or imagined risks."[13]

This neoliberal framework fails to register the lived experience of the various distinctly pleasurable elements of using: the corporeal and sensory enjoyment experienced in and through enhanced sociability, closeness, or confidence. The desire and choice to get high, especially on illicit drugs, can be read as a rejection of health, rationality, and the social institutions and representatives that mediate such desires (i.e., medical professionals, law enforcement, social workers, etc.). Frequently, the social response to the pleasure seekers' rejection of self-governance is to deny the legitimacy of the pleasure found in that act. Framed through the lens of the neoliberal subject, user agency is constrained even in harm reduction, where the user's agency is often understood as a means of empowering users not to seek pleasure but to minimize drug-related problems in their lives. Reading the use practices of both controlled and abusive users through the equation of risks and harms, as opposed to benefits, completely obscures the relevance and motivating influence of desire and pleasure. In some cases, such as celebrating an event with alcohol, most people set aside discourses of individual

WHY WE USE   137

self-control for the shared experience of pleasure. The social permission to
drink more than a moderate amount of alcohol may ignore a limit based
on good health for the sake of communal pleasure. Yet, while a user's basic
agency to make a choice to use a drug might be acknowledged, endorsing the
pursuit of pleasure through a street drug as a rational choice is less probable.
The capitalist model of the right to pleasure as an incentive or reward is not
only pervasive in the culture of consumption, but it situates using in relation to work and risk management—rather than as an intrinsic pleasure and
pursuit in itself. Drug scholars Patrick O'Malley and Mariana Valverde call
this dynamic "a presumptive right to pleasure and a duty to govern risks."[14]
In US culture, only some users of some drugs are understood to be capable
of self-governance in the pursuit of a pleasure or reward.

Drug research often reflects professional domain assumptions tied to
discourses of individual functionality, risk, and harm. In general, research
has focused on drug users through the epistemology of abuse and addiction,
focusing on recovery or harm reduction, the history of drug use and policy,
social justice, and health care—all frameworks that largely ignore or restrict
pleasure as the initial and primary motivation for using.[15] Anthropologist
David Moore sees how these trends marginalize pleasure as a topic in drug
research, a silencing that both reflects and sustains dominant cultural drug
discourses. The dominance of medicalization and addiction in drug research
is supported through "greater funding, numerical superiority in terms
of researchers and projects and the use of methodological and analytical
approaches that are accorded greater scientific credibility."[16] These priorities
impede understanding recreational drug use as beneficial in any way. Further,
the brain-disease model of addiction de-emphasizes the possibility of user
agency and control. Nora Volkow, director of the National Institute on Drug
Abuse, asserts that "our biology conspires against us with brains that are hard-
wired to increase pleasure and decrease pain."[17] Volkow's essentialist language
signals a key distinction: the brain-disease model of addiction suggests that
people are governed and manipulated by their brain chemistry's drive for
pleasure. Yet, the notion that the brain and body conspire against you is a
peculiar disassociation. If the biochemical impetus for pleasure is intrinsic
to embodied experience, then the desire to seek pleasure would seem to be
an expression of being human. The phenomenology of embodied pleasure
and the agency to seek it has remained relatively uncultivated critical ground
in terms of understanding drug use as a fundamental human experience.

Part of the problem with understanding pleasure in drug use is that
American drug narratives coalesce around addiction. Outside of alcohol

use, stories of normative drug users are not part of public drug discourses, so there is a considerable absence of information and understanding about the majority of users' experiences. Further, user experience has been tacitly if not explicitly understood as "subjugated knowledge," conveying little to no authority among professional drug discourses.[18] Howard Becker's 1953 sociological study of marijuana use for pleasure was radical and foundational in its challenge to dominant theories about the motivations for drug consumption. Becker's analysis of his interviews with fifty marijuana users led him to focus on the learned acculturation to the use of a drug as central to the ability to enjoy it. "No one becomes a user without (1) learning to smoke the drug in a way which will produce real effects; (2) learning to recognize the effects and connect them with drug use (learning, in other words, to get high); and (3) learning to enjoy the sensations he perceives." Becker points out that the positive answer to "Is it fun?" is a learned behavior in adopting a use practice.[19] His focus on the developmental nature of the meaning associated with learned behaviors (drug use) was essential in validating that marijuana users perform and interpret pleasure as embodied experience. Becker's study raised the possibility of comprehending drug use from the perspective of the users themselves, through their own understanding of their use practices.

The legalization of recreational marijuana has created some new users, groups who are going through their first user experiences. A filmmaker in Seattle made a charming and comedic video about the process that Becker identifies, filming a study group of three grandmothers who learn to smoke marijuana for the first time. The video tracks the experience of these women over the hours of their first high. They are being taught to smoke marijuana from a bong and then a vaporizer, enjoying playing Cards Against Humanity, snacking and having tea, and laughing as they report on their evolving experience. They express delight at this new state of intoxication, especially the feelings of being spaced out and relaxed. Their comments demonstrate the process of beginning to identify with and embrace the high: "I think it was easier than I thought. And I think I prefer to do the bong and not the cigarette, the joint, whatever it's called." "I feel some tingle in my brain. Don't you?" "I feel like I'm smiling." (Laughter.) "I don't feel to me as high as they look to me." (More laughter.) "I would do it again, if I ever get this bag of chips open."[20] (See fig. 4.1.) Viewers witness the women become aware of and articulate their first moments of embodied knowledge of marijuana use in a single session. While they may or may not become "users" as a regular practice, the video makes explicit that these grandmothers learn to experience,

FIGURE 4.1. Still image from video, "Grandmas Smoking Weed for the First Time," Cut Video, November, 19, 2014.

enjoy, and interpret the pleasure of being high as an embodied experience relatively quickly. Further, it conveys that their use experience is a new and welcome kind of self-knowledge.

Fifty years after Becker's study, Kane Race's *Pleasure Consuming Medicine: The Queer Politics of Drugs* provides a significant theorizing of the role of pleasure in drug use. Race's study situates drug use and pleasure as factors directly related to the politics of sexual identity, intentionally decoupling user identity and agency from discourses of medicalization and addiction. While Race's focus is on queer subculture and the complexities of gay subjectivity, HIV culture, and the consumption of drugs for self-care (ranging from the preservation of health to pleasure seeking), his critique provides a powerful model for thinking about broader cultural use practices. Race argues not only that pleasure is a human need, but that its expression "function[s] as a claim on understanding, an insistence on agency, and a sort of challenge" in the liminal spaces of subaltern identity.[21] The user agency that Race observes in a particular demographic is important not just as a means of expressing varied kinds of pleasure, but because it constitutes a meaningful socio-political identity that rejects dominant cultural definition in every way. Race's study illustrates that what straight, mainstream American culture has come to interpret as problematic behavior from outside a use practice actually fulfills significant, unanticipated roles for practitioners in that user group. Writing about these identities and communities, Race notes that "[t]hough the present legal framework produces a drug culture that is shallow, individualistic, and criminal . . . mundane but consequential practices of safety, care, and differentiation still manage to circulate in this environment, where they form part of the recreational, ethical, or practical repertoire of participants in innumerable ordinary scenes and taste communities."[22]

Intoxication and use practices are typically framed within a narrative of social restraint—measuring productivity, discipline, or self-control against pleasure, intoxication, and lack of control. Race's contention that the act of using for pleasure is both an insistence on agency and a challenge to various forms of cultural authority also pertains to all users of illicit drugs who, despite legality and other potential barriers, use for pleasure. An alternative, intentional user identity is part of the expression of agency intrinsic to various drug use practices, particularly those that are nonsocialized and/or stigmatized. For users, the question of pleasure is as relevant as the question of control. What users experience through various kinds of intoxication, and the intentionality with which they engage and perceive their actions, is central to better understanding drug-use practices.

ALTERED CONSCIOUSNESS: PERFORMING AN ALTERED SELF

The English language has no shortage of referents for intoxication, yet colloquial words and phrases fail to convey a sense of scale to differentiate between qualitative experiences. A user might be tipsy, high, loaded, stoned, tripping, blown, drunk, wasted, out of it, hammered, on the nod, gone, euphoric, or many other things. What states of being do these words signify? What do these states of being *feel* like? While intoxication is not a monolithic experience, it is nearly impossible to differentiate between these descriptors' states of altered consciousness. Intoxications feel different to users based on set, setting, and the drugs themselves. The complexity of the ways in which these elements combine to create a high, what drug historian Isaac Campos calls the "psychoactive riddle," is something that researchers have yet to be able to codify.[23] The World Health Organization describes intoxication as a "disturbance in consciousness, cognition, perception, judgment, affect, or behavior."[24] The etymology of *intoxication*, from *toxicum*—to poison— carries a discursive ambivalence that philosopher Jacques Derrida locates in Plato's understanding of the *pharmakon* as "both remedy *and* poison."[25] In this sense, the contradictory and unstable pleasures of intoxication can be intricate to explore and even more difficult to explain.

Part of the challenge in discussing the experience of intoxicating pleasure has to do with how Western cultures have codified consciousness. One's sense of subjective experience or "reality" is difficult to express, much less discuss. Many scholars have tried to identify, understand, and even map consciousness through religious, psychological, neuroscientific, and philosophical discourses, But, as writer Michael Pollan points out, "consciousness is precisely the frontier where our materialistic understanding of the brain stops."[26] That knowledge gap is a space inhabited by, among other things, cultural assumptions about altered consciousness and pleasure. Understanding users requires acknowledgement of the various ways in which the mind and body experience pleasure. Psychoactive pleasures engage far more than physiognomy. Acts of drug use for pleasure, Stuart Walton writes, engage "multiform valences of altered consciousness," which themselves represent various dimensions of aesthetics and pleasures.[27] A focus on user experience, engaging users' psychological and physical sensations, highlights salient aspects of user phenomenologies and motivations.

The effects and experiences of drug-use practices have changeable but comprehensible individual and cultural meaning.[28] One of the key challenges in describing the phenomenology of any drug-use practice is to gauge, express, and represent sensory experience. Philosopher Maurice Merleau-Ponty identifies "sensation" as a unit of experience critical to the phenomenology of perception that is often obscured by external, objectified knowledges or objects.[29] How might one begin to talk about these sensations and use practices, particularly those that bring the greatest pleasures, apart from the discourses that have criminalized, moralized, or medicalized them? What is intrinsic to a person's intentionally modified psychoactive experience? Perhaps the most fundamental aspect of many varieties of psychoactive pleasure has its roots, in some way, in the concept of *ekstasis*. The meaning of the word *ecstasy* has devolved from a referent for religious revelation to one signifying intense pleasure and the loss of control. Tracing its trajectory as it was revived by the MDMA-using dance culture, philosopher Drew Hemment notes that the meaning of the term *ecstasy* has come to be closer to Martin Heidegger's philosophical sense of *ekstasis*: a profound but also fundamental ontological human experience in which one stands apart from social contexts to contemplate one's existence.[30] Philosopher Judith Butler describes a similar sense of *ekstasis* through her reading of Georg Wilhelm Friedrich Hegel's ek-static emergent subject: "a subject who constantly finds itself outside itself, and whose periodic expropriations do not lead to a return to a former self."[31] This sense of separation or difference, being able to experience the world apart from the usual discourses and practices of life, is foundational in many drug users' description of their own experiences. The end-state of feeling and perceiving the self and the world quite differently is undoubtedly the very point of drug use practices of various kinds.

In public discourse about the use practices of particular psychoactive drugs, particularly medicalized addiction and recovery discourses, this connotation of difference is often imagined as maladaptive—detrimental to or isolating to the user. Philosopher Jacques Derrida's observation about drug use leading "to suffering and to the disintegration of the self" and endangering a social contract exemplifies this sort of supposition.[32] Yet users of many drugs frequently express that sense of difference not as a disintegration or destruction of the self so much as a welcome perceptional and behavioral shift. Drugs and other use practices facilitate a disengagement from self that can be described in a variety of ways. In Sarah MacLean's sociological study of chroming (huffing aerosol paint), users employed "metaphors of distance from lived reality and their bodies to describe the experience of chroming, suggesting that alongside escape this kind of drug use enables relocation to a new dimension and different form of subjectivity."[33] This relocation of the self into a different subjectivity is not unlike what is reported in sociologist Grazyna Zajdow's interviews with former drug addicts, who talk about the attraction and desirability of intoxication as a pleasurable "degree of difference, this degree of separateness from normal experience, a release from self—self-forgetting." For those users (or former users), the letting go or experience of not-self is not only pleasurable, it is an artful use practice that is prized. Drug use allows people to experience themselves in a sensory, rather than a rational, calculating manner. "[D]issolving the 'One in oneself,'" Zajdow writes, "becomes a transcendence through a form of . . . radical empiricism via the ingestion of drugs, the art of not being oneself."[34]

In illicit drug users' narratives, Duff found that the act or *performance* of drug use was understood to facilitate "a very particular practice of the self." Users talk about their drug use as a way "to transform the body and to transform one's subjective experience—to 'become other' sometimes very subtly and sometimes all in a rush of difference."[35] In this sense, drug use makes possible ways of being in the world that are often not possible otherwise. The performance of a different self demonstrates learning by an embodied subject who has experienced a significant *alterity*—dissimilarity from a normal state of being—as pleasurable. (For *alterity*, see glossary.) This intentional expression of the self through a sensate and pleasurable embodiment of alterity in many ways challenges the perceived irrationality of intoxication. It is possible that, as a performance of self, drug use is closer to what philosopher Richard Klein argues is to "imagine bodily pleasure to be a kind of thinking."[36] To see pleasure as thought is to recognize the rational, corporeal agency that users express and practice. In action if not ideology, the pursuit of pleasure through altered consciousness requires the basic awareness of normality, a baseline from which the change in consciousness differs. In this sense, the intoxicated self is always a transgression of norms, even when intoxication is ritualized and socially acceptable.[37]

While it is likely that this sense of alterity is expressed in as many or more ways than can imagined, there seems to be some commonality to its arc. For example, in two different psychedelic studies, researchers illustrated key elements of experiencing alterity. Neuroscientists investigating how psilocybin affects communication activity across the brain found that "psychedelics cause temporary 'ego dissolution'—in other words, diminishing one's sense of having a firm and enduring personality" by quieting the activity in the default mode network, or ego system.[38] For other study participants who experienced LSD therapy in a psychiatric setting, the drugs' phenomenological value was less in the temporary experience it elicited and more in the "integrative experience" afterward, in which patients came to self-acceptance after perceiving themselves and the word differently.[39] In contrast to the maladaptive view of drug users, in these cases discovery and reorientation through an explicit distance from self is not just the pleasure found in psychoactive drug use, but may be its essential outcome. Some clinical researchers argue for the significance of the human need for intoxicated pleasure as a fourth biological drive.[40] Potentially, the attraction of drug use is that exact knowledge that you can and will feel different—and that the sensation will feel good and be beneficial.

The transcendence of ordinary experience does not always have to be dramatically different from the day to day. Some lesser transcendent moments help identify where people find their various pleasures in altered consciousness. A recent psychoactive experience I had demonstrates a brief but powerful embodied pleasure (for me, at least) in altered consciousness. This is an experience I have had countless times, yet it is one that I did not really consider as part of my use-practice experience until writing this chapter. Prior to a root canal, my endodontist administered anesthesia, but did not offer his usual forewarning, because he had done this with me a dozen times before. On this occasion, the epinephrine cocktail hit my bloodstream and acted faster than usual. Before I could even exhale completely, I was in the throes of the experience, speeding. The familiar, heart-pounding rush of epinephrine reminded me of what I love about stimulants. The flooding of my body with an overwhelming sensation was astounding. Its blunt immediacy required a complete surrender to the sensation—which in itself felt so unexpected but good. It was also the sensation itself, heart thumping and mind racing, that were immensely pleasurable. I enjoy going fast—in cars, on my bicycle, or on amusement park rides. The punch of the epinephrine and the resulting insistent heart pounding was a condensed version of the intense joy I feel when rushing physically through space. Too soon, it was over and I was back in the usual experience of my mind and body. But for an evanescent moment, I transcended my "self" to experience an altered self that was wildly different but incredibly pleasing. I was reacquainted with an extremity of feeling so different that I seemed temporarily outside of myself.

Drug practices represent a particular kind of self-knowledge, one that becomes communal for individuals in a user culture, as Howard Becker observed. Whether conceptually or through practice, users form communities of identity based on experience and familiarity with a particular drug-use practice. For example, people who enjoy MDMA understand the arc of that drug's intoxication, what it feels like at various points throughout an episode of use. These learned expectations characterize aesthetic knowledge(s) and cultural fluency intrinsic to various actions or elements. Users' preferences and understandings regarding various drugs include both the basic or finer points of knowledge about *how* to use that drug (or how to perform a practice) and its telling phenomenological aspects, as well as how one employs a practice in various contexts. It is a shared, embodied knowledge, learned through experience. Alcohol users know the feeling or experience of drinking a strong cocktail or two (the warm wallop, the blurred sense of time and space, the understanding that more will bring a slowing of cognitive and motor ability). Drinkers learn to drink a quantity of alcohol, that quantity that brings them, personally, to the point that meets pleasure, ideally short of negative consequence. Marijuana users know what it is to be high (the quiet receding of the mental taskmaster or the inward retreat, the slowing of cognitive and motor skills, the hilarity or the paranoia). Interestingly, in the states in which "recreational" marijuana has been legalized, users who have not had experience with edible marijuana products may struggle with this lack of knowledge regarding everything from dosage to expected time to high, as well as the expected duration of the experience. In the first year of marijuana sales in Colorado and Washington, producers started including instructions on edibles to educate those for whom marijuana use is not a familiar part of their use practice. Just as Becker observed half a century ago, the corporeal agency of intoxication is a learned, social behavior. Imagine if young adults had a guide like the Cannabis Business Alliance's "Edibles Education" or the grandmothers' marijuana tutorial when learning to drink or use other drugs responsibly.[41] (See fig. 4.2) The smallest bit of guidance and oversight can make a difference.

Learned, embodied knowledge of a use practice can connect users beyond the phenomenology of that single experience. Hallucinogen users, for example, often share a particular set of sensations and knowledges, because the drugs tend to inspire radically rearranged perception.[42] Psychedelics consistently induce a state of altered perception, thought, and feeling experienced only in dreams or perhaps moments of religious trance.[43] Tripping may offer a relatively unique opportunity to let go of frameworks of perception regarding the self and the social and natural worlds, both in terms of minutiae and more broadly conceived thoughts and cultural norms. Many users conclude their first trip feeling as if they have landed in a very different place, intellectually, emotionally, and, sometimes, spiritually. This distinct sense of the aftermath, in which one incorporates an acquired way of knowing as part of the self, is possibly the most frequently articulated and valued aspect of tripping among users. For example, a sixty-one-year-old woman who tried mushrooms for the first time reported afterwards: "Your inner world changes. . . . I felt I reconnected with my real self. I got rid of a bunch of stuff that kept me from feeling like my real self. I have more clarity. More appreciation. I'm happier, lighter."[44] While this act of incorporation may be part of most psychoactive experiences of alterity, for hallucinogen users, such knowledge frequently becomes inextricable from one's perception while not using—a changed way of seeing and being.

Some critics may construe drug use as a shortcut to a particular kind of perspective or enlightenment, yet sometimes those drug-induced pathways are unique, maybe the only way to specific experiences. In fact, neuroscientist David J. Linden writes, "[t]he widespread cross-cultural (and even cross-species) drive to tamper with our brain function cannot be entirely accounted for by activation of the pleasure circuit" because most hallucinogens do not activate the medial forebrain.[45] Pleasure is central to the experience of some, but not all, psychoactive drugs, including LSD, mescaline, and ayahuasca. The drive to experience the kind of alterity available through hallucinogens, then, may broaden and complicate potential definitions of pleasure and intoxication in drug use. Tripping seems to satisfy another—related—sense of desire. Hallucinogenic experiences engage the self in ways that people

Edibles Education
Start Low, Go Slow

Start with Less than One Serving
Start with a low-dose or single serving product until you know how edibles will affect you.

Wait, Go Slow
Edibles can take up to 2 hours or longer to take effect.

Don't Mix
Edibles should not be mixed with alcohol or controlled substances.

Out of Reach
Keep away from children, pets or ANYONE under 21, and store in original packaging.

CBA CANNABIS BUSINESS ALLIANCE | cannabisalliance.org

An Introduction To Edibles Tolerance

Everyone's metabolism is different and therefore has a different reaction to cannabis edibles. It is important that you understand your edible tolerance to have a safe and enjoyable experience.

Less Than 5mg

New Consumer
If you have never experimented with edibles, you should start here. It is important to make sure your body can digest cannabis comfortably.

5mg

Occasional Consumer
This is considered a single serving. Eating more than 10mg is not recommended.

5-10mg

Frequent Consumer
Reserved only for those with a high edible tolerance or medical needs.

The information contained in this brochure is not and should not be considered legal or medical advice. Please refer to and comply with all warnings contained on your product's packaging. Seek health care if adverse effects or accidental ingestion occurs or call the poison control hotline 1-800-222-1222.

FIGURE 4.2. Edibles Education card (front and back), Cannabis Business Alliance, May 2016.

may not be able to inspire without those springboard drugs. Neuroscientist Oliver Sacks has pointed out that the "phenomenology of hallucinations" offers insight into the structures and mechanisms of the brain's functions, and that the autonomous activity of hallucination stimulates perception in ways that do not activate with unadulterated imagination.[46]

It can be tempting to dismiss perceptions of the intoxicated self as less authentic, mediated by drug or practice, and thus not truly the "self." Sociologist Pekka Sulkunen points out that drug use practice "is not only *understandable* and should be studied as meaningful; it is also *understood* by agents themselves. . . . We construct images of our practices and environment by classifying, explaining, and interpreting; in other words, we *make* them meaningful."[47] In the last decade, some scholars have sought to refocus drug use research and analysis on the pleasure-related motivations and phenomenology of drug use by looking at user narratives, patterns of consumption and behavior, and broader cultural studies of use and intoxication. Drug user narratives convey what cultural historian Sarah Shortall identifies as "an experiential rhetoric of authority." Based on observations of users and researchers, Shortall locates "invoked experience" as the key to a shared identity and as "the fullest, most open, most active kind of consciousness."[48] Users know what they seek and experience in their use practices—and they actively manage their experiences in many ways. Users inform themselves, are reflective, and weigh the risks and costs of using in general or in a specific instance. In a study of three hundred drug users, medical anthropologist Geoffrey Hunt and others found that users' management strategies were focused on achieving the most benefit while mitigating potential harms in given social situations. "[A] striking characteristic of their drug descriptions and how they negotiate pleasure and risk was the way their narratives illustrated the social nature of their drug use." At the same time, users recognized that the benefits had long lasting impact, "mental well-being and subsequent social behavior" as well as immediate pleasures.[49] The pursuit of pleasure may be a factor that assists in social integration (lessening anxiety, sharing customs) or a way of codifying experiences and time that are not work related. Younger users frequently employ various drugs over an interval of time to manage mood. After-work recreation might start with alcohol and/or marijuana, then include Ecstasy if going to a club or Adderall or meth if staying up late, and finish with marijuana or alcohol to relax at the end of the night. Even older users might use more than one drug in a celebratory evening, whether pharmaceuticals and alcohol or other drugs. This applied control brings us back to the relation between embodied subjectivity and user agency in the use practices of pleasures and intoxication. Drug use is a performance of the self that is empirical, authoritative, satisfying, and effective.

To rethink the issue of pleasure through user subjectivity requires considering forms of consciousness, alterity, and the variability of drug experiences, and, as much as possible, to acknowledge the experiential aspects of using. If one turns down the volume of inflated cultural rhetoric about the dangers of psychoactive drugs, experience may guide a different approach. In individual use practices, people experience a "performance of the self" that is intrinsic to their experience and identity. What you know to be true of your own use practices may help you recognize an embodied, experiential knowledge that conveys intentional user agency. The pleasure sought in the phenomenology of use practices, the alterity inherent to the performance of a self, and the rehearsal or rejection of cultural norms implicit in the act are familiar and unremarkable aspects of many people's lives. Your own use practices are often invisible to you—especially if they are broadly accepted and normalized. From the perspective of nonabusive users of practices that are illegal or less public, these practices are not part of a destructive identity but, rather, experiences with various personal and cultural implications.

MANAGING DRUG-USE EXPERIENCE

Despite a conflicted public discourse that has Americans fearing some drugs while consuming others in record numbers, people continue to pursue their pleasures of choice. Such pastimes—especially those involving "stronger" intoxications—are not new. For over two hundred years, Americans have found gratification and pleasure in the regular use of pharmaceutically developed drugs, from opiates (opium, morphine, heroin, and many other opioids) to stimulants (cocaine, crack, ephedrine, and crystal meth, or amphetamines like Adderall, or substituted phenethylamines, such as Ritalin), tranquilizers (Valium, Klonopin, Xanax) and antidepressants (Prozac, Celexa, Zoloft, Paxil). Where midnineteenth century medical students enjoyed ether or nitrous oxide for their "exhilarating sensations," students today use nitrous oxide ("whippits") or dextromethorphan (in cough syrup), among other drugs, to intoxicating effect.[50] Most people scarcely register their own use practices as use practices, particularly of the most commonly consumed psychoactive drugs: caffeine, alcohol, and nicotine.[51] Perhaps because these drugs have become part of a cultural context and personal use practice, controlled users accept their pleasurable and utilitarian aspects—a trust that has been learned by most users as their potential dangers have receded with practice.

While many users choose drugs and practices that are readily available (in terms of access, legality, expense, and personal costs/benefits), the proportion of users who seek highs that are not quite as available as the six-pack at the convenience store is significant. Whether users repurpose pharmaceuticals prescribed for health reasons, or seek drugs like some of what psychiatrist Adam Winstock calls "new drugs of misuse, including ketamine, γ-hydroxybutyrate (GHB), and a range of synthetic stimulants," users continuously seek to explore and manage altered consciousness with a variety of psychoactive drugs and practices.[52] Alcohol, tobacco, marijuana, caffeinated energy drinks, and MDMA are the top drugs used by US respondents to a global drug survey. But other drugs, from amphetamines, benzodiazepines, opioids, and nitrous oxide, to psilocybin/mushrooms, and LSD round out the list. Prescription-pill pleasures form an everyday cultural trope, one that is culturally accepted. In the 2014 Emmy Awards monologue about the standard industry high, host Seth Meyers teased his audience that they were so well behaved because "everyone *sits* silently in one place and waits for the *pills* to kick in."[53]

When researchers ask users about pleasure and drug use, a great deal is learned about user decision making. The Global Drug Survey (GDS) asks users to identify what they use, how, when, and why.[54] One of its reports, the drug Net Pleasure Index (NPI), is a substudy that represents the individual calculus by which users weight and rate pleasures. It identifies not just the breadth of self-reported drug use but the proportionality of the benefits and drawbacks of use practices. As part of the data gathering for use practices, the GDS team developed a set of criteria for people to use in weighing the positive and negative effects/aspects (pleasure and pain) of their use practices. The survey questions ask users to rate how drugs improve or detract from: mood and confidence, self-awareness social interactions, relief from unwanted physical or emotional sensitivity, and the ability to work, perform, and cope in life. With 22,000 self-identified respondents worldwide, the NPI sheds light on the ways in which the pleasures people experience in various drug-use practices far exceed the negative side effects they might induce.[55] (See fig. 4.3.) For the drugs with the greatest pleasure ratings and the smallest cost or "pain" ratings (MDMA, LSD, mushrooms or psilocybin, marijuana, and ketamine), pleasures far outpaced those noted for drugs like alcohol and tobacco, for which the pain/pleasure ratings were closest or nearly balanced.

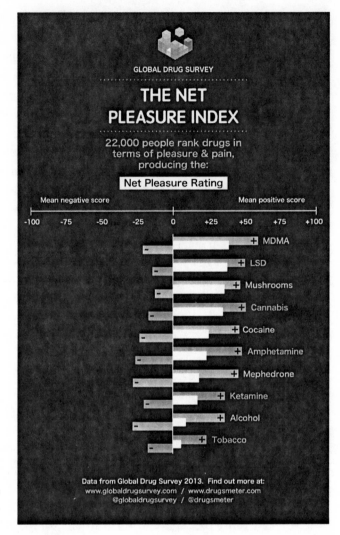

Data from Global Drug Survey 2013. Find out more at:
www.globaldrugsurvey.com / www.drugsmeter.com
@globaldrugsurvey / @drugsmeter

FIGURE 4.3.
Drug Net
Pleasure Index,
Global Drug
Survey, 2014.

Other drugs, such as cocaine and amphetamines, are somewhere closer to 25 to 30 percent net positive. Most importantly, all drugs were rated well over net positive. The closest to equilibrium between its pleasure and pain rating was tobacco, still 20 percent positive. In other words, respondents confirm that they use various drugs because of a net pleasurable experience—especially for the very drugs that are often identified as dangerous.

In the NPI's design and collected user data, a complex set of factors is revealed as a part of users' conceptualization and understanding of their use practices. For example, the raw data showed GDS that alcohol and the stimulant mephedrone appear in the top three drugs that users rated as deleterious to their work, study, and physical or mental health. Yet mephedrone also figures into the top three net-benefit or pleasure ratings for an "increase in pleasure from social interaction," and alcohol figures into the top three ratings for "helps me cope with life." MDMA, LSD, and mushrooms figure as the top three rated drugs in 70 percent of user experiences on the pleasure scale in terms of increasing mood (happiness and confidence), pleasure from social interactions, enjoyment and capacity for sex or physical activity, energy and alertness, self-awareness and understanding, or relief from pain and worry. Users make decisions based on outcomes that have real effects in their lives, outcomes they can determine and, for most users, about which they can be and are selective. In other words, what keeps users from excessive or abusive behavior with drugs is not so much legal boundaries as cultural ones: the norms and rituals they learn and employ as guiding factors in drug use. Winstock adds that users clearly weigh the benefits and costs of using in terms of "bang for buck," but also in terms of the cost/benefit ratio of use in a quotidian setting. In addition to the calculus of pleasure seeking, there is an "impact on the day-to-day" determination that users make as part of their decision making. This demonstration of informed decision making is well known to drug users but less visible in public drug discourse.

The pursuit of pleasure has various expressions, intentions, contexts, experiences, and outcomes. Use practices or drugs that do not directly lead to an intoxication or high can also be quite pleasurable. Similarly, there are outcomes of getting high, aside from intoxication itself, that bring us great pleasure. In his study of methamphetamine users, Race points out that in addition to the enhanced sexual benefits and activities that the drug facilitates, meth users cited a range of pleasures: chatting with friends for hours at home; dancing; fixing things up or cleaning obsessively; watching films, Internet browsing; creative pursuits; designing drag makeup, etc. While the drug can create obsessive periods of productive or nonproductive activity, it also becomes a given in the use practices of some users—especially HIV-positive users—who find that the different sense of the self it offers liberates them temporally from that material condition. These "contemporary practices of self-transformation" take place on many levels for many users, whether people recognize them as acts of pleasure or think of them more as self-maintenance.[56] Sometimes the pleasure of a use practice is found in psychological self-exploration, social engagement, or the learning of new ways of being in the world. Or, it can mean liberation from a normative state of being, such as anxiety, that is meaningful and comforting. Radio producer Ira Glass describes such an experience with Ecstasy:

> I am mostly a pretty worried person. In conversations, I am always worried about what to say. The first time I took ecstasy, all of that lifted away. All the anxiety, which is the baseline of my life in some way, and I had this moment of like, wait a second! Are there people who feel this way all the time? This is like a whole way to be, where you don't feel anxious? Oh my god! It was so amazing. In the months after that, it was a really helpful thing to have experienced. It remains to this day a feeling that is helpful to know about.[57]

Understanding the experience of ecstasy as an state of nonanxious being that brings about a relief from anxiety, "a feeling that is helpful to know about," may not be what people might assume about the experience of taking what is often consumed as a party drug. But for an anxious person, MDMA may create an alterity that is, in some ways, as attractive, or more so, than one's typical conscious experience. As MDMA is increasingly used in treatment of PTSD, end-of-life palliative care, and to support other human experiences, the cultural meaning of its character as a drug changes. These are reminders that intoxication is but one of many complex and gratifying ends possible in the pursuit of altered consciousness.

On the one hand, American culture has framed the pursuit of intoxicating pleasures within a work-for-reward logic: one earns the right to pleasure through work or duty. The modern American experience of leisure—whether taking a smoking break or having a postwork drink, a weekend off, or a full vacation—often involves the pursuit of altered consciousness. Sociologist Mike Featherstone calls the logic of exchange underlying use practices "calculating hedonism": users offset work effectiveness and achievement with the time, means, and ability to pursue pleasures—often consuming drugs—as leisure. In the United States, users "are encouraged to regard the enjoyment of the rewards of success as an integral part of their effort."[58] These "intoxicating commodities" are read by many scholars as a response to the increased rationalization and regulation of our lives."[59] Such drugs are part of a use practice that includes other drugs, like psychotherapeutics or hypnotics, that people use to manage their lives. But the drugs that Americans consume as rewards are, in some ways, the most culturally celebrated and approved because they are earned. They represent a shared sense of "Thank God it's

Friday," Friday evening being a time recognized to indulge in use practices that are socially sanctioned for nothing but pleasure.

On the other hand, psychoactive practices are not reserved solely for leisure time. It may be easier to see that users select and channel the effects of drugs in a rational way when one thinks about pleasure through just one part of a continuum of use-related performance management. Psychoactive drugs have long been tools of self-control and regulating experience. Caffeine, nicotine, other stimulants are conventionally used by workers to regulate attention or when incisive focus is required for a task. People work within a culture of optimization: the pressure to improve productivity has become a regular feature in professional and industrial work settings.[60] Although surveillance, evaluation, and drug testing have also become workplace norms, workers game the system. In a particular irony of contemporary American life, two of the most popular performance enhancers used to for effectiveness in the workplace are sleep aids and stimulants. Interest in work-related pursuit of cognitive enhancement, what journalist Olga Khazan has called "work doping," has given rise to a range of choices.[61] The ways in which American workers seek an edge include steroids and human growth hormone, "smart" drugs such as Adderall or modanfinil, or microdosing with psilocybin or LSD. The newer category of "nootropics," drugs and supplements that are thought to improve focus and cognitive function, like TruBrain or Optimind, serve a growing market. Some cognition-enhancing drugs have moved across the disorder spectrum and back again as tools marketed to concerns from weight loss to ADD self-management.[62] Psychoactive drugs are effective tools, apart from leisure and intoxication, and the ways in which people employ them further develops what it means to be a user.

Despite decades of drug war and medicalization, users continue to find their way to new illicit drugs, or to diverted drugs used in new applications. Fentanyl, a fast-acting and potent opiate, has surfaced in the United States and elsewhere, cut into drugs like heroin and MDMA. While it intensifies the high, it also is suspected of being responsible for the recent increase in heroin deaths. The DEA and counterpart agencies in Europe have made public service announcements warning that fentanyl is a threat to heroin users.[63] One of the fastest growing categories of recreational drugs are NBOMes, synthetic drugs made of varying constituent drugs. Another newer category of street drug, containing synthetic cannabinoids like K2 or Spice, is misnamed as these drugs bear no relation to marijuana. In 2015, 134 synthetic compounds were known to exist, but it is a fast-growing drug category. As with NBOMes, makers are synthesizing synthetic cannabinoids faster than health-care workers can identify them. There are other novel psychoactive drugs, even bath salts—synthetic cathenodes that have amphetamine-like effects. Over one hundred had been discovered in the European Union by 2015. Similarly, what is sold as Molly or MDMA is often not actual MDMA. Although drug reagent tests help users check their street purchases, many users do not employ that level of scrutiny. Some of these inexpensive drugs are popular because they cause hallucinations for fifteen to thirty hours at a time.[64]

American use practices have proven that despite various risk factors, whether engaging in the black market, taking unknown drugs, or diverting known pharmaceuticals for other purposes, people will continue to use drugs of all kinds for pleasure. Exploring what people use and do for pleasure, why, and how it affects them in the long term poses vast new territories for research. Perhaps most importantly, recognizing that pleasure is the key to why users choose to use any psychoactive drug is a necessary step toward more comprehensive understanding of drug use practices. The motivation to find pleasure is neither good nor bad; it is a fact of human existence. The consumption of psychoactive drugs has become so conventional that Americans frequently take drugs to meet cultural norms. While feeling good is one way that users employ pharmaceutical drugs, some users self-medicate to feel less bad. Mood alteration on a more substantial scale than an occasional "lift" has become a major growth area of psychoactive pharmaceutical drug use If you are a controlled user, does it matter what you use to get your work done? Does it matter if you use to feel good, or if you use drugs to avoid feeling bad? What if your friend uses drugs to have an introspective experience? Does it matter if people all use drugs because they want to celebrate and feel intoxicated? Another way to step back and rethink pleasure and drug use is not to ask what goes wrong with drug use, but, as drug historian David Herzberg has, "What goes right with drug use? What works about drug use? Where does it *not* seem to produce harm?"[65] If Americans want to develop and inculcate a culture of controlled use that teaches the social boundaries for behavior or distinctions between responsible and irresponsible use, then the models for drugs that are widely available and have been normalized will be instructive.

The most obvious, but not problem free, model for coming to terms with users and drug practices is the postprohibition legalization of an incredibly strong psychoactive drug: alcohol. Alcohol is one of the most ritualized, commonly consumed, and fetishized psychoactive drugs in the United States. With the exception of those who abstain for cultural, religious, or personal observance, alcohol is a presumed presence in American life. From artisanal cocktails and craft beer to viticulture, Americans celebrate the use of alcohol as a cultural expertise and shared pleasure. Many Americans expect alcohol to be present for drinkers of legal age at public functions, and as celebratory rites at public and private events. For some, drinking alcohol is an enjoyable daily signal that work is done. Alcohol is part of many Americans' weekly grocery shopping, meals, and events. People take trips to see how and where alcoholic beverages are made. Americans gather in places whose primary purpose is to serve alcohol, mark key life milestones with alcoholic toasts, and identify with it, as in, "women who drink whiskey." Alcoholic beverages have become meaningful in many people's lives and, for most people who use alcohol, drinking is a nonproblematic use practice. Following the logic of this example, Americans might acknowledge that alcohol prohibition may have failed in many ways, but most of all it failed to stop drinking. Allowing states to create their own policies led to state-enforced control and regulation and has, for the most part, worked well. Unless they live in a state that still has blue laws on the books, most users probably do not stop to think that there was a time, just a few generations ago, when alcohol was a contested drug in the United States.

How Americans have come to regulate and monitor alcohol use suggests a great deal about the acculturation of drinking as a use practice. Over time, Americans have created cultural and regulatory boundaries to modify and normalize alcohol use practices. These include actions like identifying what constitutes a serving of various types of alcohol, instituting minimum drinking ages, limiting the amount of alcohol consumed while legally able to drive, and penalizing "over service" to bar patrons who are drunk. Americans have recognized that alcohol has an influence on drinkers such that, past a certain point, users lose basic functionality. As a result, policies support drinkers staying within the limits of functionality. Yet Americans also recognize that people can and do drink far past that point, and so have adopted the practice of having a "designated driver" or caretaker when out drinking to excess. With some exceptions, alcohol is widely available in retail outlets and in restaurants and bars. In other words, Americans have done what they can to make consuming alcohol safe, knowing well that a small proportion of users will struggle with abuse or alcoholism. Culturally, Americans believe people will eventually learn how to use alcohol responsibly, most of the time. It is also recognized that in some drinking practices, for example college-age drinking, safe alcohol use is not always well fostered. Yet drunkenness, if occasional, is not only acceptable, it is part of many Americans' lives. It can be hard to "see" just how central drinking to excess is to mainstream American life. It is all around us. One small example, a viral tweet showing two Netflix profile icons, suggests the extent to which some Americans have fully embraced their drug-user identities. A person with the Twitter handle "Shut Up, Mike" posted: "How I significantly improved my Netflix." The image shows two Netflix profile icons: Mike and Drunk Mike. The joke, of course, is that Mike and Drunk Mike have different viewing habits. But if the film rental site's algorithm registers that Drunk Mike likes to watch, say, bromance films while Mike likes action films, then Mike's overall entertainment experience will be enhanced. It is a funny and authentic response to American use practices.

Although just over half of the US adult population consumes alcohol, the most prevalent psychoactive drug consumed is caffeine. Almost 90 percent of the US population consumes caffeine every day. It is served in most workplaces in the United States and is the focus of breaks during the workday. Caffeine is indispensable as a morning ritual for the majority of Americans—not just because they enjoy the caffeine buzz, but because they feel that they *need* it. People recognize its functionality and use it accordingly. The generation that has grown up on energy drinks also employs caffeine as a drug of utility to study or work, and marijuana or cocktails as a depressant. Energy drinks have raised the stakes of caffeine consumption as they contain up to eight times the caffeine of coffee or tea. With a twelvefold increase in energy-drink production and consumption over the last decade, and a target market of Americans ages thirteen to thirty-five, use of this caffeine source will surely become even more pervasive. Among recent applications is an "energy patch" that relieves users of actually having to consume a beverage.[66] While this increase in caffeine consumption may or may not be good for human health in the long run, it is clearly a widespread and much loved use practice, one most Americans would rather not do without.

Would the majority of psychoactive drug users change their behavior with more information about the risks and benefits of their use? It is hard to say. Some patterns of drug use have been affected by campaigns to promote information—campaigns about the increased risk of lung cancer or emphysema with smoking, for example. Public smoking laws have become more prohibitive in the last two decades: twenty-nine states now have laws requiring a smoke-free environment in workplaces, restaurants, and bars.[67] Yet a tobacco industry that seeks new ways of delivering nicotine products has found success in e-cigarettes, hookahs, and flavored nicotine products. And forty million Americans still smoke.[68] Hookah bars are popular with younger Americans, for whom the social experience is an alternative to bars. While smoking tobacco has become less prevalent, marijuana use (predominantly smoking) has remained steady. In several states, access to marijuana has become legal not just for medical marijuana patients, but for recreational users. Commanding users to change their practices has generally not been successful in the United States. Americans continue to use all kinds of drugs despite prohibitions and other barriers. They buy legal and illegal drugs and divert prescription drugs for other uses. The choice to use for pleasure is central to many Americans' lives. It can be a big part of their identities, both as consumers and as producers. For people who pursue pleasure in ways that do not hurt or derail their lives, their drug-use practices might be accepted and even embraced as expressions of intention and agency. Americans pursue these use practices because it feels good, brings relief, and offers other rewards. In this sense, people's drug use choices are intentional: they reveal how people want to live.

VOX

BONNIE
EVENING SMOKE

People think smoking pot is something you outgrow. Like teenage rebellion. Not as low as snorting or injecting God-knows-what, but definitely not something you do when you have a good job and kids. They think you should stop because it's illegal. So now I feel like I did in high school, hiding in the basement smoking when my parents were out for the night.

I've smoked pot just about every day since I was fifteen, most of my fifty-eight years. After a long day at the restaurant, it's the first thing I do—right after taking off my shoes. Sometimes I smoke before I clean the house. Or I settle into a chair under the big oak tree in my yard, spark a bowl, and sit. I like to do some thinking. There's something about getting outside that slows down the time, even in the winter. Getting high and thinking keeps me from brainlessly clicking around the TV. Pot clears my head so I can breathe at a normal pace and feel human.

Sitting out there, I think about my kids and my husband, my mom and dad, and the neighbors. I love it when thoughts I had earlier that day, the ones that got lost in the rush, come back to me. The littlest ideas can blossom. Some of the time I don't remember and sometimes I want to forget.

Don't call me a pothead (well, my husband does, but I let him). My smoke is like your glass of wine. I used to love to take mushrooms on a weekend when I could. That gave me an even bigger chunk of time for thinking. It gets harder to find that kind of time, now. I can almost always fit in my evening smoke, though, because it's the one thing that I do just for me. Like what Diane Keaton says to Woody Allen in *Annie Hall*: "You've been seeing a psychiatrist for fifteen years. You should smoke some of this. You'd be off the couch in no time." Amen to that, sister. It's gotten me through menopause without killing someone. My husband says I should share it with the ladies at church.

I understand why lots of folks have their medical marijuana cards. Sure, it can relieve pain. Some people suffer terrible back pain. It helps them get through. It's not like that for me, though. What I love most is that smoking pot helps me appreciate the smallest things. My evening smoke gives me perspective on life. I don't want to give that up and I can't think of a single reason why I should.

COSMO
WHAT COULD BE

The anxiety—a rich brew of anticipation, excitement, and fear of the unknown—begins once I make the decision to take this journey. Before I swallow the capsule, I've tested its contents and read up on what it will do once those molecules cross the blood-brain barrier and begin to take hold of my neurons. I have a pretty good idea of what to expect. But the nature of using illicit drugs precludes the luxury of the precise and pure doses of medications that I provide my patients with in my daily work as a psycho-pharmacologist.

I know that the capsules contain MDMA, but I don't know how untainted they are or what else they might contain. They could have rat poison in them for all I know, but most dealers are not interested in killing their customers. Really, of greater concern is, where will my brain go under the influence of these molecules? I'm wary, keeping my thoughts from steering into dark corners when I use psychedelics, fearful that I'll go down a hole that I will have difficulty crawling out from. Ever since I started using psychedelics twenty years ago, I have been afraid of the proverbial bad trip. I've never had one, and don't know many people who have, but sometimes, when choosing to push my internal boundaries and challenge my assumptions about the nature of the world, I know the thin line between awe and terror. These molecules have the potential to take me to that edge, and therein lies the appeal. At the same time, that also generates the fear. Why even take this risk? Because I've always felt this experience changed me in some way—sometimes significantly, sometimes subtly, but always offering enduring experiences that I have found to be instructive and positive.

My caution keeps me safe and also constrains me. I fear this less with MDMA than other molecules such as LSD or psilocybin, because I know that the flood of serotonin that comes with MDMA is almost inherently anxiolytic—it inhibits anxiety. I know I'm playing with power tools here. My father taught me to wear safety goggles and know where my fingers were when working with power saws. The preparation is no different in this case: I'm comfortable and I've surrounded myself with people whom I love and trust. Tonight, I'm curious to see what happens.

Once the capsule is swallowed, the die is cast. There is no going back and I begin to be filled with a giddy anticipation. I've taken a modest dose: one hundred milligrams of MDMA in this capsule. I know from my research that this is a threshold dose. If the powder is not pure MDMA, it's possible there's not even enough in the capsule to make an impact. But I am cautious. An hour passes, and my train is leaving the station. We are going dancing, dressed all in white, for the traditional white party at Opulent Temple, one of dozens of large-scale dance camps here at Burning Man. I am among some of my favorite people as we blend like amoebic protoplasm into the already pulsating and crowded dance floor.

The music is loud and percussive and is felt in the solar plexus as much as it is heard in the ears. It's been about an hour since I took the dose, and I have begun the psychedelic taker's ritual of asking myself, "Am I feeling it, or just having a good time?" It doesn't really matter, but tonight, I don't want a mere threshold experience, and to be really certain that I feel the full potential of this intriguing little compound: 3,4-methylenedioxymetham-phetamine. Well aware that a dose at or below one hundred milligrams might be insufficient to cause the large presynaptic dump of serotonin needed to create the desired effects, I decide to take the second capsule for a total dose of two hundred milligrams. I know the lethal dose in rodents is somewhere around fifty to one hundred milligrams per kilogram of body weight, so I'd need to take somewhere on the order of about four grams, or about twenty to forty times the dose I'm taking tonight, to put me at risk. That's nothing to an experienced raver, but for me, a timid user of psychedelics, this is the neurological equivalent of the beer bong. Still, this is a lot safer than a beer bong. I'm determined to experience the full power of these molecules. I figure if I really want to learn what this drug has to teach me, I can't just listen with one ear. I have to sit down and listen deeply.

Fast-forward twenty-five minutes, and it becomes abundantly clear that the drug is working, quite well in fact. Serotonin is being released freely, and I suspect my prolactin and oxytocin levels are rising, leaving me with increasing warmth towards my friends. I think about my amygdala quieting down, freeing me from the slight interpersonal defensiveness that we all experience, now dissolving into a warm sensation of trust. I am opening, to experience, to others, to my own feelings, quietly, but decidedly. It's a quiet euphoria, full of quiet comfort and ease. It's not the sloppy euphoria that would lead one to stick one's head out of a moving limo on the strip in Las Vegas, shouting "Whooohooo, baby!" Rather, it's a quiet warmth that makes me want to rub my hand along my friend's back, which is covered with a white fuzzy coat. It makes me want to gaze deeply into another friend's eyes for a duration that would normally be uncomfortably long, but in this context feels safe, connected, and important. I stare at the moon and think of my beloved, who is home tonight, but I feel her presence reflected back to me in the moonlight. A sense of deep gratitude washes over me.

We decide to move on to a spot where we can find more music. There is a camp, Ashram Galactica, that bills itself as a five-star hotel on the playa. Each year, they set up a Moroccan caravan tent, filled with filigree metal lanterns and antique furniture, then invite people to join them for fine drinks and dancing. What I am feeling in that moment is making a tremendous impression. My friends and I come in and out of contact with each other, as we usually do when we're out in a big group like this, but this time it's different. I have this pressing need to connect deeply. I want to look really deeply into their eyes and I don't want the connection to break. I recognize it could seem creepy, so I try to mitigate it by telling them how happy I am to be there with them and how much I love them. My observing ego catches me saying this and chides me with a question: "Really? Electronic music, fuzzy coats, and telling all your friends you love them? Could you be more cliché?" But it's true and I feel it deeply and sincerely. These feelings were not unknown to me before I took these pills. They were not created by those two hundred milligrams of MDMA. Rather, the feelings were released from my own caution and reason by those molecules. How many times have I squirmed uncomfortably when one of my more effusive friends has ended a conversation with "Love you!" and for whatever reason, I'm unable to reciprocate? It's not that I'm incapable of love, far from it. I have an embarrassment of riches of wonderful, caring people in my life, many of whom I love dearly. But for some reason I'm stingy with expressing it. Not tonight. I'm feeling it, and I'm saying it, and I realize that the sentiment is entirely real. It's deeply liberating be able to express my true feelings.

What do I take from this evening of serotonin-enhanced pleasure? Good memories, of course, stories that will probably be retold. But more importantly, I get a glimpse of a life that *could be.* A life of greater closeness and authenticity with the people that matter to me, unencumbered with my own inhibitions and reservations. Could it be anything but good if I felt closer to the important people in my life, and told them that they I am grateful for them and I love them more frequently? Do I need a drug to feel this way?

No. Does a drug help me remember this, what is important to me, and what could be, so that I keep that knowledge in the foreground a little more frequently? Yes. This experience will be recalled with ease, unlike most of our daily experience. Perhaps it is this reference point, this glimpse into an expanded world where I am reacquainted with an appreciation for both the strength of the webs that we weave and the fragility of the gossamer silk from which they are woven that makes this night truly matter.

MARK

IT'S NOT WHAT, IT'S HOW

I was always interested in the metaphysical, even as a young boy, long before I knew what the word meant. When I was a kid, I was not very physically invested in my body. I spent a lot of time in a dream-world that existed alongside the physical world we call reality. This is how I grew up: attracted to the "other" and seeing things differently. I spent years exploring various religious and spiritual experiences. Along the way, I developed an ongoing meditation practice, directly related to my extensive experiences with psychotropic drugs. Carlos Castaneda's idea that metaphysical realms were real, existing side-by-side with the physical world, was a significant influence on my thinking. I was struck by one of the teachings Castaneda received from Don Juan regarding the true purpose of the psychotropic drugs that I was using at the time. Don Juan explained that the drug was not the path, it was only a conduit; a tool to bring one to see the door between the realms. The real objective was to open the door, cross through it, and to navigate the realms without the use of drugs. This resonated strongly with me. After verifying it with my own experiences, I began a spiritual path without the use of drugs.

I started meditating—at first right after getting high, but then without any substances at all. I spent a lot of time shifting my energies upward, breathing from my center out the top of my head, trying to expand my consciousness. I would sit in meditation until it progressed beyond the physical. No longer in my body, my spirit body would actually slip outside of me, like astral projection. This was my practice. I would leave my body and interact outside of myself if that makes sense, in what was some fairly dicey terrain. I saw and did some very crazy things in that space—things you wouldn't believe if I told you. Some were amazing, others were extremely frightening. It started to get very risky. The more I traveled outside the physical plane, the more I began to fear for my safety. I was in another world and the rules of engagement were very different than those we observe in the physical plane. I didn't know how to have control of it or balance it. I also knew I needed to find a teacher to guide me so I could learn to navigate the metaphysical journey safely, fearlessly.

I was very fortunate because I found a true teacher, a blessing I attribute to the power of prayer. She was a very holy woman; a healer and deeply committed to knowing herself and the universe. She showed me that the movement of energy in meditation was not outward, but inward and the journey to know oneself was to go deeply within. This was how I began practicing a different kind of meditation: I would sit and move deeply within myself until I reached a state of calm and nonreaction, a place of equanimity. And it was wonderful! With this approach to meditation I would let go of the outside world—the worries and stresses I was experiencing and, instead, found a different place to exist in myself—to embody and order my life from. Following my meditations, I would emerge from that internal place back into the world changed, different, happier, calmer—more centered. (And of course, smelling like patchouli.)

After a few years of this focus, I began to notice that I would retreat into meditation when something happened in my life that I didn't like—whether it was the stress of struggling to make a living, my sense of failure as a person, or arguing with my ex-wife about, well, a number of things. I would go meditate, move deeply into myself, and in the process I would consciously remove the issue from my attention. I would come out of my meditation and return to the world, refreshed. The thing was, the problem would still be there. It never got resolved. I just removed myself from it and "let it go" instead of confronting it or working through it to fix it.

This became my behavioral pattern and it was noticeable to my family members, who were concerned for me at that time. They thought I was doing drugs, which is ironic, because during the five years that I was addicted to drugs, they didn't even know. At this point in my life, I was "clean," but they were worried about me. They thought that I'd joined a "meditation cult," and was being brainwashed. So they staged an intervention—which was unnecessary and, as you might imagine, very dramatic of them. But it wasn't until a few years later that I started to look at my behavior. I began to notice a pattern in my relationships and in my life. Instead of working though a disagreement with me, my ex-wife would end arguments by telling me to "go meditate and get over it." This would upset me for a number of reasons, but mostly because I realized that she knew that while I was in meditation I would remove myself from caring about the problem and give up my end of the argument.

So I did what anyone into meditation would do: I began to look at my behavior while sitting meditating. I realized that I was misusing or abusing the practice of meditation. I was using it like a drug to self-medicate—something I knew well from my own history with drug abuse. I was using meditation to disengage myself from the world and avoid of dealing with it. Even the series of positive life-goals I had established for myself years earlier when I cleaned up from addiction (to complete my education, run my own theatre company, to make my living as an artist) all fell by the wayside as I got more heavily into meditation. I remember becoming conscious of this at the time and, have received a wake-up call, I immediately began changing my life.

For years I was very distrusting of meditation and of people who meditated. It took me years to reconcile this. But I know now that I was just doing it with the wrong intention. I now meditate daily with the right intention and in balance with my interaction with the physical world we call reality.

KYLA

NOTE FROM A SOCIALLY INTEGRATED DRUG USER

I've taken dozens of different psychoactive drugs, and yet I still manage to love my grandmother, pay all of my bills, and pass a physical at the doctor's office with flying colors—no pun intended. My psychedelic list includes but is not limited to: cannabis, LSD, LSA, intramuscular ketamine, psilocybin mushrooms, DPT, TMA-2, MDMA, MBDB, MDA, MXE, salvia divinorum, mephedrone, DXM, 2C-T-2, 2C-B, and various others including natural and synthetic opiates, amphetamines, barbiturates, and benzodiazepines. I've smoked hash and opium in India, snorted cocaine in Nicaragua, chewed khat in the Middle East, drunk moonshine in rural North America, taken club drugs in Europe, and stubbed my toe in Canada.

Amid these sometimes boring, sometimes mind-blowing drug experiences, I've also been a stranger in the line at your grocery store. Between inhalations, I've been accepted to the Peace Corps, done volunteer work with children, graduated from prestigious universities, and have been—for lack of a better word—a nice person. As a matter of fact, I would say drugs have made me even nicer.

Why have they made me nicer? Well, they haven't done it on their own. By themselves, psychedelics don't actually do anything to me at all. Molecularly they look nearly identical to many of our neurotransmitters. Phylogenetically the plants are also quite normal, some being simple shrubs and lacking even the aesthetic allure of a house plant. As a result, I tend to interpret most conversations about psychedelics as conversations that are really about experiences. The rest is just interesting trivia. But the experience of taking psychedelics has changed the way I see and understand the world. No other thing on this entire planet seems to possess an equal potential to induce such unique and meaningful experiences—and not just in me. There are Zen retreats and roller-coaster rides, and the natural highs and lows of the human experience, from the death of a loved one to a marriage with our soul mate. But the difference is that with meditation we can say it is liberating; with thrill seeking we can say it is wonderfully exciting; and with the events that unfold throughout our lives we can say—usually more truthfully in hindsight—that they were marked by love, or sadness, or perhaps regret. With psychedelic experiences, once the spaceship that is your mind lands back on familiar turf, often the best description one can conjure is, "Holy shit." God has forsaken us. The experience cracks open the mind in ways that are irrevocable and good. It invokes awe and humility. True perspective. And I'll tell you, I have yet to find such a trick at the local Wal-Mart.

CONCLUSION

Perhaps we should not ask what should be done about the "drug problem," but rather what should be done about our obsession with drugs as a problem.

—REBECCA TIGER, *JUDGING ADDICTS*

THE PUBLIC DISCOURSES THAT REPRESENT DRUGS AND USERS IN the United States are frequently informed more by value judgments than by an informed sense of drugs and their users. Recently, a friend noted that, among locals, an establishment that had been renovated was referred to as a former "crack bar" or "heroin bar." This judgment was made by people who do not frequent that business, so it is more likely a comment about the perceived socioeconomic class and comportment of the patrons than an awareness of whether or not they were using various drugs. *Crack* and *heroin* have become labels that, among other things, can signal an underclass, mental illness, or the ravages of poverty. While the bar's patrons may or may not have used those drugs, the one drug they are more certainly using is alcohol. That fact may be implicit, but I find it interesting that it was missing among the influences that were credited for the behavior and appearance of that bar's patrons. This is a minor but typical example of how the politicization of drug use has created caricatures that Americans employ daily, characterizations that may or may not be accurate. Drug discourses render some use practices highly visible while making others nearly invisible. The misinformation about less frequently used drugs and their users is deeply entrenched, the product of over four decades of cultural narratives, legislation, law enforcement, and medical practices.

While legacies of prohibition and medicalization continue to frame American thinking about drugs and users, there are key changes in the domestic drug-war and drug-medicalization landscapes. Various forms of drug decriminalization are taking root across many states. Americans are coming to accept that marijuana, the most widely used drug after alcohol, caffeine, and nicotine, is a common and safe use practice. The industry that has grown up around legalized marijuana is not only starting to attract some users away from the black market and bring in new users, it is recognized as a major source of tax revenue. Awareness about licit and illicit opiate abuse has led some law-enforcement groups and cities to change their protocols to divert addicts from jail to other treatment and services. Long-fought changes in the availability and prevalence of naloxone and other drugs that block opiate overdose have changed the public conversation about the treatment of opiate users. At the same time, law enforcement, emergency medical responders, and governments are struggling with new street drugs. Fentanyl, an incredibly strong opiate, hit the American streets in the last few years, and is now a common element in many street drugs, from MDMA to heroin or cocaine. It is wreaking havoc on users who do not expect it to be in their drug of choice. Interdiction methods are becoming even less effective, because synthetic drug producers are several steps ahead of law enforcement and researchers in the creation of new drugs. Other countries have tried to outlaw such NBOMes, but cannot create and implement policy as fast as producers can resynthesize a new version of a drug. Meanwhile, prisons are overcrowded with low-level drug offenders, and the president cannot offer clemency fast enough. With the United States close to a tipping point with regard to criminalization, it may be time to think carefully about potential next steps so that we do not replace uninformed cultural assumptions and biases with a different set that may be equally as problematic.

One place to start would be with hearts and minds: to revise the notion of drugs and their users as an inherent problem. The mutability of the drug war's imagined threat over time, when considered alongside data about the millions of users who use without abuse or addiction, suggests that Americans cannot say *why* drugs in and of themselves are a threat. Former United Nations Secretary General Kofi Annan put it another way: "we need to accept that a drug-free world is an illusion."[1] Americans might begin a different kind of research and education movement to collect and share better research and information about drugs and users. If most people are users of some psychoactive substance, and the majority of them are controlled users, then drug use is a part of our lives in broader ways than Americans have been led to think. While the impetus to replace user criminalization with resources to treat addiction and harm reduction is definitely a step in the right direction, there is an unacknowledged problem with the thinking behind this effort to change policy. Not all users have a problem with drugs; in fact, most do not suffer abuse or addiction. If it is not right to penalize addicts with prison, it is also not right to insist that controlled or normative users go through recovery programs.

What it will take to change misinformation about drugs and users, especially assumptions of criminalization and inclinations toward medicalization, is a complicated, long-term series of cultural efforts. Changing hearts and minds requires, among other things, unfettered research into the short- and long-term practices of using and the effects of drugs: motivations, benefits, risks, experiences, and outcomes. If we are to fully comprehend American drug-use practices and their impacts, we must listen to users about what, how, and why they use. Prohibition has silenced users who have a great deal to share in terms of informed experience about their drug-use practices. Because we do not have a welcoming space in health care in which users can fully tell their use narratives, admitting to using drugs can have very different results, depending on the drug. These stories may affect users' health or may affect what we are prescribed as treatment. In this gaping cultural-knowledge vacuum, the United States has perpetrated horrible crimes and smaller offenses against users and their families. The cultural silencing of users is one of the most problematic, unseen outcomes of criminalization and medicalization. Making drug use practices more visible so that we become better aware of our own and others' use habits and patterns is key. More credible, diverse models that situate drug use as a normalized practice rather than a deviant behavior would better inform public drug discourse. Drug use, in itself, is not a problem, but some drugs and/or use practices can be risky, and therefore regulation of them, education about their use, and more research about long-term effects of all psychoactive substances would directly impact some of the harms and risks most associated with their use. If cultural thinking about drug use is broadened beyond addiction, we might ask: what would be useful in terms of research, health care, social practice and policy?

One thing is certain: the United States will not successfully address the issues around criminalization and medicalization with the same thinking that created them. The hegemonic hold of medicalization and criminalization has cultural effects beyond psychoactive drugs; these discourses are applied to our eating habits and food choices, how we exercise, how we raise children, etc. In other words, we are at a cultural impasse, and whether we recognize the limitations of this kind of thinking, holistically or discretely, remains to be seen. The categories that I have used for the sake of discussing the ways in which American culture engages, represents, regulates, and uses drugs are highly mutable and sometimes conflicted. The aim of this discussion is not to provide answers, but to offer perspective, some missing information, and to provoke a conversation about cultural assumptions. This book has identified

US cultural narratives about drugs and users and explored the dominance of particular ideological constructs that have become intrinsic to the discussion of drug use. The pervasive partnership of criminalization and medicalization in constructing users almost exclusively as criminals and addicts has shaped notions of licit and illicit substance use. For example, had most Americans heard the realities of illicit drug use from users other than those desperate to quit, they might have a very different impression of drug use. At the same time, some drugs have been so normalized as to be almost invisible. Again, how we respond to the use of particular drugs and their use by others likely involves a value judgment.

Social infrastructures in the United States—law enforcement, criminal justice, health care, social services, education, and other systems—are focused on drug use as criminal, and in terms of abuse or addiction. The economies of some of those industries depend on this view. Changing revenue streams and expectations around users is like turning a ship: it will be a slow process. Drug legalization in and of itself is not a panacea. While regulation of drugs assures a less contaminated and more standardized product, the other part of the question is culture: to what extent are we educated about how to use various substances? What kinds of cultural contexts and boundaries do we establish around drug use? Harm reduction measures should be widely available, and central to both policy efforts and drug-use practices. Education about harms tends to do more than anything else. Where this has been available, access to harm-reduction tools, whether clean needles and injection sites or access to medical professionals to talk about using, has offered significant benefits to users. But it is a step at the bottom of a hierarchy of social changes. Admitting that most people sometimes seek a high and accepting that this as a legitimate desire is a critical first step. Making substances safely available and understanding how dosages and other constituent elements affect immediate drug-user experience would be another. Better-informed education about drugs and users is critical for use practices and health care. Redeploying budget allocations and disburdening our law-enforcement and prison systems of a futile obligation to eradicate drug use would free resources to understand and address the issues underlying the drug war.

As Americans come to better understand their cultural proclivities for drug use, the question they might entertain is not about whether they should legalize this substance or that substance but, rather, how they conceive of and endorse the pursuit of pleasure—the desire to get high. While many other countries have adopted harm-reduction language and policy that at least assumes people are using, the United States prefers to pretend as if people are not. And that is a ridiculous position for public policy. It perpetuates a vacuum of information about authentic drug-use experiences. American culture has implicitly opposed addiction with abstention—even as over half of Americans use some kind of psychoactive drug (alcohol, tobacco, caffeine, marijuana, etc.) for pleasure, and more than 20 percent take prescribed psychotherapeutic drugs for life management. As I finished this manuscript in a café, a young college student at the next table was telling her parents about an experience working in a harm-reduction group at a rave. She clearly believed in the importance of helping users, and had a good deal of information about user distress. At the same time, when she went on to talk about various drugs that she admitted she had not tried, it was immediately apparent to me that her perceptions were shaped by the misconceptions that are part of American public drug discourses. Whether it was what street drugs might be cut with, what effects they render in users, or the experience of DMT or other hallucinogens, she could pass along only the misinformation she had been presented with as fact. Someone who has gone out of her way to offer a humane way of engaging and understanding drug users really ought to have access to better information. We can change that. It starts with conversations, questioning what we think we know about drugs and users, and listening to those whom we have silenced for too long.

NOTES

Introduction

1   *Drugs* refers to psychoactive substances that alter mental processes, cognition, or affect—anything from caffeine to alcohol to antidepressants to heroin. (See glossary.)

2   Endocannabinoids, chemicals naturally produced in the brain, create feelings of well-being. One such chemical, anandamide, is produced through massage and deep-tissue work, as well as endurance sports and other strenuous activities. Fuss et al., "A Runner's High," 13106; Chaitow, "Bodywork High," 1.

3   *Discourse* signals the language and ideas used to represent social understanding of a topic, as well as systems through which social power circulates. *Addiction*, a nonmedical term, is the cultural referent used in American discourse to refer to uncontrolled or habitual drug use. I use it to reference what is diagnosed as substance use disorder. (See glossary.)

4   Clark, "Conceptualising Addiction"; Ben-Yehuda, *The Politics and Morality of Deviance*; Conrad and Schneider *Deviance and Medicalization*.

5   Snyder, "Arrests in the United States, 1990–2010."

6   *Medicalization* refers to the cultural expansion of medical authority and practice. (See glossary.)

7   US Department of Health, Education, and Welfare, National Center for Health Statistics, Center for Disease Control, *Health, United States, 2011: With Special Feature on Socioeconomic Status and Health*, 2011, www.cdc.gov/nchs/data/hus/hus11.pdf.

8   See StreetRx.com for pricing by state and region.

9   Richard Nixon, "Remarks about an Intensified Program for Drug Abuse Prevention and Control," June 17, 1971, the American Presidency Project, www.presidency.ucsb.edu/ws/?pid=3047. The Comprehensive Drug Abuse Prevention and Control Act included the Controlled Substances Act, established the schedules for drug regulation, consolidated existing drug laws, and identified new offices to work on curbing drug abuse. The Drug Enforcement Agency (DEA) eventually brought together disparate government agencies under one office.

10 Nicholas Kristof, "Drugs Won the War," *New York Times*, June 13, 2009, www.nytimes.com/2009/06/14/opinion/14kristof.html. The annual drug war budget is estimated to be $1 billion. Drug Policy Alliance, "Drug War Statistics," 2016, www.drugpolicy.org/drug-war-statistics.

11 Between 2001 and 2010, the use of ADHD drugs tripled among Americans aged twenty to forty-four, and doubled among women aged forty-five to sixty-five. Wang, "Psychiatric Drug Use Spreads."

12 Paul Keye et al., "Fried Egg" PSA, Partnership for a Drug Free America, 1987.

13   Ritalin-SR, print advertisement, *American Journal of Psychiatry* 145, no. 1 (January 1988); Hanganu-Bresch, "Treat Her with Prozac." 181.

14   Siegel, *Intoxication*, 208; Linden, *The Compass of Pleasure*, 27.

15   In the United States, the war on drugs has literalized Michel Foucault's concept of a carceral culture of surveillance, including stop-and-frisk policing and mandatory minimum sentencing. Foucault, *Discipline and Punish*, 205.

16   Derek Waters and Jeremy Konner, *Drunk History*, Comedy Central, 2007–present.

17   Global Commission on Drug Policy, *The Negative Impact of the War on Drugs on Public Health*, 13.

18   Hart, *High Price*, 13; Linden, *The Compass of Pleasure*, 50.

19   Emphasis mine. Sullum, *Saying Yes*, 9.

20   Timothy Leary and Richard Alpert conceived of the significance of set and setting to the drug-use experience. Also Weil, *The Natural Mind*, and Zinberg and Robertson, *Drugs and the Public*. (See glossary.)

21   The United Kingdom devised a multicriteria list with sixteen measures including damage to health, drug dependency, economic costs, and crime.

22   For example, see Musto, *The American Disease*; Courtwright, *Forces of Habit*; and Erlen et al., *Federal Drug Control*.

23   For example, see Alexander, *The New Jim Crow*; Parenti, *Lockdown America*; and Goode and Ben-Yehuda, "The American Drug Panic of the 1980s."

24   Walton, *Out of It*, 258.

25   Lenson, *On Drugs*, 17.

26   Race, *Pleasure Consuming Medicine*, ix.

27   Hart's *High Price* is a notable exception. Usually such works discuss past drug use—a distance that may be real or strategic, but keeps us from having a stake as users in the present. To be absolutely clear, I have a stake in this cultural conversation as a silenced user in the present.

28   Huxley, *The Doors of Perception*, 62. For *alterity*, see glossary.

29   Pollan, *The Botany of Desire*, 170.

Chapter 1

1   Richards et al., "The Tobacco Industry's Code of Advertising."

2   Howarth, *Poststructuralism and After*, 334. For *agency*, see glossary.

3   See, for example, Judith Butler, who conceives of active subject agency as a space *between* individual choice and social inscription: neither entirely comprised of individual choice nor completely imposed. Butler, *Subjects of Desire*, 425.

4   Conceptualizing individual agency as including the power to choose helps to understand drug users as autonomous agents even as they may be subjects who resist, accept, or reproduce ideologies. (See glossary for *agency*.)

5   James Burrows, "Latke's Cookies," *Taxi*, February 5, 1981; Shelly Jensen, "Just Say Yo," *Fresh Prince of Bel Air*, February 15,1993.

6   Reeves and Campbell, *Cracked Coverage*, 344. See also Levine "The Discovery of Addiction"; Valverde, *Diseases of the Will*; and Ferentzy and Turner, *The History of Problem Gambling*.

7   Levine and Reinarman, "From Prohibition to Regulation," 462.

8   Goode and Ben-Yehuda, *Moral Panics*, 198.

9   Siff, *Acid Hype*, 408.

10   Lloyd Vries, "Candy Flavored Meth Targets New Users," CBS News, May 2, 2007.

11   Partnership for Drug Free Kids (formerly Partnership for a Drug Free America), "Meth Ado About Nothing? Flavored Meth and Cheese Heroin Stories Smack of Fear-mongering," June 22, 2007, www.drugfree.org/news-service/meth-ado-about-nothing-flavored-meth-and-cheese-heroin-stories-smack-of-fearmongering.

12   Only 0.3 percent and 0.5 percent of the US population used crack or methamphet-amine, respectively, in 2014, compared to 1.7 percent for cocaine and 13 percent for marijuana. These figures have been similar across the last decade. Data and statistics from the 2014 National Survey on Drug Use and Health (NSDUH) administered by the Substance Abuse and Mental Health Services Administration (SAMHSA) of the National Institutes of Health. See Substance Abuse and Mental Health Services Administration, *Behavioral Health Trends in the United States*.

13   Reinarman and Levine, "Crack in Context," 535; Morgan and Zimmer, "Social Phar-macology of Smokeable Cocaine."

14   Montagne, "Seeing Is Believing," 518.

15   PDFA, "I Learned It by Watching You," PSA. See Moreau, "'I Learned it by Watch-ing YOU!'"

16   PDFA, "Cocaine Rat," PSA, 1988, www.youtube.com/watch?v=7kS72J5Nlm8; Alexan-der et al., "Rat Park Chronicle."

17   PDFA, "Our Story," PSA, www.drugfree.org/about/our-history; Niesen, "Public Enemy Number One," 879.

18   Staff, "House Members Call for TV Anti-Drug Campaign," 70.

19   The ONDCP purchased network ad time in return for the inclusion of antidrug themes within specific programs. This subsidy benefitted the networks by $25 million in its first few years alone. Daniel Forbes, "Prime Time Propaganda," *Salon*, June 30, 2001, http://www.salon.com/2001/06/30/ondcp_4.

20   Congress cited the ONDCP's prepackaged "news" stories between 2002 and 2004 for being in violation of federal "propaganda and publicity" standards and the Antidefi-ciency Act. GAO Letter, 2005, B-303495, www.gao.gov/decisions/appro/303495.htm.

21   The $3.2 million paid for two thirty-second spots made this the largest single-event advertising expenditure in US government history. Zara Gelsey, "Pricey Prime Time Propaganda: Anti-Drug Adverts and the Super Bowl," February 1, 2002, www.the conversation.org/archive/alchemind.html.

22   Ogilvy and Mather, "I Helped" PSA, 2002.

23   Ogilvy and Mather, "AK-47" PSA, 2002.

24   The antidrug, antiterror campaign continued in a series of 2003 print PSAs. See also Hickman, "Target America," 222.

25   Allison North Jones, "Strong Views on Ads Linking Drug Use to Terrorism," *New York Times*, April 2, 2002, www.nytimes.com/2002/04/02/business/media-business-advertising-strong-views-pro-con-ads-linking-drug-use-terrorism.html.

26   Mark Souder, House of Representatives Subcommittee on Criminal Justice, Drug Policy, and Human Resources, March 27, 2003, Serial No. 108-17, www.congress.gov/

congressional-report/106th-congress/house-report/1053/1; Grimm "A Dubious Pitch," 44.

27 President Bush, "Address to the Nation on the September 11 Attacks," September 11, 2001, in *Selected Speeches of President George W. Bush*, 2001–2008, https:// georgewbush-whitehouse.archives.gov/infocus/bushrecord/documents/Selected_ Speeches_George_W_Bush.pdf.

28 Frank Davies, "Provocative White House Antidrug Ads Stir Debate," *Philadelphia Inquirer*, March 17, 2002.

29 Keh, "Drug Money in a Changing World," 4.

30 Hornik et al., "Evaluation of the National Youth Anti-Drug Media Campaign"; Witte and Allen, "A Meta-Analysis of Fear Appeals."

31 Beau Kilmer, Jonathan P. Caulkins, Rosalie Liccardo Pacula, and Peter H. Reuter, "The US Drug Policy Landscape," Rand Corporation Report 2012, www.rand.org/pubs/ occasional_papers/OP393.html.

32 Ira Teinowitz, "White House to End Drugs and Terror Ads," *Ad Age*, April 1, 2003, http://adage.com/article/news/white-house-end-drugs-terror-ads/37193.

33 The Montana Meth Project (MP) has become The Meth Project (TMP) as Colorado, Georgia, Hawaii, Idaho, Montana, and Wyoming have joined the campaign.

34 "Meth mouth" is a term used to describe the dental problems seen in some methamphetamine abusers, although evidence on its etiology is anecdotal. It may be a misnomer because the presentation of decay (e.g., buccal surfaces, smooth surfaces) is indicative of generalized drug-induced hyposalivation. Goodchild and Donaldson, "Methamphetamine Abuse and Dentistry," 583. Neuroscientist Carl Hart points out that there is no empirical evidence to support the claims of "meth mouth" and, as Adderall is the same drug, it would be surprising that there is no such disease in those users if "meth mouth" were caused by methamphetamine. Hart, *High Price*, 304. Also, Forest, "Methamphetamine and Oral Health," 445.

35 Naomi Murakawa argues that the victimhood of meth users depicted in the media has as much to do with fear "for" (versus fear "from") white drug users. Murakawa, "Toothless," 220–22. For an in-depth reading of TMP's images, see Linnemann et al., "'With Scenes of Blood and Pain.'" See also Cobbina, "Race and Class Differences."

36 Linnemann and Wall, "'This Is Your Face on Meth,'" 316.

37 Kristeva, *Powers of Horror*, 9, 4, 13.

38 Murakawa, "Toothless," 223.

39 Deputy Bret King created the Faces of Meth. *Frontline*, PBS, February 14, 2016, www .pbs.org/wgbh/pages/frontline/meth/body/faces.html.

40 Deputy Thomas Allman created Face2Face. Christine Byers, *St. Louis Post-Dispatch*, December 26, 2009, www.stltoday.com/news/students-face-up-to-meth-computer -simulations-showing-how-they/article_f709e858-3562-5e91-b0d8-1370b4d4fa3d.html.

41 Clinical psychologist David Erceg-Hurn reported that The Meth Project used poor research methods and ignored negative data from its own studies (2008). He criticized the project's research methods and failure to report data. For example, before the ads, 84 percent of teens saw a "great" or "moderate" risk of dying from meth use; after, that percentage was unchanged. The percentage of teens strongly disapproving of regular meth use actually declined from 98 percent to 91 percent. Interestingly, the ads were

very effective in promoting meth mouth: the perceived risk of tooth decay grew from 69 percent to 82 percent. Erceg-Hurn, "Drugs, Money, and Graphic Ads." See also Ryan S. King, "The Next Big Thing? Methamphetamine in the United States," Sentencing Project, 2006, https://static.prisonpolicy.org/scans/sp/methamphetamine_report.pdf.

42 Linnemann and Wall, "'This Is Your Face on Meth'"; Witte and Allen, "A Meta-Analysis of Fear Appeals"; Cuipers, "Three Decades of Drug Prevention Research"; Linneman et al., "'With Scenes of Blood and Pain.'"

43 Substance Abuse and Mental Health Services Administration. *Behavioral Health Trends in the United States: Results from the 2014 National Survey on Drug Use and Health.*

44 E. J. Schultz, "Whatever Happened to the Ad War on Drugs?," *AdAge*, March 24, 2014, http://adage.com/article/news/happened-ad-war-drugs/292262.

45 Joe Gabriel, "Aesthetics and the Failure of the FDA's Cigarette Warning Labels," *Points* blog, March 20, 2012, https://pointsadhsblog.wordpress.com/2012/03/20/aesthetics-and-the-failure-of-the-fdas-cigarette-warning-labels.

46 "The Inaugural Global Commission on Drug Policy report in 2011 called on all countries, but especially the United States, to challenge rather than reinforce common misconceptions about drug use and users." GDCP, *War on Drugs*, 18.

47 Porter, "Direct-to-Consumer (DTC) Pharmaceutical Marketing"; Donohue, "A History of Drug Advertising"; Angell, *The Truth About Drug Companies*, 123.

48 Aikin et al., "Patient and Physician Attitudes and Behaviors Associated with DTC Promotion of Prescription Drugs."

49 Sepracor, Inc., Lunesta print ad campaign, 2005; Sanofi Aventis, Ambien CR television spot, aired 2006.

50 AbelsonTaylor for Takeda, "Your Dreams Miss You," 2005, aired in 2006.

51 J. Heinrich, "Prescription Drugs: FDA Oversight of Direct-to-Consumer Advertising Has Limitations," GAO, 2002, www.gao.gov/new.items/d03177.pdf; Avorn et al., "Scientific Versus Commercial Sources of Influence on the Prescribing Behavior of Physicians"; Bell et al., "Direct-to-Consumer Prescription Drug Advertising and the Public."

52 Milt Freudenheim, "Showdown Looms in Congress Over Drug Advertising on TV," *New York Times*, January 22, 2007, www.nytimes.com/2007/01/22/business/media/22drug.html; Aikin et al., "Patient and Physician Attitudes and Behaviors Associated with DTC Promotion of Prescription Drugs," 6.

53 J. Heinrich, "Prescription Drugs: FDA Oversight of Direct-to-Consumer Advertising Has Limitations," GAO, 2002, www.gao.gov/new.items/d03177.pdf; Porter, "Direct-to-Consumer (DTC) Pharmaceutical Marketing," 63.

54 Montagne, "Mass Media Representations as Drug Information for Patients."

55 Thomas Abrams, FDA Letter Facsimile, FDA Downloads, "Drugs, Guidance, Compliance, Regulatory Information," September 25, 2008.

56 Vyvanse generated over $1 billion in 2014; Shire's CEO expects it to earn $10 billion by 2020. Thomas, "Shire, Maker of Binge-Eating Drug Vyvanse, First Marketed the Disease."

57 Nicolas Bombourg, "Attention Deficit Hyperactivity Disorder (ADHD) Therapeutics—Pipeline Assessment and Market Forecasts to 2018," *PRI Newswire*, October 27,

2011, www.prnewswire.com/news-releases/attention-deficit-hyperactivity-disorder-adhd-therapeutics—pipeline-assessment-and-market-forecasts-to-2018-132679803.html; Dina Gusovsky, "A Start-up Making Play for Billions in ADHD Drug Market," *CNBC*, May 21, 2015.

58 Ed Silverman, "Gulp! A Shire Campaign to Promote Vyvanse for Binge Eating is Questioned," *Wall Street Journal*, February 25, 2015; Porter, "Direct-to-Consumer (DTC) Pharmaceutical Marketing," 63.

59 Rubin, "Merchandising Madness," 369.

60 J. Heinrich, "Prescription Drugs: FDA Oversight of Direct-to-Consumer Advertising Has Limitations," GAO, 2002, www.gao.gov/new.items/d03177.pdf; Rosenthal et al., "Promotion of Prescription Drugs to Consumers"; Gellad and Lyles, "Direct-to-Consumer Advertising of Pharmaceuticals," 475.

61 Justin Wm. Moyer, "American Medical Association Urges Ban on TV Drug Ads," *Washington Post*, November 19, 2015, www.washingtonpost.com/news/morning-mix/wp/2015/11/19/american-medical-association-urges-ban-on-tv-drug-ads/?utm_term=.4e4a3eba8ec6.

62 Lauren Silverman, "Social Media Help Diabetes Patients (and Drug Makers) Connect," National Public Radio, December 3, 2012, www.npr.org/sections/health-shots/2012/12/03/166241115/social-media-helps-diabetes-patients-and-drugmakers-connect.

63 Goodman et al., *Consuming Habits*, 258.

64 Chanel pill dresses "Pills and Tablets as Embroidery," *Vogue*, Spring/Summer 2007, http://www.vogue.com/fashion-shows/spring-2007-ready-to-wear/chanel/slideshow/collection#66; Karen Hill, "Betsey Johnson Gives a New 'Prescription' For Her Spring/Summer 2014 Collection," *Marie Claire*, August 29, 2013, www.marieclaire.com/fashion/news/a8019/betsey-johson-prescription.

65 Shapiro, *Waiting for the Man*; Snoop Dogg with Pharrell Williams, "Let's Get Blown," *Rhythm and Gangsta*, Geffen, 2004; Cypress Hill, "Hits from the Bong," Columbia, 1992; Afroman, "Because I Got High," Columbia, 2001; Lil' Kim with Notorious B.I.G., "Drugs," *Hardcore*, Atlantic, 1996; The Pharcyde, "Pack the Pipe," *Bizarre Ride II the Pharcyde*, Delicious Vinyl, 1992; Notorious B.I.G. with Chuck D, "Ten Crack Commandments," *Life After Death*, Big Beat Records, 1997; 50 Cent, "Corner Bodega (Coke Spot)," *Power of the Dollar*, Columbia, Unreleased, 2000; 50 Cent, "Ghetto Qu'ran," *Power of the Dollar*, Columbia, Unreleased, 2000; Ice-T, "6 'N the Mornin'," *Rhyme Pays*, Sire/Warner Brothers, 1987.

66 Josh Homme, Nick Oliveri, Queens of the Stone Age, "Feel Good Hit of the Summer," Interscope, 2000.

67 Steven Soderbergh, *Traffic*, USA Films, 2000.

68 Vince Gilligan, director and writer, "Pilot," *Breaking Bad*, AMC, January 20, 2008.

69 Michael Slovis, director, and Gennifer Hudson, writer, "Cornered," *Breaking Bad*," AMC, August 21, 2011.

70 Darren Aronofsky, director, *Requiem for a Dream*, Artisan Entertainment, 2000.

71 Jeff Stark, "It's a Punk Movie," *Salon*, October 13, 2000, www.salon.com/2000/10/13/aronofsky.

72 Graham, *Representations of the Post/Human*, 53.

73 Sam Esmail, director and writer, "eps1.0_hellofriend," *Mr. Robot*, USA, August 2015.

74 Allen Coulter, director, Liz Brixius, Linda Wallem, and Evan Dunsky, writers, "Pilot," *Nurse Jackie*, Showtime, June 8, 2009.

75 Paul Feig, director, John Hilary Shepherd, writer, "Nosebleed," *Nurse Jackie*, Showtime, August 3, 2009.

76 Seth Mann, director, Evan Dunsky and Liz Brexius, writers, "The Wall," *Nurse Jackie*, Showtime, April 22, 2012.

77 Elliot's case is complex; he self-medicates for mental illness. He becomes far more dysfunctional when he takes too much Adderall in season two in order to rid himself of his internal alter ego, Mr. Robot. Sam Esmail, "eps2.1_k3rnel-pan1c.ksd," *Mr. Robot*, Season 2 Episode 3, USA, July 20, 2016.

78 Stephens "Addiction to Melodrama," 859–60, 869.

79 David Trainer, director, Bonnie and Terry Turner, writers, "That Disco Episode," *That '70s Show*, Fox Broadcasting Company, November 8, 1998.

80 Matt Groening, "Weekend at Burnsie's," *The Simpsons*, Fox Broadcasting Company, April 7, 2002; Matt Groening, "My Three Suns," *Futurama*, Twentieth Century Fox Home Entertainment, May 4, 1999.

81 Mike Judge, Greg Daniels, "Peggy's Turtle Song," *King of the Hill*, Fox Broadcasting Company, May 10, 1998. At the end of the episode, prior to the credits, Fox offered information about ADD.

82 Neil Burger, director, *Limitless*, Intermedia Film, 2011.

Chapter 2

1 Nancy Reagan, quoted in Herrington, *The White House Conference for a Drug Free America, Final Report, June 1988*.

2 "Subcommittee Report on Terrorism, Narcotics, and International Relations, of the Committee on Foreign Relations, United States Senate," National Security Agency archive, December 1988, www.cfr.org/drug-trafficking-and-control/senate -sub committee-report-drugs-law-enforcement-foreign-policy-kerry-committee -report/p28122.

3 Eleanor Clift, "Reagan Outlines Goals in Anti-Drug Crusade: President, Cabi- net May Take Tests as Example in Increased National Effort to Curb Trafficking," *Los Angeles Times*, August 5, 1986, http://articles.latimes.com/1986-08-05/news/ mn-1343_1_drug-abuse.

4 Reagan, "Speech on the Campaign against Drug Abuse" (1986), *Public Papers of the Presidents of the United States*; Elwood, *Rhetoric in the War on Drugs*, 30.

5 "The Larry King Show," Cable News Network, June 15, 1989, quoted in "Crackmire," *New Republic*, September 11, 1989, p. 7.

6 Knight Ridder Newspapers, "Drug Czar: Go After Casual Users, Parents," *Chi- cago Tribune*, May 4, 1989, http://articles.chicagotribune.com/1989-05-04/ news/8904090784_1_drug-users-drug-czar-casual-users.

7 Eric Weiner, "The Nation; In the War on Drugs, Planes Are a Big Enemy," *New York Times*, October 8, 1989, sec. Week in Review.

8 Clift, "Reagan Outlines Goals in Anti-Drug Crusade."

9   Reeves and Campbell, *Cracked Coverage*, 162–63.

10   Peter Kerr, "Anatomy of the Drug Issue: How, After Years, It Erupted," *New York Times*, November 17, 1986, sec. U.S., www.nytimes.com/1986/11/17/us/anatomy-of-the -drug-issue-how-after-years-it-erupted.html?pagewanted=all.

11   Abelson and Miller, "A Decade of Trends in Cocaine Use in the Household Population," 37–40.

12   Reinarman and Levine, "The Crack Attack," 154, 157.

13   Walter Miller and James Lynch, *The Growth of Youth Gang Problems in the United States: 1970–98*, US Department of Justice, Office of Justice Programs, Office of Juvenile Justice and Delinquency Prevention, 2001, https://cops.usdoj.gov/html/cd_rom/ solution_gang_crime/pubs/TheGrowthofYouthGangProblemsinUS.pdf.

14   Reese and Danielian, "A Closer Look at InterMedia Influences in Agenda Setting," 34.

15   Ronald Reagan, "Remarks on Signing the Anti-Drug Abuse Act of 1986," October 27, 1986, www.reaganlibrary.archives.gov/archives/speeches/1986/102786c.htm.

16   Goode and Ben-Yehuda, *Moral Panics*, 62; Michael Oreskes, "Drug War Underlines Fickleness of Public," *New York Times*, September 6, 1990, A22.

17   Peter Kerr, "Anatomy of the Drug Issue: How, After Years, It Erupted," *New York Times*, November 17, 1986, sec. U.S., www.nytimes.com/1986/11/17/us/anatomy-of-the -drug-issue-how-after-years-it-erupted.html?pagewanted=all.

18   Courtwright, "The Controlled Substances Act."

19   Anti-Drug Abuse Act of 1988, H.R. 5210, www.congress.gov/bill/100th-congress/ house-bill/5210.

20   Ryan S. King, "Disparity by Geography: The War on Drugs in America's Cities," the Sentencing Project, 2008, 1–41, www.sentencingproject.org/publications/ disparity-by-geography-the-war-on-drugs-in-americas-cities.

21   "National Drug Control Strategy, Progress in the War on Drugs 1989–1992," ONDCP, 1993, www.ncjrs.gov/pdffiles1/ondcp/140556.pdf.

22   Garriott, *Policing Methamphetamine*, 2.

23   Reinarman and Levine, *Crack in America*, 18–51 and 37.

24   Drug Control Policy Reauthorization Act of 1998, H11225, https://obamawhitehouse .archives.gov/ondcp/reauthorization-act.

25   Ian Rothkerch, "What Drugs Have Not Destroyed, the War on Them Has," *Salon*, June 29, 2002, www.salon.com/2002/06/29/simon_5.

26   Sterling, "Drug Policy," 54; Garriott, *Policing Methamphetamine*, 11.

27   Alexander, *The New Jim Crow*, 104.

28   Carroll Doherty et al., "America's New Drug Landscape," Pew Research, April 2, 2014, 1–4, www.people-press.org/files/legacy-pdf/04-02-14%20Drug%20Policy%20 Release.pdf.

29   Reinarman and Levine, *Crack in America*, 334–35.

30   Manderson, "Possessed," 36.

31   Sacco and Finklea, "Reauthorizing the Office of National Drug Control Policy," 9–12.

32   Seddon, "Court-Ordered Treatment," 156.

33   Justin Scheck, "Strapped Police Run on Fumes and Federal Pot-Fighting Cash," *Wall Street Journal*, July 3, 2010, www.wsj.com/articles/SB1000142405274870364830457521238 2612331758.

34 The Department of Justice fund receives revenue from the Drug Enforcement Agency and the Federal Bureau of Investigation; the US Treasury fund receives revenue from the Coast Guard and US Customs.

35 Theshia Naidoo, "Asset Forfeiture," International Drug Policy Reform Conference, 2015; Jonah Engle, *Above the Law*, report for the Drug Policy Alliance, 2014; Carpenter et al., *Policing for Profit: The Abuse of Civil Asset Forfeiture*.

36 Robert Rodriguez, "Quinn Wants Drug Dealer to Pay—Literally—for Crimes," NBC, September 18, 2001, www.nbcchicago.com/blogs/ward-room/quinn-drug-crimes -128045768.html.

37 Alexander, *The New Jim Crow*, 88–89; Stevens, "Our 'Broken System' of Criminal Justice."

38 Nicole Porter and Tyler Clemons, "Drug-Free Zone Laws," the Sentencing Project, 1–3. http://sentencingproject.org/wp-content/uploads/2015/12/Drug-Free-Zone-Laws .pdf; Christie Thompson, "What Happens When an Entire City Becomes a Drug-Free School Zone," April 14, 2014, https://thinkprogress.org/what-happens-when-an-entire -city-becomes-a-drug-free-school-zone-46c5cb8760f9#.gpnbeke3j.

39 FBI Uniform Crime Reporting, Arrest Tables 2014, https://ucr.fbi.gov/ crime-in-the-u.s/2010/crime-in-the-u.s.-2010/persons-arrested.

40 Stevens, "Our 'Broken System' of Criminal Justice," 56; Staff, "Report of the Sentencing Project to the United Nations Human Rights Committee Regarding Racial Disparities in the United States Criminal Justice System," August 20, 2013, http://sentencingproject .org/wp-content/uploads/2015/12/Race-and-Justice-Shadow-Report-ICCPR.pdf.

41 King, "Disparity by Geography: The War on Drugs in America's Cities."

42 Alexander, *The New Jim Crow*, 60, 74–75, 90; Pettit and Western, "Mass Imprisonment and the Life Course," 155.

43 FBI Uniform Crime Reporting, Arrest Tables 2014.

44 The FBI defines violent crimes as murder, nonnegligent manslaughter, forcible rape, robbery, and aggravated assault. FBI Uniform Crime Reporting, Arrest Tables 2014; Federal Bureau of Prisons, Inmate Statistics, "Offenses," 2016, www.bop.gov/about/ statistics/statistics_inmate_offenses.jsp.

45 "Federal Drug Sentencing Laws Bring High Cost, Low Return," PEW Research Brief, August 27, 2015, www.pewtrusts.org/en/research-and-analysis/issue-briefs/2015/08/ federal-drug-sentencing-laws-bring-high-cost-low-return.

46 E. Ann Carson, "Prisoners in 2014," US Department of Justice, 1–5, www.bjs.gov/ content/pub/pdf/p14.pdf.

47 "Federal Drug Sentencing Laws Bring High Cost, Low Return," PEW Research Brief, August 27, 2015.

48 Administrative Office of the US Courts, *Judicial Business of the U.S. Courts Series*, Table D-5, 1980–2014, www.uscourts.gov/statistics/table/d/judicial-business/2014/09/30; Bureau of Justice Statistics, *Federal Criminal Case Processing, 1982–93*, Table 18 (1988), www.bjs.gov/content/pub/pdf/Fccp93.pdf; Bureau of Justice Statistics, *Federal Justice Statistics 2012—Statistical Tables*, Table 7.11, www.bjs.gov/content/pub/pdf/fjs12st.pdf.

49 Adam Liptak, "Justices, 5-4, Tell California to Cut Prisoner Population," *New York Times*, May 23, 2011, www.nytimes.com/2011/05/24/us/24scotus.html.

50 GCDP, *War on Drugs*.

51 Ibid., 15.

52   Neill Franklin, Executive Director, Law Enforcement against Prohibition, interview with Ingrid Walker, January 8, 2016.

53   Susan E. Collins et al., "LEAD Program Evaluation: Recidivism Report," March 27, 2015, http://static1.1.sqspcdn.com/static/f/1185392/26121870/1428513375150/LEAD_EVALUATION_4-7-15.pdf.

54   "No Entry: A National Survey of Criminal Justice Diversion Programs and Initiatives," Center for Health and Justice, December 2013, www2.centerforhealthandjustice.org/sites/www2.centerforhealthandjustice.org/files/publications/CHJ%20Diversion%20Report_web.pdf.

55   Conor Friedersdorf, "Federal Judge: My Drug War Sentences Were 'Unfair and Disproportionate," *Atlantic*, June 29, 2015, www.theatlantic.com/politics/archive/2015/06/federal-judge-my-drug-war-sentences-were-unfair-and-disproportionate/397130.

56   Anne Holland, "Black Market Threat to Rec Sales Lower than Expected: Exclusive Data," *Marijuana Business Daily*, March 3, 2014, http://mjbizdaily.com/black-market-threat-to-rec-sales-lower-than-expected-exclusive-data-2.

57   The drug war's total budget in 2014, which included treatment, prevention, domestic law enforcement, and interdiction, was over $25.5 billion dollars. Jeffrey Miron and Katherine Waldock, "The Budgetary Impact of Ending Drug Prohibition," Cato Institute, September 27, 2010, www.cato.org/publications/white-paper/budgetary-impact-ending-drug-prohibition; "FY 2015 Budget and Performance Summary," ONDCP, 2014, https://obamawhitehouse.archives.gov/sites/default/files/ondcp/about-content/fy2015_summary.pdf; Kristen Finklea, "Reauthorizing the ONDCP: Issues for Consideration," December 21, 2010, 9–12, http://defense-legislation.blogspot.com/2010/12/reauthorizing-office-of-national-drug.html.

58   Christopher Ingraham, "Colorado's Legal Weed Market: $700 Million in Sales Last Year, $1 Billion by 2016," *Chicago Tribune*, February 12, 2015, www.chicagotribune.com/news/nationworld/chi-colorado-marijuana-profits-2016-20150212-story.html; Katie Smith, "Washington Expects Sales Tax Revenues to Surge to $1 Billion," *Bloomberg News*, October 23, 2015, www.bloomberg.com/news/articles/2015-10-23/washington-expects-pot-sales-tax-revenue-surge-to-1-billion.

59   Tom Huddleston, "Legal Marijuana Sales Could Hit $6.7 Billion," *Fortune*, February 1, 2016, http://fortune.com/2016/02/01/marijuana-sales-legal.

60   Alison Schrager, "The Economic Case for the US to Legalize All Drugs," *Quartz*, June 7, 2013, http://qz.com/91642/the-economic-case-for-the-us-to-legalize-all-drugs.

61   The Original Silk Road: June 2011–October 2013, created by Ross Ulbricht, the "Dread Pirate Roberts." Researchers and practitioners at the 2015 International Drug Policy Reform Conference made a compelling argument for the positive effects of this market. "The Future of Digital Spaces, Drug Sales, and Drug Policy," International Drug Policy Reform Conference, Washington, DC, 2015. See also Caudevilla et al., "Results of an International Drug Testing Service for Cryptomarket Users."

Chapter 3

1   See, for example, Conrad and Schneider, *Deviance and Medicalization*; Conrad, *Medicalization of Society*; Greco, "Psychosomatic Subjects and the 'Duty to Be Well,'" 357.

2   Clarke et al., "Biomedicalization," 47.

3   US National Center for Health Statistics, "Health, United States, 2014," 79, www.cdc
     .gov/nchs/data/hus/hus14.pdf.

4   Becker et al., "Non-medical Use, Abuse, and Dependence on Sedatives and Tranquil-
     izers among U.S. Adults," 280.

5   Decorte, "Blinding Ourselves with Science," 36.

6   Campbell, *Discovering Addiction*; Keane, *What's Wrong with Addiction?*; Granfield and
     Reinarman, *Expanding Addiction*; Herzberg, *Happy Pills in America*; Courtwright,
     Forces of Habit; DeGrandpre, *The Cult of Pharmacology*; Musto, *The American Disease*;
     Goodman et al., *Consuming Habits*; Acker, *Creating the American Junkie*; Roizen, *The
     American Discovery of Alcoholism*.

7   The NSDUH offers even starker statistics. Aside from alcohol and marijuana (with
     addiction rates of 6.4 percent and 13 percent, respectively), well under 6 percent of
     users of any drug suffer addiction (substance abuse disorder). The Global Commis-
     sion on Drug Policy confirms 10 percent or less as the worldwide statistic for illicit
     drug addiction. See results from the 2014 National Survey on Drug Use and Health;
     GCDP, *War on Drugs*.

8   Pincus et al., "Prescribing Trends."

9   Goodman et al., *Consuming Habits*, xviii.

10   Herzberg, *Happy Pills in America*, 89–90.

11   Foucault, Michel, *Technologies of the Self*, 18.

12   Conrad, *The Medicalization of Society*, 9.

13   Clark, "Conceptualising Addiction," 57, 62; Rinaldi et al., "Clarification and Standard-
     ization of Substance Abuse Terminology."

14   "Addiction" is not used by either professional diagnostic manual: the American
     Psychiatric Association's *Diagnostic and Statistical Manual of Mental Disorders IV*
     (DSM-4) or Hasin et al., *International Classification of Disease* (ICD-10). (See glossary
     for *addiction*.)

15   See, for example, Levine, "The Discovery of Addiction"; Keane, "Drugs that Work," 6.

16   Conrad and Schneider, *Deviance and Medicalization*, 8, 250–51.

17   Peretti-Watel, "Epidemiology as a Model," 56.

18   Most recent revisions: DSM-5, 2013; Hasin et al., *International Classification of Dis-
     ease* (ICD-10).

19   DSM-2, 1968.

20   DSM-5, 2013.

21   The WHO Expert Committee on Drug Dependence's definitional evolution reflects
     the social politics of naming drug abuse, diagnostically and descriptively. Nomencla-
     ture shifts include: 1949, Habit-Forming Drugs; 1950, Drugs Liable to Produce Addic-
     tion; 1964, Addiction-Producing Drugs; 1966, Dependence-Producing Drugs; 1969,
     Drug Dependence; and to the present, Expert Committee on Drug Dependence. All
     reports available at www.who.int/substance_abuse/right_committee/en.

22   Edwards et al., "Nomenclature and Classification of Drug- and Alcohol-Related Prob-
     lems," 230. See also Reinarman, "Addiction as Accomplishment," 311–12; and Bell and
     Salmon, "Pain, Physical Dependence, and Pseudoaddiction." Definitional differences
     between the DSM-5 and ICD-10 exceed language issues: studies that investigated

diagnostic concordance by applying both criteria to the same individuals found both minor and significant differences. First, "Harmonisation of ICD-11 and DSM-V," 382.

23   Both research and public debate on addiction are "consistently informed by epidemio-logical data, to such an extent that discussions tend to focus more on the data than on their interpretations." Peretti-Watel, "Epidemiology as a Model," 56.

24   McLellan et al., "Drug Dependence, a Chronic Medical Illness."

25   Vaccarino and Rotzinger, *Neuroscience of Psychoactive Substance Use and Dependence: Summary*. How researchers engage with the diagnostic tools presents a secondary set of issues. In a study of the issues related to the use of the ICD-10 and DSM-4, the variability of dependence diagnoses had to do with treatment researchers' attitudes about what was required for research purposes. Hasin et al., "Prevalence, Correlates, Disability, and Comorbidity of DSM-IV Alcohol Abuse and Co-dependence in the United States."

26   Peele, *The Meaning of Addiction*, 25.

27   Keane, *What's Wrong with Addiction?*, 44–45.

28   The DSM-5 Open Letter Committee of the Society for Humanistic Psychology, Division 32 of the American Psychological Association, June 6, 2012, http://dsm5-reform .com/2012/06/response-to-the-final-dsm-5-draft-proposals-by-the-open-letter -committee.

29   Dr. Howard B. Moss, cited in Ian Urbina, "Addiction Diagnoses May Rise under Guideline Changes," *New York Times*, May 11, 2012, www.nytimes.com/2012/05/12/us/ dsm-revisions-may-sharply-increase-addiction-diagnoses.html.

30   Ibid.

31   Reinarman, "Addiction as Accomplishment," 308.

32   Peele, *The Meaning of Addiction*, 26.

33   Campbell, *Discovering Addiction*, 3.

34   Keane, *What's Wrong with Addiction?*, 61.

35   Abigail Zuger, "A General in the Drug War," *New York Times*, June 13, 2011, www .nytimes.com/2011/06/14/science/14volkow.html.

36   Douglas Quenqua, "An Addiction Vaccine, Tantalizingly Close," *New York Times*, October 3, 2011, www.nytimes.com/2011/10/04/health/04vaccine.html.

37   Kalivas and Volkow, "The Neural Basis of Addiction," 1413.

38   Vaccarino and Rotzinger, *Neuroscience of Psychoactive Substance Use and Dependence: Summary*.

39   Gil Kerlikowske, "Obama Administration Releases 21st Century Drug Policy Strategy," White House press release, April 17, 2012, https://obamawhitehouse.archives.gov/blog/ 2012/04/17/drug-policy-21st-century-0.

40   Hart, *High Price*, 302.

41   Hickman, "Target America," 215; Bogren and Winter, "Knowledge Production, Communication and Utilization." Campbell writes that the new optics of addiction neuroscience are "not simply a new way of seeing, but a new way of explaining what was seen." Campbell, "Toward a Critical Neuroscience of 'Addiction,'" 90; Campbell, *Discovering Addiction*, 208.

42   Bishop, "Research Review: Neuroscientific Studies of Intervention for Language Impairment in Children."

43 Hansen, "Pharmaceutical Evangelism and Spiritual Capital," 120; Clark, "Chemistry Is the New Hope."

44 Page, "What Can't Functional Neuroimaging Tell the Cognitive Scientist?," 442.

45 Heyman, *Addiction: A Disorder of Choice.*

46 Flanagan, "What's It Like to Be an Addict?" 289.

47 Hart, *High Price*, 269, 272, 273–74; Lewis, *The Biology of Desire*, 33–34.

48 Caroline Cassels, "APA 2009: Alcoholism Is Not What It Used to Be, Expert Says," *Medscape*, May 28, 2009, www.medscape.com/viewarticle/703483.

49 Heyman, *Addiction*, 21. See also Reznicek, *Blowing Smoke.*

50 Acker, "How Crack Found a Niche in the American Ghetto," 70.

51 Kushner, "Toward a Cultural Biology of Addiction," 19.

52 Valentine, "Intoxicating Culture," 438; John Monterosso and Barry Schwartz, "Did Your Brain Make You Do It?" *New York Times*, July 27, 2012, www.nytimes.com/2012/07/29/opinion/sunday/neuroscience-and-moral-responsibility.html.

53 Granfield and Cloud, "The Elephant That No One Sees."

54 Keane, *What's Wrong with Addiction?*, 161–62.

55 Lewis, *The Biology of Desire*, 12.

56 Alexander and Roberts, *High Culture*, 3.

57 Conrad, *The Medicalization of Society: On the Transformation of Human Conditions into Treatable Disorders.*

58 Meyers, *The Clinic and Elsewhere*, 12, 82, 95.

59 Martin, "The Pharmaceutical Person."

60 National Institute of Drug Abuse, "Dr. Nora Volkow on Addiction: A Disease of Free Will," www.drugabuse.gov/videos/dr-nora-volkow-addiction-disease-free-will.

61 Sedgwick, "The Epidemics of the Will," 582.

62 Kushner, "Toward a Cultural Biology of Addiction," 9; Carey Goldberg, "At the White House, Learning How Not to Talk about Addiction," WBUR, December 13, 2013, http://commonhealth.legacy.wbur.org/2013/12/language-substance-abuse-addiction. Also, Kelly et al., "Determining the Relative Importance of the Mechanisms of Behavior Change within Alcoholics Anonymous," 289–99.

63 Alexander and Roberts, *High Culture*, 4.

64 DeGrandpre, *The Cult of Pharmacology*, 120–21.

65 The NSDUH defines *dependence or abuse* for psychoactive substances using criteria from the DSM-4, including: symptoms such as withdrawal, tolerance, trouble with the law, and interference in major obligations at work, school, or home during the past year. While the NSDUH is the primary data source on drug use in the United States and is used by many social researchers and policy makers, it is problematic for a variety of reasons, including: aggregation of abuse and dependence; a lack of trend data due to a shift in focus from 2000 on; and questions and reporting categories that are inconsistent across substances and study years. Most problematic is that the NSDUH reports figures that cite estimates as if they are genuine statistics. The percentage from a 65,000-person sample is applied to the entire nation and reported as if the whole United States population has been surveyed. Further, the report moves back and forth between its sample and the nation, making it difficult to cite data with any sense of whether it is an estimate or an actual figure based on user reportage. That said, it is the

main source of national data, so I use it with these caveats. Special thanks to Dr. Elin Bjorling for her expertise in reviewing and analyzing this NSDUH data. See Substance Abuse and Mental Health Services Administration, *Behavioral Health Trends in the United States*.

66 Linden, *The Compass of Pleasure*, 50.

67 Substance Abuse and Mental Health Services Administration, *Behavioral Health Trends in the United States*, 16.

68 Conway et al., "Lifetime Comorbidity of DSM-IV Mood and Anxiety Disorders and Specific Drug Use Disorders"; Hasin et al., "Prevalence, Correlates, Disability, and Comorbidity of DSM-IV Alcohol Abuse and Co-dependence in the United States"; Petry et al., "Comorbidity of DSM-IV Pathological Gambling and Other Psychiatric Disorders"; Substance Abuse and Mental Health Services Administration, *Results from the 2011 National Survey on Drug Use and Health*.

69 Eoin Cannon, "The Democracy of Addicts, if Not Addiction," *Points*, September 20, 2012, https://pointsadhsblog.wordpress.com/2012/09/20/the-democracy-of-addicts-if-not-of-addiction/.

70 Granfield and Cloud, "The Elephant that No One Sees," 45–61.

71 Hart, *High Price*, 258.

72 "Alcoholism Isn't What It Used To Be," *NIAAA Spectrum* 1, no. 1 (2009), www.spectrum.niaaa.nih.gov/archives/v1i1Sept2009/features/Alcoholism.html; Becker and Fiellin, "Non-medical Use," 280–87.

73 Biernacki, *Pathways from Heroin Addiction*.

74 Granfield and Cloud, "The Elephant That No One Sees"; Klingemann and Sobell, *Promoting Self-Change from Problem Substance Use*, 64–75.

75 See, for example, Reznicek, *Blowing Smoke*, 92; Granfield and Cloud, "The Elephant That No One Sees."

76 Kim Sue, "Does Public Health Really Want to Own Addiction?" *Points* blog, May 29, 2013, https://pointsadhsblog.wordpress.com/2013/05/29/does-public-health-really-want-to-own-addiction; Peretti-Watel, "Epidemiology as a Model," 53.

77 Raikhel and Garriott, *Addiction Trajectories*, 28. Gilles Deleuze identifies drug use as having two domains: vital experimentation and deadly experimentation—and seeks to identify a turning point between them: "Vital experimentations occurs when a trial grabs you, takes control of you, establishing more and more connections, and opens you to connections." Deleuze, *Two Regimes of Madness*, 153.

78 A reference to Courtwright's observation, "What we think about addiction very much depends on who is addicted." Courtwright, *Dark Paradise*, 4.

Chapter 4

1 Katherine Dorsett Bennett, "Gotta Watch: Kid Feels Dizzy, Hilarity Ensues," CNN, May 30, 2012, http://news.blogs.cnn.com/2012/05/30/gotta-watch-kid-feels-dizzy-hilarity-ensues.

2 South, *Drugs*, 4–5.

3 Goodman, "Excitantia," 122.

4 Courtwright, "Addiction and the Science of History," 489.

5   Carlos Zarate, National Institutes of Health, cited in Jon Hamilton, "Club Drug Relief from Depression?" NPR, January 30, 2012, www.npr.org/sections/health-shots/2012/01/30/145992588/could-a-club-drug-offer-almost-immediate-relief-from-depression.

6   Walton, *Out of It*, 258.

7   The DSM-5 recognizes ten classes of psychoactive drugs: alcohol, caffeine, cannabis, hallucinogens (phencyclidine or similarly acting arylcyclohexylamines), other hallucinogens like LSD, inhalants, opioids, sedatives, hypnotics, anxiolytics, stimulants (including amphetamine-type drugs, cocaine, and other stimulants), and tobacco.

8   Boon, *The Road of Excess*, 48.

9   O'Malley and Valverde, "Pleasure, Freedom and Drugs," 33.

10 MacLean, "Volatile Bodies," 381.

11 Bancroft, "Nudge Policy," 172.

12 O'Malley and Valverde, "Pleasure, Freedom and Drugs," 27–28.

13 Duff, "The Pleasure in Context," 383–85. See also Bunton and Coveney, "Drugs' Pleasures," 10, 161.

14 O'Malley and Valverde, "Pleasure, Freedom and Drugs," 39.

15 Fraser and Valentine, *Substance and Substitution*, 410–11.

16 Moore, "Erasing Pleasure from Public Discourse on Illicit Drugs."

17 Volkow quoted in Abigail Zuger, "A General in the Drug War," *New York Times*, June 13, 2011, http://www.nytimes.com/2011/06/14/science/14volkow.html. Bunton and Coveney add, "[S]o many injunctions to healthy behaviours seem to be concerned with restricting or overcoming our seemingly 'natural' inclinations toward certain pleasures." Coveney and Bunton, "In Pursuit of the Study of Pleasure," 163.

18 Moore, "Erasing Pleasure from Public Discourse on Illicit Drugs," 354.

19 Becker, "Becoming a Marihuana User," iv.

20 "Grandmas Smoking Weed for the First Time," Cut Video, November 19, 2014, www.youtube.com/watch?v=IRBAZJ4lFoU.

21 Race, *Pleasure Consuming Medicine*, ix–xii.

22 Ibid., xiii.

23 Campos, *Home Grown*, 8.

24 World Health Organization, "Management of Substance Abuse," www.who.int/substance_abuse/terminology/acute_intox/en.

25 Derrida, "The Rhetoric of Drugs," in Alexander and Roberts, *High Culture: Reflections on Addiction and Modernity*, 24.

26 Pollan, *The Botany of Desire*, 152.

27 Walton, *Out of It*, 258.

28 Valentine, "Intoxicating Culture," 438–39.

29 Merleau-Ponty and Carman, *Phenomenology of Perception*, 12, 82–83.

30 Hemment, "E is for *Ekstasis*," 1–2.

31 Butler, *Subjects of Desire*, xxi.

32 Derrida, "The Rhetoric of Drugs," 7.

33 MacLean, "It Might Be a Scummy-Arsed Drug but It's a Sick Buzz,'" 312.

34 Zajdow, "'It Blasted Me into Space,'" 223, 227.

35 Duff, "The Pleasure in Context," 386–87.

36 Klein, "What Is Health and How Do You Get It?," 23.

37 Sulkunen, "Between Culture and Nature," 266.

38 Tagliazucchi et al., "Enhanced Repertoire of Brain Dynamical States during the Psychedelic Experience," 542–56; Carhart-Harris, "Neural Correlates of the Psychedelic State as Determined by fMRI Studies with Psilocybin."

39 Shortall, "Psychedelic Drugs and the Problem of Experience," 191–92.

40 Siegel. *Intoxication,* 2–3.

41 "Edibles Education," card from Cannabis Business Alliance, CO, 2015.

42 Nichols, "Psychedelics," 266.

43 Jaffe, "Drug Addiction and Abuse," 528.

44 "Mom Eats Mushrooms," Patreon video, http://boingboing.net/2016/02/25/watch-61 -year-old-takes-magic.html.

45 Linden, *The Compass of Pleasure,* 47–48.

46 "Oliver Sacks, Exploring How Hallucinations Happen," *Fresh Air*, NPR interview, November 6, 2012, www.npr.org/2012/11/06/164360724/oliver-sacks-exploring-how -hallucinations-happen.

47 Sulkunen, "Between Culture and Nature," 261.

48 Shortall, "Psychedelic Drugs and the Problem of Experience," 204.

49 Hunt et al., " Drug Use and Meanings of Risk and Pleasure," 84, 87, 93.

50 Gabriel, "Anesthetics and the Chemical Sublime," 78, 93.

51 Courtwright, *Forces of Habit,* 19.

52 Winstock, "New Recreational Drugs and the Primary Care Approach to Patients Who Use Them," 288.

53 Aaron Couch, "Emmys: Seth Meyers Zings Network TV, 'Big Bang' Salaries in Opening Monologue," *Hollywood Reporter*, August 15, 2014.

54 The Global Drug Survey is self-selected by respondents, and its questions are directed at a wider set of indicators and use habits than abuse and addiction. The NSDUH tends to focus on the latter, but both surveys show similar data points with different emphases. (See figure 3.2 in chapter 3.)

55 The Net Pleasure Index depicts the net for positive and negative aspects of drug use. The relationship between frequency of use and typical dose used helps define any relationship between patterns of use and overall pleasure (or pain). "People are asked to score each drug they have used on 10 items exploring positive drug effects each scored out of 10 (NPI+ve) and then 10 items exploring negative drug effects each scored out of 10." Interview with Adam Winstock, September 10, 2014. See also the Global Drug Survey website: "Net Pleasure Index," "Drug Pleasure Ratings," *Global Drug Survey*, 2014, www.globaldrugsurvey.com/past-findings/the-net-pleasure-index-results.

56 Race, *Pleasure Consuming Medicine,* x–xi, 183.

57 Spencer, "Ira Glass: 'The First Time I Took Ecstasy, My Anxiety Lifted Away.'".

58 Featherstone, "The Body in Consumer Culture," 38.

59 Coveney and Bunton, "In Pursuit of the Study of Pleasure," 172; Bancroft, "Nudge Policy, Embodiment, and Intoxication Problems"; Haydock, "The Rise and Fall of the 'Nudge' of Minimum Unit Pricing," 260–69.

60 Keane, "Drugs that Work," 107–8.

61 Olga Khazan, "The Rise of Work Doping," *Atlantic*, August 27, 2015, www.theatlantic .com/health/archive/2015/08/the-rise-of-work-doping/402373.

62   See discussion of Vyvanse in chapter 1. Adderall, one of the leading ADHD drugs, originated as Obertrol, a weight-loss pill, owned by a company bought out by Shire after Adderall hit the market. Alan Schwartz, "The Selling of Attention Deficit Disorder," *New York Times*, web edition, December 14, 2013, www.nytimes.com/2013/12/15/health/the-selling-of-attention-deficit-disorder.html?pagewanted=all&_r=0.

63   Nadia Whitehead, "How the Prescription Painkiller Fentanyl Became a Street Drug," NPR, August 26, 2015, www.npr.org/sections/health-shots/2015/08/26/434867357/how-the-prescription-painkiller-fentanyl-became-a-street-drug.

64   Comment by Ross Bell of the New Zealand Drug Foundation on a panel with Mitchell Gomez and Joseph Palamar, 2015 International Drug Policy Reform Conference, Washington, DC. See also "Spotlight on NBOMes: Potent Psychedelic Issues," *Erowid Extracts 24*, July 2013, https://erowid.org/chemicals/nbome/nbome_article1.shtml.

65   David Herzberg at the Alcohol and Drugs History Society plenary session, Bowling Green, Ohio, 2015.

66   Laszlo P. Somogyi, *Caffeine Intake by the US Population*, Food and Drug Administration, cited by James Hamblin, "Caffeine 'Addiction': A Tortured Love," *Atlantic*, November 12, 2013, www.theatlantic.com/video/index/281364/caffeine-addiction-a-tortured-love.

67   American Nonsmokers' Rights Foundation, 2015, www.no-smoke.org.

68   Substance Abuse and Mental Health Services Administration, *Behavioral Health Trends in the United* States.

Conclusion

1   Kofi Annan, "Why It's Time to Legalize Drugs," *Spiegel International Online*, February 2, 2016, www.spiegel.de/international/world/kofi-annan-on-why-drug-bans-are-ineffective-a-1078402.html.

GLOSSARY

addiction. This term is employed broadly in American public discourse to refer to or uncontrolled drug use. It persists although the concept and terminology related to what is often imagined or diagnosed as addiction has been changeable. From habituation to dependence and abuse, American understanding of what it means to abuse a drug to the point of dysfunction has been challenging to identify and articulate. Currently, the diagnostic term for what is colloquially referred to as *addiction* is "substance use disorder with various areas of consideration: impaired control, social impairment, risky use, and pharmacological criteria (i.e., tolerance and withdrawal)." Chapter 3 explores the definitions of and terminology surrounding addiction and drug abuse at length to better understand how addiction and drug abuse have become the major focus of health care, criminal justice, and other social contexts related to drug users.

agency. This theoretical term describes the individual subject's ability to act and have influence in her or his social context. That action may be an expression of, response to, or intervention in a cultural meaning or construct, and any particular action in which the individual generates a habit, choice, or judgment expresses agency. Agency operates at a basic level: the ability to imagine oneself as having an active social role in a particular context. Conceptualizing individual agency as including the power to choose helps to understand drug users as autonomous agents even as they are social subjects who operate within social contexts and accept and reproduce ideologies. Some poststructuralist theorists contend that even actors dominated by cultural ideologies are aware of power relationships and consciously make decisions about their actions within those contexts: to comply, resist, or subvert certain practices, discourses, and identities. Further, subjectivity is experienced in a myriad of ways, including physically. Experiencing agency corporeally through their choices begins to explain drug user's practices and why most users can and do express various kinds of agency in their choices to use psychoactive drugs.

alterity. This philosophical term describes an otherness from the self, conceived of as a separate entity whose otherness denotes exclusion from structures of power and privilege. It can denote the subjectivity of that other, a way of perceiving, such as the point of view of a subaltern in a colonial state. It can also mean a potentially unknowable "other" that is in dialectic with the self—an alienation of aspects of the self that do not conform to cultural norms, such as those expressing mental illness, which produces a different kind of disenfranchisement. Some drug users have, through criminalization or medicalization, been rendered "other" from mainstream US culture in ways that fulfill both ways of understanding alterity. Chapter 4 explores another alterity, a sought-after and pleasurable state for some drug users.

controlled use. This phrase describes a wide range of drug-use practices that are non-problematic, specifically in terms of addiction (falling short of diagnostic parameters for substance abuse disorder), and are thus user controlled. Controlled use may be light drug use or it can mean getting high or drunk frequently. It may be regular, occasional, or episodic. Such drug use is typically selective in terms of managing the user's mood or attention, whether for recreational or other self-management purposes. Controlled use is, in some cases, culturally normalized—as in coffee or alcohol use. Importantly, a controlled-use practice is possible for every psychoactive drug.

discourse. In cultural studies, *discourse* refers to a cultural dynamic in language and ideology that produces and reproduces meanings as particular ways of understanding an issue. A discourse is group of statements that provide a language for expressing a particular kind of knowledge. A discourse is also one of the systems through which social, economic, and political power circulates. Discourses often convey a hegemonic power, a cultural acceptance of a dominant ideology that makes social inequalities or hierarchies appear natural.

drugs. This term is used specifically to describe psychoactive substances that alter mental processes, cognition, or affect—from caffeine or alcohol to antidepressants or heroin. This includes alcohol, nicotine, and pharmaceutical medicines as well as illicit drugs. In its online "Lexicon of Alcohol and Drug Terms," the World Health Organization notes that "this term [psychoactive] and its equivalent, psychotropic drug, are the most neutral and descriptive terms for the whole class of substances, licit and illicit, of interest to drug policy. 'Psychoactive' does not necessarily imply dependence-producing, and in common parlance, the term is often left unstated, as in 'drug use' or 'substance abuse.'"

medicalization. This theoretical term describes the expansion of medical authority and practice across greater areas of social influence and individual lives. Specifically, it refers to a pathologization of humans as organisms who require medical oversight to be well. Peter Conrad originated this concept, pointing to the understanding of human issues as medical problems and the secondary effect of medicalization in creating products and markets to address them. Chapter 3 examines the cultural effects of medicalization.

phenomenology. While phenomenology enjoys a vast philosophical discourse, here it is employed in a limited manner. At its most basic sense, phenomenology is the nature of first-person human experience, particularly how one experiences phenomena. It raises issues of subjectivity and intentionality, actions, consciousness in terms of sensory perception, emotions, actions. Here it is used as a term that describes one's experience (psychological, emotional, physical, sensory) related to drug-use practices.

set and setting. *Set* refers to the mindset, attitude, or personality structure of an individual at the time of drug use. *Setting* refers to the actual physical and social context for drug use. *Set and setting* refers to the various factors that can influence psychoactive drug use. Psychologists who have informed these terms include Timothy Leary, Richard Alpert, Andrew Weil, Norman Zinberg, Howard Shaffer, et al.

subjectivity. This theoretical term refers to the individual identity shaped by social and political dynamics and discourses in a particular social context. An individual's subjectivity is formed through interactions with the norms and practices of a social context. She is subject to expectations of those social discourses about her specific identity (perhaps gender, race, sexuality, class) that then shape her ability to act as an agent. She may internalize or adopt some of these identifying elements, such as the expectations of dressing to signal gender (femininity, masculinity). For drug users, subjectivity is significantly framed by discourses of criminalization, medicalization, and addiction.

use practice. The phrase *use practices* signals pursuits that stimulate brain chemistry to noticeably alter consciousness. This includes drug use or other practices that affect the brain's endogenous opioids and endocannabinoids to alter mental processes, cognition, or affect, such as ultrarunning, trance dancing, meditation, and yoga.

SELECTED BIBLIOGRAPHY

Abelson, Herbert, and Judith Miller. "A Decade of Trends in Cocaine Use in the Household Population." *Cocaine Use in America: Epidemiologic and Clinical Perspectives. NIDA Research Monograph* 61 (1985): 35–49.

Acker, Caroline. *Creating the American Junkie: Addiction Research in the Classic Era of Narcotic Control.* Baltimore: Johns Hopkins University Press, 2002.

———. "How Crack Found a Niche in the American Ghetto: The Historical Epidemiology of Drug Related Harm." *BioSocieties* 5, no. 1 (2010): 70–88.

Aikin, Kathryn J., John L. Swasy, and Amie C. Braman. "Patient and Physician Attitudes and Behaviors Associated with DTC Promotion of Prescription Drugs—Summary of FDA Survey Research Results." *U.S. Department of Health and Human Services Food and Drug Administration Center for Drug Evaluation and Research* 24 (2004): 1–9.

Alexander, Anna, and Mark S. Roberts, eds. *High Culture: Reflections on Addiction and Modernity.* Albany: State University of New York Press, 2003.

Alexander, Bruce K., Patricia Hadaway, and Robert Coambs. "Rat Park Chronicle." *British Columbia Medical Journal* 22, no. 2 (1980): 32–45.

Alexander, Michelle. *The New Jim Crow: Mass Incarceration in the Age of Colorblindness.* New York: The New Press, 2011.

American Psychiatric Association. *Diagnostic and Statistical Manual of Mental Disorders.* 2nd ed. Washington, DC: American Psychiatric Association, 1968.

———. *Diagnostic and Statistical Manual of Mental Disorders.* 4th ed. Washington, DC: American Psychiatric Association, 2000.

———. *Diagnostic and Statistical Manual of Mental Disorders.* 5th ed. Washington, DC: American Psychiatric Association, 2013.

Angell, Marcia. *The Truth about Drug Companies.* New York: Random House Trade Paperbacks, 2005.

Avorn, J., M. Chen, and R. Hartley. "Scientific Versus Commercial Sources of Influence on the Prescribing Behavior of Physicians." *American Journal of Medicine* 73, no. 1 (July 1982): 4–8.

Bancroft, Angus. "Nudge Policy, Embodiment, and Intoxication Problems." In *Intoxication and Society: Problematic Pleasures of Drugs and Alcohol,* edited by Jonathan Herring et al., 172–90. Basingstoke, UK: Palgrave Macmillan, 2013.

Baudrillard, Jean, and Marc Guillaume. Translated by Ames Hodges. *Radical Alterity.* Cambridge, MA: MIT Press, 2008.

Becker, Howard. "Becoming a Marihuana User." *American Journal of Sociology* 59, no. 3 (1953): 235–42.

———. *Outsiders: Studies in the Sociology of Deviance.* New York: The Free Press, 1963.

Becker, William C., David A. Fiellin, and Rani A. Desai. "Non-medical Use, Abuse, and Dependence on Sedatives and Tranquilizers among U.S. Adults: Psychiatric and Socio-Demographic Correlates." *Drug and Alcohol Dependence* 90, no. 2 (2007): 280–87.

Bell, Kristen, and Amy Salmon. "Pain, Physical Dependence, and Pseudoaddiction: Redefining Addiction for 'Nice' People?" *International Journal of Drug Policy* 20, no. 2 (2009): 170–78.

Bell, Robert A., Richard L. Kravitz, and Michael S. Wilkes. "Direct-to-Consumer Prescription Drug Advertising and the Public." *Journal of General Internal Medicine* 14, no. 11 (1999): 651–57.

Bell, Sheri. "Commodifying Health: An Analysis of the Effects of Western Medical Consumerism on Malaria Treatments in Africa." *Journal of the University of Manitoba Anthropology Students' Association* 29, no. 3 (2011): 1–11.

Benavie, Arthur. *Drugs: America's Holy War.* New York: Routledge, 2009.

Bents, Robert, and Erik Marsh. "Patterns of Ephedra and Other Stimulant Use in Collegiate Hockey Athletes." *International Journal of Sport Nutrition, Exercise, and Metabolism* 16, no. 7 (2006): 636–43.

Ben-Yehuda, Nachman. *The Politics and Morality of Deviance: Moral Panics, Drug Abuse, Deviant Science, and Reversed Stigmatization.* Albany: State University of New York Press, 1990.

———. "The Sociology of Moral Panics: Toward a New Synthesis." *The Sociological Quarterly* 27, no. 4 (1986): 495–513.

Best, Joel, ed. *Images of Issues: Typifying Contemporary Social Problems.* Hawthorne, NY: Aldine de Gruyter, 1995.

Biernacki, Patrick. *Pathways from Heroin Addiction: Recovery without Treatment.* Philadelphia: Temple University Press, 1986.

Birkeland, Sarah, Erin Murphy-Graham, and Carol Weiss. "Good Reasons for Ignoring Good Evaluation: The Case of the Drug Abuse Resistance Education (D.A.R.E.) Program." *Evaluation and Program Planning* 28, no. 3 (2005): 247–56.

Bishop, D. V. M. "Research Review: Neuroscientific Studies of Intervention for Language Impairment in Children: Interpretive and Methodological Problems." *Journal of Child Psychology and Psychiatry* 54, no. 3 (2013): 247–59.

Bloom, Paul. *How Pleasure Works: The New Science of Why We Like What We Like.* New York: Norton, 2010.

Bogren, Alexandra, and Katarina Winter. "Knowledge Production, Communication and Utilization: Studying Biomedical Alcohol Research." *Drugs and Alcohol Today* 13, no. 1 (2013): 28–35.

Boon, Marcus. *The Road of Excess: A History of Writers on Drugs.* Cambridge, MA: Harvard University Press, 2005.

Bourdieu, Pierre. *The Logic of Practice.* Translated by Richard Nice. Redwood City, CA: Stanford University Press, 1992.

———. *Pascalian Meditations.* Translated by Richard Nice. Redwood City, CA: Stanford University Press, 2000.

Bunton, Robin, and John Coveney. "Drugs' Pleasures." *Critical Public Health* 21, no. 1 (2011): 9–23.

Butler, Judith. *Subjects of Desire*. Reprint edition. New York: Columbia University Press, 1999.

Campbell, Nancy. *Discovering Addiction: The Science and Politics of Substance Abuse Research*. Ann Arbor: University of Michigan Press, 2007.

———. "Toward a Critical Neuroscience of 'Addiction.'" *BioSocieties* 5, no. 1 (2010): 89–104.

Campos, Isaac. *Home Grown: Marijuana and the Origins of Mexico's War on Drugs*. Chapel Hill: University of North Carolina Press, 2012.

Carhart-Harris, Robin. "Neural Correlates of the Psychedelic State as Determined by fMRI Studies with Psilocybin." *Proceedings of the National Academy of Sciences of the United States of America* 109, no. 6 (2014): 2138–43.

Carpenter, D. M., Lisa Knepper, Angela C. Erickson, and Jennifer McDonald. *Policing for Profit: the Abuse of Civil Asset Forfeiture*. 2nd ed. Arlington, VA: Institute for Justice, 2015.

Caudevilla, Fernando, Mireia Ventura, Iván Fornís, Monica J. Barratt, Claudio Vidal, Pol Quintana, Ana Muñoz, and Nuria Calzada. "Results of an International Drug Testing Service for Cryptomarket Users." *International Journal of Drug Policy* 35 (2016): 38–41.

Chaitow, Leon. "Bodywork High: The Cannabinoids Connection." *Massage Today* 8, no. 2 (2008). www.massagetoday.com/mpacms/mt/article.php?id=13752.

Chossudovsky, Michel. "Heroin Is 'Good for Your Health': Occupation Forces Support Afghan Narcotics Trade." *Global Research*, April 29, 2007. www.globalresearch.ca/heroin-is-good-for-your-health-occupation-forces-support-afghan-narcotics-trade/5514.

Clark, Claire. "'Chemistry Is the New Hope': Therapeutic Communities and Methadone Maintenance, 1965–71." *Social History of Alcohol and Drugs* 26, no. 2 (2012): 192–216.

Clark, Marilyn. "Conceptualising Addiction: How Useful Is the Construct." *International Journal of Humanities & Social Science* 1, no. 13 (2011): 55–64.

Clark, Walter. "Cultural Changes in Drinking and Trends in Alcohol Problem Indicators: Recent U.S. Experience." In *Alcohol in America: Drinking Practices and Problems*, 7th ed., edited by Michael Hilton, 47–91. Albany: State University of New York Press, 1991.

Clarke, Adele, Janet Shim, Laura Mamo, Jennifer Fosket, and Jennifer Fishman. "Biomedicalization: Technoscientific Transformations of Health, Illness, and US Biomedicine." *Biomedicalization: Technoscience, Health, and Illness in the US* 68, no. 2 (2003): 161–94.

Cobbina, Jennifer Ernestina. "Race and Class Differences in Print Media Portrayals of Crack Cocaine and Methamphetamine." *Journal of Criminal Justice and Popular Culture* 15, no. 2 (2008): 145–67.

Cockburn, J., and S. Pit. "Prescribing Behaviour in Clinical Practice: Patients' Expectations and Doctors' Perceptions of Patients' Expectations—A Questionnaire Study." *BMJ (Clinical Research Ed.)* 315, no. 7107 (1997): 520–23.

Conrad, Peter. *The Medicalization of Society: On the Transformation of Human Conditions into Treatable Disorders*. Baltimore: Johns Hopkins University Press, 2007.

Conrad, Peter, and Joseph Schneider. *Deviance and Medicalization: From Badness to Sickness*. Philadelphia: Temple University Press, 1992.

Conway, Kevin P., Wilson Compton, Frederick S. Stinson, and Bridget F. Grant. "Lifetime Comorbidity of DSM-IV Mood and Anxiety Disorders and Specific Drug Use Disorders: Results from the National Epidemiologic Survey on Alcohol and Related Conditions." *Journal of Clinical Psychiatry* 67, no. 2 (2006): 247–57.

Courtwright, David. "Addiction and the Science of History." *Addiction* 107, no. 3 (2012): 486–92.

———. "The Controlled Substances Act: How a 'Big Tent' Reform Became a Punitive Drug Law." *Drug and Alcohol Dependence* 76, no. 1 (2004): 9–15.

———. *Dark Paradise: A History of Opiate Addiction in America before 1940.* Cambridge, MA: Harvard University Press, 1982.

———. *Forces of Habit: Drugs and the Making of the Modern World.* Cambridge, MA: Harvard University Press, 2001.

Coveney, John, and Robin Bunton. "In Pursuit of the Study of Pleasure: Implications for Health Research and Practice." *Health* 7, no. 2 (2003): 161–79.

Cuijpers, Pim. "Three Decades of Drug Prevention Research." *Drugs: Education, Prevention and Policy* 10, no. 1 (2003): 7–20.

Davenport-Hines, Richard. *The Pursuit of Oblivion: A Global History of Narcotics.* New York: W. W. Norton & Company, 2004.

Davies, John. *The Myth of Addiction.* 2nd ed. Netherlands: Harwood Academic Publishers, 1997.

Decorte, Tom. "Blinding Ourselves with Science: The Chronic Infections of Our Thinking on Psychoactive Substances." In *Drugs and Culture: Knowledge, Consumption, and Policy,* edited by Geoffrey Hunt, Maitena Milhet, and Henri Bergeron, 33–51. Farnham: Ashgate Publishing, 2011.

DeGrandpre, Richard. *The Cult of Pharmacology: How America Became the World's Most Troubled Drug Culture.* Durham, NC: Duke University Press, 2006.

Deleuze, Gilles. *Two Regimes of Madness: Texts and Interviews, 1975–1995.* Translated by David Lapoujade. Los Angeles: MIT Press, 2006.

Derrida, Jacques. "The Rhetoric of Drugs." Translated by Michael Israel. *Differences: A Journal of Feminist Cultural Studies* 5, no. 1 (1993): 1–24.

Donohue, Julie. "A History of Drug Advertising: The Evolving Roles of Consumers and Consumer Protection." *The Milbank Quarterly* 84, no. 4 (2006): 659–99.

Duff, Cameron. "The Pleasure in Context." *International Journal of Drug Policy* 19, no. 5 (2008): 384–92.

Dufton, Emily. "Points Roundtable, 'Becoming a Marihuana User': Nancy Campbell." *Points: The Blog of the Alcohol & Drugs History Society,* September 1, 2015. https://pointsadhsblog.wordpress.com/2015/09/01/points-roundtable-becoming-a-marihuana-user-nancy-campbell.

Eddy, Mark. "War on Drugs: The National Youth Anti-Drug Media Campaign." *Congressional Research Service: Library of Congress* (June 17, 2003): 1–6.

Edwards, G., A. Arif, and R. Hadgson. "Nomenclature and Classification of Drug- and Alcohol-Related Problems: A WHO Memorandum." *Bulletin of the World Health Organization* 59, no. 2 (1981): 225–42.

Elwood, William N. *Rhetoric in the War on Drugs: The Triumphs and Tragedies of Public Relations.* Santa Barbara, CA: Greenwood Publishing Group, 1994.

Erceg-Hurn, David M. "Drugs, Money, and Graphic Ads: A Critical Review of the Montana Meth Project." *Prevention Science: The Official Journal of the Society for Prevention Research* 9, no. 4 (2008): 256–63.

Erlen, Jonathon, Joseph F. Spillane, Rebecca Carroll, William Mcallister, and Dennis B. Worthen. *Federal Drug Control: The Evolution of Policy and Practice.* New York: CRC Press, 2004.

Erowid, E. "Spotlight on NBOMes: Potent Psychedelic Issues." *Erowid Extracts*, July 2013. https://erowid.org/chemicals/nbome/nbome_article1.shtml.

Esterl, Mike, Karishma Mehrotra, and Valerie Bauerlein. "America's Smokers: Still 40 Million Strong." *Wall Street Journal*, July 16, 2014, sec. Business.

Featherstone, Mike. "The Body in Consumer Culture." *Theory, Culture and Society* 1, no. 2 (1982): 18–33.

Ferentzy, Peter, and Nigel Turner. *The History of Problem Gambling: Temperance, Substance Abuse, Medicine, and Metaphors.* New York: Springer-Verlag, 2013.

First, Michael. "Harmonisation of ICD-11 and DSM-V: Opportunities and Challenges." *British Journal of Psychiatry* 195, no. 5 (2009): 382–90.

Flanagan, Owen. "What's It Like to Be an Addict?" In *Addiction and Responsibility*, edited by Jeffrey Poland and Georgia Graham. Cambridge, MA: MIT Press, 2011.

Forest, D. "Methamphetamine and Oral Health: Reality or Myth." *Journal Dentaire du Québec* 42 (2005): 445.

Foucault, Michel. *Discipline and Punish: The Birth of the Prison.* Translated by Alan Sheridan. 2nd ed. New York: Vintage Books, 1995.

———. *The History of Sexuality, Vol. 2: The Use of Pleasure.* Translated by Robert Hurley. Reissue edition. New York: Vintage Books, 1990.

———. *The History of Sexuality, Vol. 3: The Care of the Self.* Translated by Robert Hurley. Reprint edition. New York: Vintage Books, 1988.

———. *Power/Knowledge: Selected Interviews and Other Writings, 1972–1977.* 1st American ed. New York: Pantheon, 1980.

———. *Technologies of the Self: A Seminar with Michel Foucault.* Edited by Luther Martin, Huck Gutman, and Patrick Hutton. Amherst: University of Massachusetts Press, 1988.

Fraser, Suzanne, and Kylie Valentine. *Substance and Substitution: Methadone Subjects in Liberal Societies.* London: Palgrave Macmillan, 2008.

Friedman, Samuel. "The Political Economy of Drug-User Scapegoating—and the Philosophy and Politics of Resistance." *Drugs, Education, Prevention, and Policy* 5, no. 1 (1998): 15–32.

Fuss, Johannes, Jörg Steinle, Laura Bindila, Matthias K. Auer, Hartmut Kirchherr, Beat Lutz, and Peter Gass. "A Runner's High Depends on Cannabinoid Receptors in Mice." *Proceedings of the National Academy of Sciences* 112, no. 42 (2015): 13105–8.

Gabriel, Joseph. "Anesthetics and the Chemical Sublime." *Raritan: A Quarterly Review* 20, no. 1 (2010): 69–74.

Garriott, William. *Policing Methamphetamine: Narcopolitics in Rural America.* New York: New York University Press, 2011.

Gellad, Ziad F., and Kenneth W. Lyles. "Direct-to-Consumer Advertising of Pharmaceuticals." *American Journal of Medicine* 120, no. 6 (2007): 475–80.

Global Commission on Drug Policy. *The Negative Impact of the War on Drugs on Public Health: The Hidden Hepatitis C Epidemic.* Global Commission on Drug Policy, 2013, www.globalcommissionondrugs.org/reports.

————. *Taking Control: Pathways to Drug Policies that Work.* Global Commission on Drug Policy, 2014, www.globalcommissionondrugs.org/reports.

————. *War on Drugs: Report of the Global Commission on Drug Policy.* Global Commission on Drug Policy, 2011. www.globalcommissionondrugs.org/reports.

Goetz, Edward G. "The US War on Drugs as Urban Policy." *International Journal of Urban and Regional Research* 20, no. 3 (2009): 539–49.

Goodchild, Jason H., and Mark Donaldson. "Methamphetamine Abuse and Dentistry: A Review of the Literature and Presentation of a Clinical Case." *Quintessence International* 38, no. 7 (2007): 583–90.

Goode, Erich. "The American Drug Panic of the 1980s: Social Construction or Objective Threat?" *Substance Use & Misuse* 25, no. 9 (1990): 1083–98.

Goode, Erich, and Nachman Ben-Yehuda. *Moral Panics: The Social Construction of Deviance.* 2nd ed. Chichester, UK; Malden, MA: Wiley-Blackwell, 2009.

Goodman, Jordan. "Excitantia: Or, How Enlightenment Europe Took to Soft Drugs." In *Consuming Habits: Global and Historical Perspectives on How Cultures Define Drugs,* 2nd ed., edited by Jordan Goodman, Paul Lovejoy, and Andrew Sherratt, 126–41. London: Routledge, 2007.

Goodman, Jordan, Paul Lovejoy, and Andrew Sherratt, eds. *Consuming Habits: Global and Historical Perspectives on How Cultures Define Drugs.* 2nd ed. London: Routledge, 2007.

Graham, Elaine L. *Representations of the Post/Human: Monsters, Aliens and Others in Popular Culture.* New Brunswick, NJ: Rutgers University Press, 2002.

Gramsci, Antonio. *Selections from the Prison Notebooks.* New York: International Publishing Co., 1971.

Granfield, Robert, and William Cloud. "The Elephant that No One Sees: Natural Recovery among Middle Class Addicts." *Journal of Drug Issues* 26, no. 1 (1996): 45–61.

Grandfield, Robert, and Craig Reinarman, eds. *Expanding Addiction: Critical Essays.* New York: Routledge, Taylor & Francis Group, 2015.

Greco, Monica. "Psychosomatic Subjects and the 'Duty to Be Well'. Personal Agency Within." *Economy and Society* 22, no. 3 (1993): 357–72.

Grimm, Matthew. "A Dubious Pitch." *American Demographics* 24, no. 5 (2002): 44–46.

Grossberg, Lawrence. *Cultural Studies in the Future Tense.* Durham, NC: Duke University Press, 2010.

Hall, Stuart. "The West and the Rest: Discourse and Power." In *Modernity: An Introduction to Modern Societies,* edited by David Held, Don Hubert, and Kenneth Thompson, 201–2. Hoboken, NJ: Wiley-Blackwell, 1996.

Hanganu-Bresch, Cristina. "Treat Her with Prozac: Four Decades of Direct-to-Physician Antidepressant Advertising." In *Drugs and Media: New Perspectives on Communication, Consumption, and Consciousness,* edited by Robert MacDougall, 166–92. London: Bloomsbury, 2012.

Hansen, Helena. "Pharmaceutical Evangelism and Spiritual Capital: An American Tale of Two Communities of Addicted Selves." In *Addiction Trajectories,* edited by Eugene Raikhel and William Garriott, 108–25. Durham, NC: Duke University Press, 2013.

Hart, Carl. *High Price: A Neuroscientist's Journal of Self-Discovery that Challenges Everything You Know about Drugs and Society.* New York: Harper Collins, 2013.

Hasin, Deborah S., Frederick S. Stinson, Elizabeth Ogburn, and Bridget F. Grant. "Prevalence, Correlates, Disability, and Comorbidity of DSM-IV Alcohol Abuse and Co-dependence in the United States: Results from the National Epidemiologic Survey on Alcohol and Related Conditions." *Archives of General Psychiatry* 64, no. 7 (2007): 830–42 .

Haydock, William. "The Rise and Fall of the 'Nudge' of Minimum Unit Pricing: The Continuity of Neoliberalism in Alcohol Policy in England." *Critical Social Policy* 34, no. 2 (2014): 260–79.

Hemment, Drew. "E Is for Ekstasis." *New Formations: A Journal of Culture, Theory and Politics* 31 (1997): 23–38.

Herrington, Lois Haight. *The White House Conference for a Drug Free America, Final Report, June 1988.* Washington, DC: US Government Printing Office, 1988.

Herzberg, David. *Happy Pills in America: From Miltown to Prozac.* Baltimore: Johns Hopkins University Press, 2009.

Heyman, Gene. *Addiction: A Disorder of Choice.* Cambridge, MA: Harvard University Press, 2009.

Hickman, T. A. "Target America: Visual Culture, Neuroimaging, and the 'Hijacked Brain' Theory of Addiction." *Past & Present* 222, no. 9 (2014): 207–26.

Hornik, Robert, Lela Jacobsohn, Robert Orwin, Andrea Piesse, and Graham Kalton. "Effects of the National Youth Anti-Drug Media Campaign on Youths." *American Journal of Public Health* 98, no. 12 (2008): 2229–36.

Hornik, Robert, et al. "Executive Summary." In *Evaluation of the National Youth Anti-Drug Media Campaign: Fifth Semi-annual Report of Findings.* Washington, DC: National Institute on Drug Abuse, November 2002.

Howarth, David R. *Poststructuralism and After: Structure, Subjectivity and Power.* London: Palgrave Macmillan, 2013.

Hunt, Geoffrey P., Kristin Evans, and Faith Kares. "Drug Use and Meanings of Risk and Pleasure." *Journal of Youth Studies* 10, no. 1 (2007): 73–96.

Huxley, Aldous. *The Doors of Perception: Heaven and Hell.* New York: Harper Collins, 1954.

Jaffe, Jerome. "Drug Addiction and Drug Abuse." In *Goodman and Gilman's The Pharmacological Basis of Therapeutics,* 8th ed., 522–73. New York: Pergamon Press, 1990.

Kalivas, Peter, and Nora Volkow. "The Neural Basis of Addiction: A Pathology of Motivation and Choice." *American Journal of Psychiatry* 162, no. 8 (2005): 1403–13.

Keane, Helen. "Drugs that Work: Pharmaceuticals and Performance Self-Management." In *The Drug Effect: Health, Crime and Society,* edited by Suzanne Fraser and David Moore, 106–21. Port Melbourne: Cambridge University Press, 2011.

———. *What's Wrong With Addiction?* New York: New York University Press, 2002.

Keh, Douglas. "Drug Money in a Changing World." *Report of the International Narcotics Control Board* (1999): 49–51.

Kellner, Douglas. *Media Culture: Cultural Studies, Identity and Politics Between the Modern and the Postmodern.* London: Routledge, 1995.

Kelly, John F., Bettina Hoeppner, Robert L. Stout, and Maria Pagano. "Determining the Relative Importance of the Mechanisms of Behavior Change within Alcoholics Anonymous: A Multiple Mediator Analysis." *Addiction* 107, no. 2 (2012): 289–99.

Kirsch, Irving. "Antidepressants and the Placebo Effect." *Zeitschrift für Psychologie* 222, no. 3 (2014): 128–34.

Kleiman, Mark, Jonathan Caulkins, and Angela Hawken. *Drugs and Drug Policy: What Everyone Needs to Know*. Oxford: Oxford University Press, 2011.

Klein, Richard. "What Is Health and How Do You Get It?" In *Against Health: How Health Became the New Morality*, edited by Jonathan Metzl and Anna Rutherford Kirkland, 15–25. New York: New York University Press, 2010.

Klingemann, Harold, and Linda Sobell. *Promoting Self-Change from Problem Substance Use*. Boston: Kluwer Academic Publishers, 2001.

Kramer, Peter. *Listening to Prozac: A Psychologist Explores Antidepressant Drugs and the Remaking of the Self*. New York: Penguin Books, 1993.

Kristeva, Julia. *Powers of Horror: An Essay on Abjection*. Translated by Leon S. Roudiez. Reprint ed. New York: Columbia University Press, 1982.

Kushner, Howard. "Toward a Cultural Biology of Addiction." *BioSocieties* 5, no. 1 (2010): 8–24.

Leary, Timothy, Ralph Metzner, and Richard Alpert. *The Psychedelic Experience: A Manual Based on the Tibetan Book of the Dead*. New Hyde Park, NY: University Books, 1964.

Lenson, David. *On Drugs*. Minneapolis: University of Minnesota Press, 1999.

Levine, Harry. "The Discovery of Addiction: Changing Conceptions of Habitual Drunkenness in America." *Journal of Studies on Alcohol* 39, no. 2 (1978): 143–74.

Levine, Harry, and Craig Reinarman. "The Politics of America's Latest Drug Scare." In *Freedom at Risk: Secrecy, Censorship and Repression in the 1980s*, edited by Richard O. Curry, 1–6. Philadelphia: Temple University Press, 1988.

———. "From Prohibition to Regulation: Lessons from Alcohol Policy for Drug Policy." *The Milbank Quarterly* 69, no. 3 (1991): 461–94.

Lewis, Marc. *The Biology of Desire: Why Addiction Is Not a Disease*. New York: Public Affairs, 2015.

Linden, David. *The Compass of Pleasure: How Our Brains Make Fatty Foods, Orgasm, Exercise, Marijuana, Generosity, Vodka, Learning, and Gambling Feel So Good*. New York: Penguin Books, 2011.

Linnemann, Travis, Laura Hanson, and L. Susan Williams. "'With Scenes of Blood and Pain': Crime Control and the Punitive Imagination of The Meth Project." *British Journal of Criminology* 53, no. 4 (2013): 605–23.

Linnemann, Travis, and Tyler Wall. "'This Is Your Face on Meth': The Punitive Spectacle of 'White Trash' in the Rural War on Drugs." *Theoretical Criminology* 17, no. 3 (2013): 315–34.

MacCoun, Robert, and Peter Reuter. *Drug War Heresies: Learning from Other Vices, Times, and Places*. Cambridge: Cambridge University Press, 2001.

MacLean, Sarah. "'It Might Be a Scummy-Arsed Drug but It's a Sick Buzz': Chroming and Pleasure." *Contemporary Drug Problems* 32, no. 2 (2005): 295–318.

———. "Volatile Bodies: Stories of Corporal Pleasure and Damage in Marginalised Young People's Drug Use." *International Journal of Drug Policy* 19, no. 5 (2008): 375–83.

Manderson, Desmond. "Possessed: Drug Policy, Witchcraft and Belief." *Cultural Studies* 19, no. 1 (2005): 35–62.

Manning, Paul, ed. *Drugs and Popular Culture*. Cullompton, Devon, England; Portland, OR: Willan, 2007.

Mark, Arlene. "Adolescents Discuss Themselves and Drugs Through Music." *Journal of Substance Abuse Treatment* 3, no. 4 (1986): 243–49.

Martin, Emily. "The Pharmaceutical Person." *BioSocieties* 1, no. 3 (2006): 273–87.

Maté, Gabor. *In the Realm of the Hungry Ghosts: Close Encounters with Addiction*. Berkeley: North Atlantic Books, 2010.

McKenna, Terrence. *Food of the Gods: The Search for the Original Tree of Knowledge: A Radical History of Plants, Drugs, and Human Evolution*. New York: Bantam Doubleday, 1993.

McLellan, Thomas, David C. Lewis, Charles P. O'Brien, and Herbert D. Kleber. "Drug Dependence, a Chronic Medical Illness: Implications for Treatment, Insurance, and Outcomes Evaluation." *Journal of the American Medical Association* 284, no. 13 (2000): 1689–95.

Merleau-Ponty, Maurice, and Taylor Carman. *Phenomenology of Perception*. Translated by Donald Landes. London: Routledge, 2013.

Meyers, Todd. *The Clinic and Elsewhere: Addiction, Adolescents, and the Afterlife of Therapy*. Seattle: University of Washington Press, 2013.

Montagne, M. "Mass Media Representations as Drug Information for Patients: The Prozac Phenomenon." *Substance Use & Misuse* 36, no. 9–10 (2001): 1261–74.

———. "Seeing Is Believing, Looks Are Deceiving: What Does One See in Images of Drugs and Drug Use(rs)?" *Substance Use & Misuse* 50, no. 4 (2015): 517–19.

Moore, David. "Erasing Pleasure from Public Discourse on Illicit Drugs: On the Creation and Reproduction of an Absence." *International Journal of Drug Policy, Pleasure and Drugs* 19, no. 5 (2008): 353–58.

Moreau, Joseph. "'I Learned It by Watching YOU!' The Partnership for a Drug-Free America and the Attack on 'Responsible Use' Education in the 1980s." *Journal of Social History* 49, no. 3 (2016): 710–37.

Morgan, John P., and Lynn Zimmer. "Social Pharmacology of Smokeable Cocaine: Not All It's Cracked Up to Be." In *Crack in America: Demon Drugs and Social Justice*, edited by Craig Reinarman and Harry G. Levine, 131–70. Berkeley: University of California Press, 1997.

Mukherjee, Siddhartha. "Post-Prozac Nation: The Science and History of Treating Depression." *New York Times Magazine*, April 19, 2012, sec. News.

Murakawa, Naomi. "Toothless." *Du Bois Review: Social Science Research on Race* 8, no. 1 (2011): 219–28.

Musto, David. *The American Disease: Origins of Narcotic Control*. 3rd ed. Oxford: Oxford University Press, 1999.

Nadelmann, Ethan. Plenary address, International Drug Reform Policy Conference, Washington, DC, November 18, 2015.

Nichols, David. "Psychedelics." *Pharmacological Reviews* 68, no. 2 (2016): 264–355.

Niesen, Molly. "Public Enemy Number One: The US Advertising Council's First Drug Abuse Prevention Campaign." *Substance Use & Misuse* 46, no. 7 (2011): 872–81.

Nutt, David, Leslie King, and Lawrence Phillips. "Drug Harms in the UK: A Multicriteria Decision Analysis." *Lancet* 376, no. 9752 (2010): 1558–65.

Ortner, Sherry. "Subjectivity and Cultural Critique." *Anthropological Theory* 5, no. 1 (2005): 37–66.

O'Malley, Pat, and Mariana Valverde. "Pleasure, Freedom and Drugs: The Uses of 'Plea-sure in Liberal Governance of Drug and Alcohol Consumption." *Sociology* 38, no. 1 (2004): 25–42.

Page, Mike. "What Can't Functional Neuroimaging Tell the Cognitive Scientist?" *Cortex* 42, no. 3 (2006): 428–43.

Palumbo, Francis, and C. Daniel Mullins. "Development of Direct-to-Consumer Prescrip-tion Drug Advertising Regulation." *Food & Drug Law Journal* 57, no. 3 (2002): 423–44.

Parenti, Christian. *Lockdown America: Police and Prisons in the Age of Crisis.* New York: Verso Books, 1999.

Peele, Stanton. "Addiction as a Cultural Concept." *Annals of the New York Academy of Sci-ences* 602, no. 1 (1990): 205–20.

———. *The Meaning of Addiction: Compulsive Experience and Its Interpretation.* Lexington: Lexington Books, 1985.

Peretti-Watel, Patrick. "Epidemiology as a Model: Processing Data through a Black Box." In *Drugs and Culture: Knowledge, Consumption, and Policy*, edited by Geoffrey Hunt, Maitena Milhet, and Henri Bergeron, 53–70. Farnham: Ashgate Publishing, 2011.

Pettit, Becky, and Bruce Western. "Mass Imprisonment and the Life Course: Race and Class Inequality in US Incarceration." *American Sociological Review* 69, no. 2 (2004): 151–69.

Petry, Nancy M., Frederick S. Stinson, and Bridget F. Grant. "Comorbidity of DSM-IV Pathological Gambling and Other Psychiatric Disorders: Results from the National Epidemiologic Survey on Alcohol and Related Conditions." *Journal of Clinical Psy-chiatry* 66, no. 5 (2005): 564–74.

Pincus, Harold et al. "Prescribing Trends in Psychotropic Medications: Primary Care, Psychiatry, and Other Medical Specialties." *Journal of the American Medical Associa-tion* 279, no. 7 (1998): 526–31.

Pollan, Michael. *The Botany of Desire: A Plant's-Eye View of the World.* New York: Random House, 2001.

Porter, Dayna. "Direct-to-Consumer (DTC) Pharmaceutical Marketing: Impacts and Policy Implications." *SPNHA Review* 7, no. 1 (2011): 62–63.

Race, Kane. *Pleasure Consuming Medicine: The Queer Politics of Drugs.* Durham, NC: Duke University Press, 2009.

Raikhel, Eugene, and William Garriott. *Addiction Trajectories.* Durham, NC: Duke Uni-versity Press, 2013.

Rasmussen, Nicolas. *On Speed: The Many Lives of Amphetamine.* New York: New York University Press, 2008.

Ratner, Carl. "Agency and Culture." *Journal for the Theory of Social Behaviour* 30, no. 4 (2000): 413–34.

Reagan, Ronald. Book 1 of *Public Papers of the Presidents of the United States: Ronald Reagan, 1981–1989.* Washington, DC: Office of the Federal Register, 1999.

Reese, Stephen D., and Lucig H. Danielian. "A Closer Look at InterMedia Influences in Agenda Setting: The Cocaine Issue of 1986." In *Communication Campaigns about Drugs: Government, Media, and the Public*, edited by Pamela J. Shoemaker , 47–66. New York: Routledge: 1989.

Reeves, Jimmie, and Richard Campbell. *Cracked Coverage: Television News, the Anti-Cocaine Crusade, and the Reagan Legacy.* Durham, NC: Duke University Press, 1994.

Reinarman, Craig. "Addiction as Accomplishment: The Discursive Construction of Disease." *Addiction Research & Theory* 13, no. 4 (2005): 307–20.

———. "On the Cultural Domestication of Intoxicants." In *Intoxication and Society: Problematic Pleasures of Drugs and Alcohol,* edited by Jonathan Herring, Ciaran Regan, Darin Weinberg, and Phil Withington, 153–71. London: Palgrave Macmillan, 2013.

Reinarman, Craig, and Harry G. Levine. "The Crack Attack: America's Latest Drug Scare, 1986–1992." In *Images of Issues: Typifying Contemporary Social Problems,* edited by Joel Best, 2nd ed., 147–86. Chicago: Aldine Transaction, 1995.

———. "Crack in Context: Politics and Media in the Making of a Drug Scare." *Contemporary Drug Problems* 16 (1989): 535–77.

———, eds. *Crack in America: Demon Drugs and Social Justice.* Berkeley: University of California Press, 1997.

Reznicek, Michael. *Blowing Smoke: Rethinking the War on Drugs without Prohibition and Rehab.* Lanham, MD: Rowman and Littlefield, 2012.

Richards, John et al. "The Tobacco Industry's Code of Advertising in the United States: Myth and Reality." *Tobacco Control* 5, no. 4 (1996): 295–311.

Rinaldi, Robert, Emanual Steindler, Bonnie Wilford, and Desiree Goodwin. "Clarification and Standardization of Substance Abuse Terminology." *Journal of the American Medical Association* 259, no. 4 (1988): 555–57.

Roberts, Donald F., Lisa Henriksen, and Peter G. Christenson. *Substance Use in Popular Movies and Music.* Washington, DC: US Government Printing Office, 1999.

Rocca, Walter A., Barbara P. Yawn, Jennifer L. St. Sauver, Brandon R. Grossardt, and L. Joseph Melton. "History of the Rochester Epidemiology Project: Half a Century of Medical Records Linkage in a US Population." *Mayo Clinic Proceedings* 87, no. 12 (2012): 1202–13.

Roizen, Ronald. *The American Discovery of Alcoholism.* Berkeley: University of California Press, 1991.

Room, Robin. "The Cultural Framing of Addiction." *Janus Head* 6, no. 2 (2003): 221–34.

Rosenthal, Meredith B., Ernst R. Berndt, Julie M. Donohue, Richard G. Frank, and Arnold M. Epstein. "Promotion of Prescription Drugs to Consumers." *New England Journal of Medicine* 346, no. 7 (2002): 498–505.

Rounsaville, B., R. Spitzer, and J. Williams. "Proposed Changes in DSM-III Substance Use Disorders: Description and Rationale." *American Journal of Psychiatry* 143, no. 4 (1986): 463–68.

Rubin, Lawrence C. "Merchandising Madness: Pills, Promises, and Better Living Through Chemistry." *Journal of Popular Culture* 38, no. 2 (2004): 369–83.

Sacco, Lisa N., and Kristin Finklea. "Reauthorizing the Office of National Drug Control Policy: Issues for Consideration." *Journal of Drug Addiction, Education, and Eradication* 10, no. 4 (2014): 1–15.

Schwartz, Alan, and Kristin Swenson. *Lifestyle Drugs and the Neoliberal Family.* New York: Peter Lang, 2013.

Seddon, Tony. "Court-Ordered Treatment, Neo-liberalism and Homo Economicus." In *The Drug Effect: Health, Crime and Society, edited by Suzanne Fraser and David Moore*, 155–170. Cambridge: Cambridge University Press, 2011.

Sedgwick, Eve. "The Epidemics of the Will." In *Zone 6: Incorporations*, edited by Jonathan Crary and Stanford Quinter. Cambridge, MA: MIT Press, 1992.

Shapiro, Harry. *Waiting for the Man: The Story of Drugs and Popular Music*. London: Quartet Books, 1988.

Shaw, Deborah. "'You Are Alright, But . . .': Individual and Collective Representations of Mexicans, Latinos, Anglo-Americans and Africans in Steven Soderbergh's Traffic." *Quarterly Review of Film and Video* 22, no. 3 (2005): 211–23.

Shepard, Edward. "The Economic Costs of D.A.R.E." *Institute of Industrial Relations Research Paper* 22 (2001): 1–20.

Sherry B. Ortner. *Anthropology and Social Theory: Culture, Power, and the Acting Subject*. Durham, NC: Duke University Press, 2006.

Shortall, Sarah. "Psychedelic Drugs and the Problem of Experience." *Past & Present* 222, no. 9 (2014): 187–206.

Siegel, Ronald. *Intoxication: Life in Pursuit of Artificial Paradise*. New York: Dutton, 1989.

Siff, Stephen. *Acid Hype: American News Media and the Psychedelic Experience*. Urbana: University of Illinois Press, 2015.

Singh, Illina. "Not Robots: Children's Perspectives on Authenticity, Moral Agency and Stimulant Drug Treatments." *Journal of Medical Ethics* 39, no. 6 (2013): 359–66.

Snyder, Howard. "Arrests in the United States, 1990–2010." *Bureau of Justice Statistics* (2012): 1–26.

Somogyi, Laszlo P. *Caffeine Intake by the US Population*. Thousand Oaks, CA: Food and Drug Administration and Oakridge National Laboratory, 2012.

South, Nigel, ed. *Drugs: Cultures, Controls and Everyday Life*. Thousand Oaks, CA: SAGE, 1998.

Spencer, D. C. "Habit(us), Body Techniques and Body Callusing: An Ethnography of Mixed Martial Arts." *Body & Society* 15, no. 4 (2009): 119–43.

Spencer, Ruth. "Ira Glass: 'The First Time I Took Ecstasy, My Anxiety Lifted Away.'" *Guardian*, May 3, 2014, sec. Television and Radio.

Spillane, Joseph. "The Forgotten Drug War: One Million Drug Addicts (Washington, DC, 1919)." *Points: The Blog of the Alcohol & Drugs History Society*, September 23, 2015. https://pointsadhsblog.wordpress.com/2015/09/23/the-forgotten-drug-war-one-million -drug-addicts-washington-d-c-1919.

———. "The Points Interview—Michael Reznicek." *Points: The Blog of the Alcohol & Drugs History Society*, May 25, 2012. https://pointsadhsblog.wordpress.com/2012/05/25/the -points-interview-michael-reznicek.

Staff. "House Members Call for TV Anti-Drug Campaign." *Broadcasting and Cable* 111 (1986): 70–71.

Stephens, Robert P. "Addiction to Melodrama." *Substance Use & Misuse* 46, no. 7 (2011): 859–71.

Sterling, Eric. "Drug Policy: A Challenge of Values." *Journal of Religion & Spirituality in Social Work* 23, no. 1 (2004): 51–81.

Stevens, John Paul. "Our 'Broken System' of Criminal Justice." *New York Review of Books*, November 10, 2011, 56–59.

Sturken, Marita, and Lisa Cartwright. *Practices of Looking: An Introduction to Visual Culture*. 2nd ed. Oxford: Oxford University Press, 2009.

Substance Abuse and Mental Health Services Administration. *Behavioral Health Trends in the United States: Results from the 2014 National Survey on Drug Use and Health*. HHS Publication No. SMA 15-4927, NSDUH Series H-50. Rockville, MD: Substance Abuse and Mental Health Services Administration, 2015.

———. *Results from the 2011 National Survey on Drug Use and Health: Mental Health Findings*. HHS Publication No. SMA 12-4725, NSDUH Series H-45. Rockville, MD: Substance Abuse and Mental Health Services Administration, 2012.

Sulkunen, Pekka. "Between Culture and Nature: Intoxication in Cultural Studies of Alcohol and Drug Use." *Contemporary Drug Problems* 29, no. 2 (2002): 253–76.

Sullum, Jacob. *Saying Yes: In Defense of Drug Use*. New York: Tarcher, 2003.

Tagliazucchi, Enzo, Robin Carhart-Harris, Robert Leech, David Nutt, and Dante R. Chialvo. "Enhanced Repertoire of Brain Dynamical States during the Psychedelic Experience." *Human Brain Mapping* 35, no. 11 (2014): 5442–56.

Thomas, Katie. "Shire, Maker of Binge-Eating Drug Vyvanse, First Marketed the Disease." *New York Times*, February 24, 2015, sec. B1.

Tiger, Rebecca. *Judging Addicts: Drug Courts and Coercion in the Justice System*. New York: New York University Press, 2012.

Tunnel, Kenneth. "The OxyContin Epidemic and Crime Panic in Rural Kentucky." In *The American Drug Scene*, edited by James Inciardi and Karen McElrath, 225–58. Oxford: Oxford University Press, 2008.

Vaccarino, Franco, and Susan Rotzinger. *Neuroscience of Psychoactive Substance Use and Dependence: Summary*. Geneva: World Health Organization, 2004.

Valentine, Kylie. "Intoxicating Culture." *Contemporary Drug Problems* 38, no. 3 (2011): 429–40.

Valentine, Kylie, and Suzanne Fraser. "Trauma, Damage and Pleasure: Rethinking Problematic Drug Use." *International Journal of Drug Policy* 19, no. 5 (2008): 410–16.

Valverde, Mariana. *Diseases of the Will: Alcohol and the Dilemmas of Freedom*. Cambridge: Cambridge University Press, 1998.

Vastag, Brian. "Pay Attention: Ritalin Acts Much Like Cocaine." *Journal of the American Medical Association* 286, no. 8 (2001): 905–06.

Volkow, Nora. "Prescription Drug Abuse." *National Institute on Drug Abuse: The Science of Drug Abuse & Addiction*, September 22, 2010.

Volkow, Nora D. et al. "Effects of Modafinil on Dopamine and Dopamine Transporters in the Male Human Brain: Clinical Implications." *Journal of the American Medical Association* 301, no. 11 (2009): 1148–54.

Waldroupe, Amanda. "Portland's 'War on Drugs' Impact Area," *Street Roots News*, August 3, 2011.

Walton, Stuart. *Out of It: A Cultural History of Intoxication*. New York: Harmony Books, 2001.

Wang, Shirley. "U.S. News: Psychiatric Drug Use Spreads—Pharmacy Data Show a Big Rise in Antipsychotic and Adult ADHD Treatments." *Wall Street Journal*, November 16, 2011, sec. A3.

Weil, Andrew. *The Natural Mind: An Investigation of Drugs and the Higher Consciousness.* Boston: Houghton Mifflin, 1972.

Whitaker, Robert. *Anatomy of an Epidemic: Magic Bullets, Psychiatric Drugs, and the Astonishing Rise of Mental Illness in America.* New York: Broadway Books, 2010

Williams, Raymond. *Keywords: A Vocabulary of Culture and Society.* Oxford: Oxford University Press, 1985.

Winstock, Adam. "New Recreational Drugs and the Primary Care Approach to Patients Who Use Them." *British Medical Journal* 344, no. 288 (2012): 1–10.

Witte, K., and M. Allen. "A Meta-Analysis of Fear Appeals: Implications for Effective Public Health Campaigns." *Health Education and Behavior: The Official Publication of the Society for Public Health Education* 27, no. 5 (2000): 591–615.

Yates, Rowdy, and Margaret Malloch. *Tackling Addiction: Pathways to Recovery.* London: Jessica Kingsley Publishers, 2010.

Zajdow, Grazyna. "'It Blasted Me into Space': Intoxication and an Ethics of Pleasure." *Health Sociology Review* 19, no. 2 (2010): 218–29.

Zinberg, Norman E., and John A. Robertson. *Drugs and the Public.* New York: Simon and Schuster, 1972.

INDEX

Page numbers in italics refer to illustrations.

A

abjection, 35; of drug users, 39, 51

Acker, Caroline, 113

ADD, 179n81; stimulant use and, 53–54

Adderall (ADHD drug), 42, 176n34, 189n62; advertising for, 41; socially permissible, 100; in television, 52, 179n77

addiction: abstention and, 171; to alcohol, 112–13, 117, 118; bio-behavioral view of, 106; biological, 98, 103, 108; brain disease model of, 104, 106, 109–12, 114, 115, 137; versus casual use, 11–12; causes of, 99, 113; as colloquial term, 98–99, 122, 183n14; as compulsion, 102; contingency management in, 112; continuum in, 105, 107; craving in, 107, 108; cultural understanding of, 98, 100, 103, 113–15, 173n3; definitions of, 102–9; demographics of, 116; diagnosis of, 103, 104–9, 113–14, 183nn21–22, 184n25; discourses of, 4, 10–11, 83, 99, 115–18, 121; as disease, 104, 106, 107, 125; "drug dependence syndrome" definition of, 105; drug maintenance therapies for, 111; drug use as, 100, 102, 103; dysfunction of, 13; enforcement-only approach to, 93; epidemiological data for, 184n23; essentialism of, 111–12; fatalism in, 93; in film, 48–49; frequency of, 116–18; ideologies of, 11, 109–16; as lifetime identity, 114; medical definitions of, 98; medicalization of, 11, 98, 109, 114–15, 142; to meth, 36; methadone treatment for, 109; as mode of learning, 112; multidimensionality of, 102, 113; multigenerational, 93; narratives of, 48–49, 137; neuroscience of, 111–12, 184n41; overestimation of, 16, 118, 123; as overindulgence, 122; pharmaceutical response to, 108; police calls concerning, 91–92; "polythetic syndrome" definition of, 105; psychological, 103, 113; psychotherapy for, 112; public perception of, 52, 99; qualifying behavior for, 102; rates of, 99, 116–18, 168, 183n7; recovery discourses for, 142; recovery movements in, 104, 111; and recreational drug use, 53; research on, 103, 109–16, 135; response to stimuli, 112; risks of, 116; role of dopamine in, 109; self-delusion concerning, 114; social issues of, 24, 104, 106, 107, 113; state disciplining of, 102–3; static identities in, 109, 114; subjectivity of, 48; in television, 49–51; treatment of, 99–100, 109–16, 168; triggers for, 113; "unmasking" of, 108; user agency in, 107, 109–16, 122; user identification with, 103, 111, 113; vaccine for, 109; in visual media, 48–53. *See also* dependence, drug

addicts: arrests of, 93; numbers of, 99, 116–18; as objects, 115; recognizing, 116–20; recovering, 114

ADHD drugs, 8, 173n11. *See also* Adderall; Vyvanse

advertising: cigarette, 23–24; direct-to-consumers (DTC), 7–8, 37–43, 55; propharmaceutical, 14, 37, 96

advertising, antidrug, 27–37; cost of, 36, 37; "Drugs and Terror," 30–32; fear-based, 35–36. *See also* public-service announcements

African Americans: profiling of, 76; war on drugs against, 65, 68

Afroman, "Because I Got High," 44

agency: in alcohol use, 135; in direct-to-consumer advertising, 38, 55; of drug

problem-causing, 100, 102; prostitu-
tion for, 34, 42; repurposing of, 153–54;
scope of, 173n1; "set and setting" of, 13,
174n20; social/medical approval of, 100;
"soft" and "hard," 18; testing for, 89–90
drugs, illicit, xii; arrests for, 4; contradictory discourses of, 97; controlled use
of, 10; health care providers and, 97;
as human-rights issue, 83; legalization
of, 84, 85–86, 170; media narratives of,
7–8; moralistic conception of, 15–16;
online markets for, 86; oversimplified
narratives of, 4; pleasure in, 121, 136,
140, 170; research on, 81; scheduling of,
82; support for overcoming, 124; trends
in use, 81
"Drugs and Terror" advertising campaign,
30–32; controversial aspects of, 32–33
Drugstore Cowboy (film), drug use in, 14
drug trade: effect on poor, 85; power
dynamics of, 85–86; regulation of, 86
drug use: as abuse, 83, 99; as addiction, 100,
102, 103; alterity in, 142–43; in American music, 44–45; association with
terrorism, 30–33, 175n24; barriers to,
157; biological determinism of, 106–7;
conceptual frameworks for, 123; cost-
benefit ratio for, 151; cultural engagement with, 15, 21–27, 45, 120, 141, 169;
cultural inconsistencies concerning,
122–23; desire in, 8–9, 13, 46; diagnostic
terminology for, 104–9; difference in,
142; and drug possession, 70; education
for, 168, 170; embodied knowledge in,
145; embodied subjectivity through,
134; empiricism of, 142; epistemological
stance toward, 121; ethnicity and, 76;
experience ratings for, 149–50; fallacies concerning, 11; harm-reduction
measures, 85–86, 111, 123, 170; health
approach to, 84; iatric, 14; incorporation in, 145; learned behaviors of,
138; learned expectations of, 144; as
lifestyle, 121; managing experience
of, 148–57; media representations
of, 14–15, 27–35; medical/addiction
dichotomy of, 98; and national security,
32; neoliberal framework for, 136;
participant-observer perspective on, 17;

performance of, 142, 148; phenomenology of, 148; physiological/psychological
experience of, 106–8; pleasure-seeking
in, 9–10, 14, 55, 60, 148, 157; polarization
concerning, 5, 9; politicization of, 167;
in popular culture, 15, 21–27, 43–55, 61,
70, 135; reasons for, 120–22; research
on, 16, 17, 80–81, 109–16, 137, 154, 169;
rethinking, 12–17; risk in, 9, 116, 135,
169; romanticization of, 14, 51–52; in
science fiction, 54–55; self-knowledge
in, 144; as self-maintenance, 151; sexual
benefits of, 151; sexual identity and, 139;
social, 13, 70, 98, 132; socially integrated,
164–65; spectrum of, 123; trends in, 79,
80; ways of knowing, 17; zero tolerance
for, 71. See also substance use
drug use, controlled, xi–xii, addiction
and, 98, 107; data concerning, 11–12;
in DTC advertising, 55; effects of,
132; failure of, 51; of illicit drugs, 10;
invisibility of, 87, 119, 169; lifestyles of,
18; normative, 20, 121, 138, 148, 170;
pleasure in, 148; political context of, 69;
in popular culture, 21; of psychoactive
drugs, 5, 10, 119; responsible, 12; socialization of, 12, 154
drug use, recreational, xii; as abuse, 99;
addiction and, 53; after-work, 147;
agency in, 55; in criminalization culture, 18; health care providers and,
97; invisibility of, 87; moralistic conception of, 15; of pharmaceuticals, 96;
pleasure in, 55, 60; in popular culture,
45; in PSAs, 36; as self-destructive,
98; stigmatization of, 97; in war on
drugs, 22
"drug use disorder," 105, 107, 114, 123; sociopolitical identity in, 115
drug users: abject, 39, 51; as addicts, 16;
agency of, 14, 17, 32, 103, 109, 120–23,
133–40, 174n4; as amoral, 71; anxiety
over, 25–26; autonomy loss among, 136;
in carceral state, 61, 76; children, 63;
conceptualization of practices, 150–51;
cultural representation of, 21–27;
danger of, 32; decision-making by, 151;
diversity among, 18–19; information
campaigns for, 156; intentionality of,

136–37; serotonin-enhanced, 161; social construction of, 17; thinking as, 143; user agency and, 134–40; varied expressions of, 151–52. *See also* desire; drug use, recreational

police, drug-related calls of, 91–93. *See also* arrests, drug-related; criminalization; war on drugs

Pollan, Michael, 20, 141

"polythetic syndrome" (addiction), 105

possession: arrests for, 72, 76–77; of controlled substances, 69–70; by immigrants, 76; of marijuana, 75–76; penalties for, 75–76. *See also* drug offenders

prescription drugs: increased use of, 4; withdrawal from, 126–27. *See also* pharmaceuticals

Prescription Drug User Fee Act, 40

prisons: criminalization's support of, 15, 76; overcrowded, 78. *See also* incarceration; war on drugs

prohibition, drug, 135; legacies of, 167. *See also* drug control

Prozac (antidepressant), 126; advertising for, 8

psilocybin, 143

psychedelics, xii; bad trips from, 159. *See also* hallucinogens

psychoactive drugs: addiction to, 99; agency through, 10; in American society, 3, 42; awareness of abuse, 97–98; classification of, 187n7; conflicting ideologies of, 3–5; controlled use of, 5, 10, 119; cultural discourses of, 118; DTC ads for, 38, 41–43; legislation regulating, 66–67; medicalization of, 4; misconceptions concerning, 11, 21; for mood management, 102; normalization of, 11, 18; overgeneralization concerning, 118; for performance management, 153; pleasure in, 16, 123, 132–34, 145, 154; ritualized use of, 122; social inequities concerning, 5; social narratives of, 8; social use of, 131, 135; "unhealthy users" of, 108; use rates for, 171

psychotherapeutic drugs, increased use of, 7

psychotherapy, for addiction, 112

PTSD, MDMA for, 152

public-service announcements (PSAs), antidrug, 7–8, 15, 22, 27–37; cocaine in, 28, 29; congressional support for, 28; frightening narratives of, 27–28; ineffectiveness of, 33; print, 32; as propaganda, 36; recreational drugs in, 36; straight talk in, 27. *See also* advertising; antidrug narratives

Q

Queens of the Stone Age, "Feel Good Hit of the Summer," 44–45

Quinn, Governor Pat, 74

R

Race, Kane, 17, 151; *Consuming Medicine*, 139–40

Reagan, Nancy, 61–62

Reagan administration, antidrug policies of, 14, 15, 27, 61–66

Reinarman, Craig, 107–8

Requiem for a Dream (film), 50; addiction narrative of, 48–49; drug-taking montages of, 52; as monster movie, 49

Rescue Me (television series), alcohol use on, 25

Ritalin-SR, advertising for, 8

Roberts, Mark, 114

Rubin, Laurence, 42

S

Sacks, Oliver, 147

Scarface (film), 47; cocaine use in, 14

Schrager, Allison, 85

Schumer, Charles, 65

science fiction, drug use in, 54–55

Scott, Jeremy, 43

Seddon, Toby, 72

Sedgwick, Eve Kosofsky, 115

self: abject, 35; altered, 144; distance from, 143; frameworks of perception for, 145; medicalization of, 95, 115; performance of, 140–48; technologies of, 101

self-care, drugs for, 139

self-diagnosis, 101

self-knowledge: communal, 144; medicalized, 95

self-medication: culture of, 3, 121; for mood alteration, 154; motivation for, 132

71–72, 75–79; cultural narrative of, 23; discourse of, 6, 87; drug czar of, 67; economic impact of, 71, 72; expansion of, 67; failure of, 19; federal authority in, 67–68; fundamentalism of, 71; funding of, 71, 74, 76; hysteria in, 63–64; ideologies of, xi, 61, 62–63, 82, 87; infrastructure of, 71; legal focus of, 62; militarization of, 69, 76; moral logic of, 52, 71; mutability of, 168; political aspects of, 61–66, 71; power structures of, 87; punitive, 66; recreational use in, 22; second era of, 69; as social policy, 66–70; societal effects of, 7; socioeconomic costs of, 86–87; stereotypes of, xii, 21, 83; surveillance in, *73*, 78, 174n15; in visual media, 46, 47. *See also* arrests; criminalization; drug control
Washington State, drug legalization in, 85
The Wayans Bros. (television series), anti-drug scripts of, 30
Weeds (television series), drug narrative of, 46, 47

Weil, Andrew, 8
whippits (inhalant), 148
Willenbring, Mark, 118–19
The Wire (television series), drug narrative of, 46–47
World Health Organization (WHO), 103; on addiction, 104–5; drug use data of, 12; Expert Committee on Drug Dependence, 183n21; on intoxication, 140; on social issues, 110. See also *International Classification of Diseases* (ICD)

X
xenophobia, drug use and, 63

Y
"Your Dreams Miss You" (Rozerem advertisement), 38–39, *39*

Z
Zajdow, Grazyna, 142
Zoloft, side effects of, 41

ABOUT THE AUTHOR

INGRID WALKER IS ASSOCIATE PROFESSOR OF AMERICAN STUDIES at the University of Washington, Tacoma, where she researches and teaches about the politics of contemporary culture in the United States. Her controversial TEDx Talk, "Drugs and Desire," explores the stigmas surrounding psychoactive drugs, from caffeine to hallucinogens. Her writing has appeared in the *Journal of Popular Culture, NANO,* publications of the Alcohol and Drug History Association, and the edited volumes *Conspiracy Nation* and *The Gangster Film Reader.*

CPSIA information can be obtained
at www.ICGtesting.com
Printed in the USA
LVOW11s1824031017
551035LV00006B/1072/P